K423.1

Dictionary of Catchphrases

Dictionary of Catchphrases

NIGEL REES

CASSELL

Cassell Publishers Limited
Wellington House
125 Strand
London WC2R 0BB
England

First published 1995
© Nigel Rees 1995

Distributed in the United States
by Sterling Publishing Co., Inc.
387 Park Avenue South, New York, New York 10016–8810

Distributed in Australia
by Capricorn Link (Australia) Pty Ltd
2/13 Carrington Road, Castle Hill, NSW 2154

British Library Cataloguing-in-Publication Data
A catalogue record for this book is available from the British Library

ISBN 0–304–34563–6

Printed and bound in Great Britain by Biddles Ltd

Preface

Whether you call it a 'catch-phrase', a 'catch phrase' or, as I prefer, a 'catchphrase', what we are talking about here is a phrase in frequent use and one which, for some reason, appeals to the public fancy. The catchphrase catches on because it is a more colourful and enjoyable way of expressing an idea or feeling than the conventional, straightforward one.

Perhaps it rhymes or alliterates and is fun to speak. Perhaps it is the sort of phrase that can be employed in all sorts of situations and circumstances. In other words, a catchphrase is useful – even if this usefulness only exists to the extent that you can make a *double entendre* out of it. When a catchphrase verges on the cliché, it may be a bit maddening. But, above all, it is a bit *silly*, and that is of the nature of the beast.

The first book I wrote about catchphrases was entitled *Very Interesting. . .But Stupid!* (1980) and was restricted to phrases that had caught on in the world of entertainment. In the *Cassell Dictionary of Catchphrases*, I have only included show business phrases that have stood the test of time, as well as adding some of the more recent ones. Chiefly, I have extended the range of the book to embrace non-show business phrases – the sort that have arisen in everyday speech and become popular in that way. I have not tried to produce a comprehensive collection in this small space, but have selected what seem to be the most enduring catchphrases and the ones about which there is something useful to be said. I have tried to explain their meanings and origins, as well as attempting to suggest when and where they might first have caught on.

Lastly, it might be useful if I were to define briefly what I mean by the various categories of popular phrase that give rise to or describe the catchphrases to be found in this dictionary:

Catchphrase: in its purest form, simply a phrase that has 'caught on' with the public and is, or has been, in frequent use. It might have originated with a named entertainer – like **Loadsamoney!** On the other hand, it might *not* be traceable to a particular source – like **Bob's your uncle!**

Cliché: a worn or hackneyed phrase. 'Winter of discontent' was a bright phrase when Shakespeare first minted it in *King Richard III* but it has become devalued by frequent repetition in other, political, contexts. 'At the end of the day' must also once have been rather a good way of describing something, but not now. I could not argue that 'in the final analysis', for example, was ever a good phrase. There are some who would say that the clichés of journalism are used in such a way that they amount to a special language – journalese – which does not deserve to be condemned. I disagree.

Format phrase: a basic phrase or sentence structure capable of infinite variation by the insertion of new words.

Idiom: a picturesque expression that is used to convey a metaphorical meaning different to its literal one – or, as *The Oxford Dictionary of Current Idiomatic English* puts it, that has a meaning 'not deducible from those of the separate words'. For example, if I say someone is a 'square peg in a round hole' it is obvious he or she cannot literally be such a thing. My hearers will know exactly what I mean, although I have not told them directly. Like the term 'catchphrase', 'idiom' could be applied to most of the phrases in this book, but I have tried to restrict its use to those which conform to the above definition.

Saying: this is what is sometimes called 'a well-known phrase or saying' (as in 're-arrange these words into a well-known phrase or saying') but, unlike a formal 'quotation', is probably not attributable to a precise source, be it speaker, book or show. Proverbial expressions most commonly fall into this category.

Slogan: a phrase designed to promote a product, idea or cause – or which has this effect. However, at times I have employed it rather loosely to cover any phrase that is used in advertising – in headlines, footnotes, but not necessarily in a selling line that names the product. Thus 'body odour/B.O.' could hardly be described as a slogan in itself, but as an advertising line it did help to promote a product.

Stock phrase: a regularly used phrase that cannot be said to have 'caught on' like a full-blooded catchphrase.

I must repeat that there is considerable overlap between these categories. Indeed, it is possible for a phrase to be several things at once – catchphrase, slogan, idiom, or whatever.

Please note that the catchphrases are listed in 'word by word order' – that is to say, in alphabetical order according to how the letters occur in the first and following words.

A
a

abandon hope all ye who enter here! a popular translation of the words written over the entrance to Hell in Dante's *Divina Commedia* (*c* 1320). However, 'All hope abandon, ye who enter here!' would be a more accurate translation of the Italian *'lasciate ogni speranza, voi ch'entrate!'*

accidents will happen in the best-regulated families catchphrase used to cover any domestic upset, and allusively such matters as pregnancy. The more basic proverbial expression, 'Accidents will happen' was known by the 1760s, the full version by the 1810s. Best known in the form delivered by Mr Micawber in Charles Dickens, *David Copperfield* (1850): ' "Copperfield," said Mr. Micawber, "accidents will occur in the best-regulated families; and in families not regulated by...the influence of Woman, in the lofty character of Wife, they may be expected with confidence, and must be borne with philosophy".'

act your age! (also **be your age!**) grow up, behave in a manner more befitting your years. Probably from the US and in use by the 1920s. An elaboration heard in the UK (1985) – **act your age, not your shoe size** (normal shoe sizes in the UK are in the range 4–12).

after you, Claude!/no – after you, Cecil! an enduring exchange of phrases for overcoming some social awkwardness like deciding who should go first through a door. From the BBC radio show *ITMA* (1940s), where it was spoken by actors Horace Percival and Jack Train playing two over-polite handymen, Cecil and Claude.

age before beauty! as with the previous one, a useful phrase when inviting another person to go through a door before you.

1

Possibly of American origin and certainly known there by the 1920s. Variants and responses include **dirt/dust before the broom!**; **shit before shovel!**; **shepherd before sheep!**; and the **dog follows its master/dogs follow their master!**

age of miracles is not past!, the   ironic comment when an unexpected event occurs, especially involving an act of good manners. Sometimes the **age of chivalry is not past!** Both expressions are negative forms of proverbs: 'the age of miracles is past' was known by the early 1600s and 'the age of chivalry is gone' by the 1790s.

aha, me proud beauty!   I've got you where I want you! A phrase suggestive of nineteenth-century melodrama or, at the very least, of parodies of the style.

ain't it a shame, eh? ain't it a shame?   catchphrase of the nameless man (played by Carleton Hobbs) in the BBC radio show *ITMA* (1940s) who told banal tales ('I waited for hours in the fish queue. . .and a man took my plaice') and always prefaced and concluded them with 'ain't it a shame?'

alive and well and living in ——   response to the queries **whatever happened to ——?** and **where are they/you now?** 'Alive and well' was known by the 1910s; the full version by 1968 when the Belgian song-writer and singer Jacques Brel became the subject of an off-Broadway musical show entitled *Jacques Brel is Alive and Well and Living in Paris.*

all/any publicity is good publicity   an almost proverbial saying, certainly current by the 1960s, but probably as old as the public relations industry itself. Often used defensively when the speaker has been the subject or victim of adverse publicity. Alternative forms include: **there's no such thing as bad publicity**, **there's no such thing as over-exposure – only bad exposure**, and, **don't read it – measure it**. In Dominic Behan's *My Brother Brendan* (1965), the Irish playwright is quoted as saying: 'There is no such thing as bad publicity except your own obituary.' James Agate in *Ego 7* (for 19 February 1944) quotes Arnold Bennett, 'All praise is good', and adds, 'I suppose the same could be said about publicity.' The idea behind this catchphrase also occurs in **any publicity, good or bad, is better than none, provided they spell your name right** (from the 1930s – but certainly current by the 1960s). As, 'I don't care what the papers say about me as long as they spell my name right', this saying has been attributed to the American Tammany leader 'Big Tim' Sullivan.

all balls and bang me arse!   an intensifier of the basic **all balls!** meaning 'sheer nonsense'. British use, probably since the 1910s.

all behind like the cow's tail, (I'm/we're)   for when one is getting behind with one's schedule. Known since the nineteenth century. A ritual addition.

all bitter and twisted   about someone who is psychologically mixed-up and shows it. Sometimes made light of in the form 'all twitter and bisted'. Since the 1940s, at least.

all contributions gratefully received   as with **please give generously/all you can**, a standard phrase from charitable appeals for money. But also used jokingly to accept gifts of almost anything – another helping of food, even a sexual favour.

——, all day!   response to the question 'What day is it?' or 'What's the date?' For example, 'Tuesday/the 13th...all day!' In use since the late nineteenth century.

all done with mirrors   a way of describing how anything has been accomplished when the method is not obvious. Originally, a way of explaining how conjuring tricks and stage illusions were performed when some of them, indeed, were done using mirrors. A suspicion of trickery is implicit in the phrase. *They Do It With Mirrors* is the title of an Agatha Christie thriller (1952). In use by 1900.

all dressed up and nowhere to go   phrase describing a particular dilemma. From a song popularized by the American comedian Raymond Hitchcock in *The Beauty Shop* (New York, 1914) and *Mr Manhattan* (London, 1915): 'When you're all dressed up and no place to go,/Life seems dreary, weary and slow.' The words gained further emphasis when they were used by William Allen White to describe the Progressive Party following Theodore Roosevelt's decision to retire from presidential competition in 1916. He said it was: 'All dressed up with nowhere to go'.

all dressed up like a Christmas tree   gaudily attired – not a compliment. Since the late nineteenth century.

all fur coat and no knickers   *see* **all kid gloves and no drawers.**

all gas and gaiters   to do with the church, especially the higher clergy. Bishops wore gaiters and all clergymen may have a tendency to create hot air. *All Gas and Gaiters* was the title of a BBC TV comedy series about the clergy (1966–70). The phrase comes from Charles Dickens, *Nicholas Nickleby* (1838–9).

all gong and no dinner   what one would say of a person who was loud-mouthed and somewhat short on achievement – all talk and no action. It may be a fairly recent coinage.

all hands on deck!   everybody help – obviously of naval origin – but now applicable in any emergency, domestic or otherwise. Nineteenth century?

all human life is there   originally, a quotation from Henry James, 'Madonna of the Future' (1879): 'Cats and monkeys, monkeys and cats – all human life is there.' Used notably as an advertising slogan for the British Sunday newspaper, the *News of the World*, in the late 1950s.

all I know is what I read in the papers   I'm just an ordinary guy. From a saying much used by Will Rogers, the American cowboy humorist of the 1920s. For example, from *The Letters of a Self-Made Diplomat to His President* (1927): 'Dear Mr Coolidge: Well all I know is just what I read in the papers.'

all jam and Jerusalem   a popular misconception of the local Women's Institute groups in the UK is that their members are solely concerned with making jam, with flower arranging, and with singing the Blake/Parry anthem 'Jerusalem'. The faintly mocking encapsulation 'all jam and Jerusalem' is said to date from the 1920s. Simon Goodenough's history of the movement was entitled *Jam and Jerusalem* (1977).

all kid gloves and no drawers describing a certain kind of woman, and possibly of London Cockney origin in the 1930s. Another version encountered in the 1980s was **all fur coat and no knickers.**

all mouth and trousers describing a type of man who is 'all talk', but possibly implying that he is also only interested in sexual matters (compare the earlier **all prick and breeches**). Since the 1950s?

all my eye and Betty Martin nonsense, and so described since the 1780s, at least. The shorter expressions 'all my eye' or 'my eye' pre-date this. Various attempts have been made to identify the original Betty Martin – including the suggestion that she was an actress whose favourite expression is supposed to have been 'My eye!' or that the name was a British sailor's garbled version of words heard in an Italian church: *'O, mihi, beate Martine'* (Oh, grant me, blessed St Martin. . .).

all over the place like a madwoman's —— in disarray, in a mess – in the form 'all over the place like a mad woman's shit/knitting/ custard/lunch box'. There is a strong possibility that the phrase originated in Australia. The writer Germaine Greer recalls that, when she was growing up in Australia in the 1940s, 'all over the place like a madwoman's underclothes' was her mother's phrase to describe, say, an untidy room. Hence, Greer used *The Mad Woman's Underclothes* as the title of a book of her assorted writings (1986).

all piss and wind empty, vacuous – of a man prone to bombast and no achievement. Apparently derived from the earlier (about 1800) saying, 'All wind and piss like a barber's cat'.

all prick and breeches *see* **all mouth and trousers.**

all right for some! some people have all the luck! – a good-humoured expression of envy. 'I'm just off to the West Indies for an all-expenses paid holiday' – 'All right for some!' Twentieth century.

5

all right, you did hear a seal bark! an expression of resigned, good-humoured defeat, in response to someone else's far-fetched claim of long standing. The origin lies in the caption to a James Thurber cartoon of a husband and wife in bed. She says, 'All Right, Have It Your Way – You Heard a Seal Bark' and there is, indeed, a seal to hand (1932).

all-singing, all-dancing the meaning of this catchphrase has developed to the stage where – chiefly in the fields of financial services and computing – it indicates that what you are getting is a multi-purpose something or other, with every possible feature, which may or may not 'perform' well. Originally, in 1929, the phrase was a descriptive slogan for the first ever Hollywood musical, MGM's *Broadway Melody*, which was promoted with posters bearing the words: '*The New Wonder of the Screen!* ALL TALKING ALL SINGING ALL DANCING *Dramatic Sensation.*'

all systems go! in a state of readiness to begin any enterprise. From the US space programme of the 1960s.

all we want is the facts, ma'am (or **just the facts, ma'am**) don't give us your opinions, let us just have the unvarnished details of what happened. In parody of the American TV series *Dragnet* (1951–8), largely the creation of Jack Webb (1920–82) who produced, directed and starred in it. As Police Sergeant Joe Friday he had a deadpan, staccato style which was much parodied. The show first appeared on radio in 1949 and was said to draw its stories from actual cases dealt with by the Los Angeles police – hence the famous announcement: 'Ladies and gentlemen, the story you are about to hear is true. *Only the names have been changed to protect the innocent.*'

although I says it as shouldn't phrase of excuse before uttering an indiscretion. Since the seventeenth century.

always merry and bright almost the sobriquet or the bill matter of the British comedian Alfred Lester (1872–1925) – who was always lugubrious. As 'Peter Doody', a jockey in the Lionel Monckton/Howard Talbot/Arthur Wimperis musical comedy *The Arcadians* (1909), he had the phrase as his motto in a song, 'My Motter'.

amaze me!   *see* **astonish me!**

America, love it or leave it   *see* **put up or shut up!**

—— **and all that**   and all that sort of thing. Apparently the phrase
was in the language before it was popularized by Robert Graves
in the title of his autobiographical volume *Goodbye To All That*
(1929) – a farewell to his participation in the First World War and
to an unhappy period in his private life – and by Sellar and
Yeatman in their cod volume of English history *1066 And All That*
(1930).

and awa-a-aay we go!   a show business catchphrase from the
Jackie Gleason Show on US television (1952–70). The rotund
comedian hosted variety acts, and used this phrase to lead into
the first sketch. He had a special pose to accompany it – head
turned to face left, one leg raised ready to shoot off in the same
direction.

and how!   an intensifying phrase of agreement, almost certainly
of American origin from, say, the 1920s. 'Would you like
another beer?' – 'Yes, I would – and how!'

and I don't mean maybe!   an intensifying phrase, to show that the
speaker has just issued a command and has not simply expressed
a wish. American origin, 1920s. The second line of the song 'Yes,
Sir, That's My Baby' (1922–5) is: '. . .No, sir, don't mean maybe'.

and no mistake!   an intensifying phrase of affirmation, dating
from the 1810s.

and now for something completely different...   catchphrase first
delivered by Eric Idle in the second edition of *Monty Python's
Flying Circus* (BBC TV, 12 October 1969), though it had also
featured in part of the comedy team's earlier series *At Last the
1948 Show* (ITV, 1967). Used as the title of the team's first
cinema feature in 1971. Normally, it was delivered by John
Cleese as a dinner-jacketed BBC announcer, seated before a
microphone placed on a desk in some unlikely setting. The
phrase was taken from the slightly arch 'link' much loved by

magazine programme presenters, particularly on BBC radio, though the children's BBC TV series *Blue Peter* is sometimes said to have provoked the *Python* use of the phrase.

and so forth, and so fifth! a would-be humorous elaboration of 'and so forth', dating from the mid-twentieth century.

and so to bed! Samuel Pepys's famous signing-off line for his diary appears first on 15 January 1660. However, on that particular occasion, they are not quite his last words. He writes: 'I went to supper, and after that to make an end of this week's notes in this book, and so to bed'. Then he adds: 'It being a cold day and a great snow, my physic did not work so well as it should have done'. *And So To Bed* was the title of a play (1926) by J.B. Fagan, which was then turned into a musical (by Vivian Ellis, 1951). As a catchphrase, it can be taken to mean 'and that's the end of it', though conceivably it could also have a lubricious suggestiveness.

and so we say farewell... a phrase from rather second-rate cinema travelogues made by James A. Fitzpatrick which were a supporting feature of cinema programmes from 1925 onwards. With the advent of sound, the commentaries to 'Fitzpatrick Traveltalks' became noted for their closing words: 'And it's from this paradise of the Canadian Rockies that we reluctantly say farewell to Beautiful Banff.../And as the midnight sun lingers on the skyline of the city, we most reluctantly say farewell to Stockholm, Venice of the North.../With its picturesque impressions indelibly fixed in our memory, it is time to conclude our visit and reluctantly say farewell to Hong Kong, the hub of the Orient...'.

Frank Muir's and Denis Norden's notable parody of the genre – 'Bal-ham – Gateway to the South' – first written for radio *c* 1948 and later performed on record by Peter Sellers (1958) accordingly contained the words, 'And so we say farewell to this historic borough...'.

and that ain't hay! and that's not to be sniffed at/that isn't negligible, usually with reference to money. The title of the 1943 Abbott and Costello film which is said to have popularized this (almost exclusively US) exclamation was *It Ain't Hay*. But in the same year, Mickey Rooney exclaimed 'And that ain't hay!' as he went into the big 'I Got Rhythm' number (choreographed by Busby Berkeley) in the film *Girl Crazy* (the scene being set, appropriately, in an agricultural college).

and that's the way it is   sign-off phrase by the authoritative and avuncular American TV anchorman, Walter Cronkite who anchored the CBS TV *Evening News* for nineteen years. On the final occasion, he said: 'And that's the way it is, Friday March 6, 1981. Goodnight.'

and the band played on...   things went on as usual. A phrase from a song 'The Band Played On', written by John F. Palmer in 1895.

and the best of luck!   a phrase of ironic encouragement. Frankie Howerd, the British comedian, claimed in his autobiography, *On the Way I Lost It* (1976), to have given this phrase to the language in the late 1940s when he introduced BBC radio's *Variety Bandbox*. However, as **and the best of British luck!**, it may already have been in existence as a Second World War army phrase meaning the exact opposite of what it appears to say – that is, the very worst form of luck, no luck.

and the next object is...   phrase from the BBC radio quiz *Twenty Questions* (1947–76) in which a mystery voice (most notably Norman Hackforth's) would inform listeners in advance about the object the panellists would then try to identify by asking no more than twenty questions. Hackforth would intone in his deep, fruity voice: 'And the next object is "The odour in the larder" [or some such poser].'

and there's more where that came from!   the origins of this phrase probably lie in some music-hall comedian's patter, uttered after a particular joke has gone well. Charles Dickens in Chapter 11 of *Martin Chuzzlewit* (1843–4) shows that the phrase was established in other contexts first: 'Mr Jonas filled the young ladies' glasses, calling on them not to spare it, as they might be certain there was plenty more where that came from.'

In the twentieth century it has been popularized by the BBC radio *Goon Show* (1950s). It was sometimes said by Major Denis

Bloodnok (Peter Sellers) and occasionally by Wallace Greenslade (a BBC staff announcer who, like his colleague, John Snagge, was allowed to let his hair down on the show).

and they all lived happily ever after   traditional ending to a fairy tale. It is present in five of *The Classic Fairy Tales* gathered in their earliest known English forms by Iona and Peter Opie (1974). The concluding words of Winston Churchill's *My Early Life* (1930) are: '. . .September 1908, when I married and lived happily ever afterwards.'

and with that, I return you to the studio!   the standard outside broadcast commentator or reporter's line, given new life when used by 'Cecil Snaith' (Hugh Paddick), the hush-voiced BBC man in the radio show *Beyond Our Ken* (early 1960s). Always used after he had described some disaster in which he had figured.

another day, another dollar!   what one says to oneself at the conclusion of toil. Of American origin, but now as well known in the UK where there does not appear to be an equivalent expression using 'pound' instead of 'dollar'. Popular in the US by 1910 and in the UK by the 1940s.

another fine mess   *see* **here's another nice mess. . .**

another little drink wouldn't do us any harm!   a boozer's jocular justification for another snort. The actual origin is in a song with the phrase as title, written by Clifford Grey to music by Nat D. Ayer, and sung by George Robey in the London show *The Bing Boys Are Here* (1916). The song includes a reference to the well-known fact that Prime Minister Asquith was at times the worse for drink when on the Treasury Bench:

Mr Asquith says in a manner sweet and calm:
And another little drink wouldn't do us any harm.

answer is a lemon!, the   non-answer to a question or a refusal to do something requested of one. Probably of American origin by about 1910. A lemon is acidic, and there are several other American phrases in which a lemon denotes something that is not working properly.

10

answer is in the plural and they bounce, the   that is to say, 'balls!' Said to have been the response given by the architect Sir Edwin Lutyens to a Royal Commission. However, according to Robert Jackson, *The Chief* (1959), when Gordon (later Lord) Hewart was in the House of Commons, he was answering questions on behalf of David Lloyd George. For some time, one afternoon, he had given answers in the customary brief parliamentary manner – 'The answer is in the affirmative' or 'The answer is in the negative'. After one such non-committal reply, several members arose to bait Hewart with a series of rapid supplementary questions. He waited until they had all finished and then replied: 'The answer is in the plural!'

any colour you like, so long as it's black   there is no choice. This saying originated with Henry Ford who is supposed to have said it about the Model T Ford which came out in 1909. Hill and Nevins in *Ford: Expansion and Challenge* (1957) have him saying: 'People can have it any colour – so long as it's black'. However, in 1925, the company had to bow to the inevitable and offer a choice of colours.

any more, Mrs Moore?, is there/have you   elaborations of 'any more?' from the British music-hall song (late nineteenth century):

> Don't have any more, Mrs Moore,
> Mrs Moore, please don't have any more;
> If you have too much you can't stop, they say,
> And enough is as good as a feast any day;
> If you have any more, Mrs Moore,
> Then you'll have to take the house next door;
> Too many double gins give a woman double chins –
> So don't have any more, Mrs Moore.

any publicity...   *see* **all/any publicity...**

any time, any place, anywhere   absolutely anywhere. A phrase popularized by British advertisements for Martini which has used it as a slogan since the early 1970s. The exact phrase 'any time, any place, anywhere' had occurred earlier, however, in the song 'I Love To Cry at Weddings' in the musical *Sweet Charity* (1966).

11

In April 1987, a woman called Marion Joannou was jailed at the Old Bailey, London, for protecting the man who had strangled her husband. She was nicknamed 'Martini Marion' because, apparently, she would have sex 'any time, any place, anywhere'.

anyone for tennis? an enquiry seen as typical of the 'teacup' theatre of the 1920s and 1930s (as also in the forms **who's for tennis?** and **tennis, anyone?**). An approximation occurs in the first act of George Bernard Shaw's play *Misalliance* (1910) in which a character asks: 'Anybody on for a game of tennis?' For many years it was held that the first line Humphrey Bogart had spoke on the stage in the early 1920s was 'Tennis, anyone?', but he denied it.

anything for a laugh casual reason given for doing something a little out of the ordinary. Since the 1930s: in P.G. Wodehouse, *Laughing Gas* (1936): ' "Anything for a laugh" is your motto.' In the 1980s it was combined with the similar phrases **good for a laugh** and **game for anything** to produce the title of the British TV show *Game For a Laugh*, which consisted of various stunts.

anything goes! there are no rules and restrictions here, you can do whatever you like (compare the much older **this is/it's liberty hall**). Popularized by the song and musical show with the title written by Cole Porter (1934).

are there any more at home like you? a chatting-up line dating back to the musical comedy *Floradora* (1899) which contains a song written by Leslie Stuart entitled, 'Tell Me, Pretty Maiden (Are There Any More At Home Like You?)'. The singer Tom Jones may be heard saying it to a member of the audience on the record album *Tom Jones Live at Caesar's Palace Las Vegas* (1971).

are we downhearted? – no! a phrase usually thought of in connection with the early stages of the First World War had political origins before that. Joseph Chamberlain (1838–1914) said in a 1906 speech: 'We are not downhearted. The only trouble is, we cannot understand what is happening to our neighbours.' The day after he was defeated as candidate in the Stepney Borough Council election of 1909, Clement Attlee, the future British

Prime Minister, was greeted by a colleague with the cry, 'Are we downhearted?' (He, being Attlee, replied, 'Of course we are.')

On 18 August 1914, the *Daily Mail* reported: 'For two days the finest troops England has ever sent across the sea have been marching through the narrow streets of old Boulogne in solid columns of khaki...waving as they say that new slogan of Englishmen: "Are we downhearted? ... Nooooo!" "Shall we win? ... Yessss!" ' The phrase was later incorporated in a song by Lawrence Wright and Worton David in 1917.

are yer courtin'?   Wilfred Pickles introduced the first edition of his homely, travelling BBC radio show *Have a Go* in 1946. Within twelve months, it had an audience of twenty million and ran for another twenty years. It was a simple quiz which enabled the host, accompanied by his wife, to indulge in folksy chatting to contestants, at some length. Talking to spinsters, of any age from nineteen to ninety, Pickles would invariably ask if they were courting.

are you sitting comfortably? Then I'll/we'll begin   the customary way of beginning stories on BBC radio's daily programme for small children, *Listen with Mother* (1950–82). Julia Lang was the first person to say it. Like any good catchphrase, it was capable of being used as a *double entendre*.

are you with me?   *see* **no, I'm/we're with the Woolwich!**

aren't we all?   a collusive phrase that has become simply a jokey retort or a way of coping with an unintentional *double entendre*: 'I'm afraid I'm coming out of my trousers' – 'Aren't we all, dear, aren't we all?' In Frederick Lonsdale's play with the title *Aren't We All?* (1924), the Vicar says, 'Grenham, you called me a bloody old fool' and Lord Grenham replies, 'But aren't we all, old friend?' By 1929, Ray Henderson had composed the song 'I'm a Dreamer, Aren't We All'.

aren't you the lucky one?   congratulatory phrase from the 1920s, but one tinged with mockery and no envy.

arm and a leg, an   a measurement of (high) cost, as in 'That'll cost you an arm and a leg'. Probably of American origin, mid-twentieth century. Compare B.H. Malkin's 1809 translation of Le Sage's *Gil Blas*: 'He was short in his reckoning by an arm and a leg.'

arrivederci! *see* **if you want me, Thingmy...**

as busy as a one-armed paperhanger a colourful, and fairly outrageous, American comparison known by the 1940s. Similar coinages include: **as useless as a chocolate kettle** (British); **as scarce as rocking-horse manure** (Australian); **as inconspicuous as Liberace at a wharfies' picnic** (Australian/American); **as easy as juggling with soot** (American – as are also the following); **as jumpy as a one-legged cat in a sand-box; as much chance as a fart in a wind-storm; as much use as a one-legged man at an arse-kicking contest; as likely as a snow-storm in Karachi.**

as 'e bin in, whack? question repeatedly put to Dave Morris, manager of BBC radio's *Club Night* in the 1950s. 'E never 'ad, of course.

as every schoolboy knows patronizing remark likely to be made by the knowledgeable but now only as a conscious archaism. Used straight by Robert Burton in *The Anatomy of Melancholy* (1621). Lord Macaulay, the historian, was still at it in 1840: 'Every schoolboy knows who imprisoned Montezuma, and who strangled Atahualpa' (essay on 'Lord Clive').

as if I cared... a catchphrase from the 1940s BBC radio series *ITMA*. 'Sam Fairfechan' (Hugh Morton) would say, 'Good morning, how are you today?' and immediately add, 'as if I cared...'. This may be seen as a reflection on Welsh heartlessness.

as it happens verbal cement used notably by the British disc-jockey Jimmy Savile (later Sir James Savile OBE, for his charitable works). Rather like an 'um' or an 'er', it helps to pad out a sentence. Savile was, however, sufficiently aware of this to entitle his autobiography *As It Happens* (1974).

as the bishop said to the actress! (sometimes *vice versa*) a verbal interjection that encourages the finding of a *double entendre* (e.g. 'In *A Midsummer Night's Dream*, I've never seen a female

"Bottom' "/'...as the Bishop said to the actress'). Established by 1935. A pleasant variation was introduced in the BBC radio comedy show *Educating Archie* (1950s). The schoolgirl character, Monica (Beryl Reid), would say **as the art mistress said to the gardener!**

as the girl said to the sailor! like the previous entry, a catchphrase used to create or emphasize a *double entendre*. Probably British use only, twentieth century.

as the man said (or **like the man said**) an emphasizing, additional phrase to lend a kind of authority to what has just been said. An Americanism of the 1950s/60s.

as the saying is a phrase well established by the sixteenth century. A marking-time phrase, often used to excuse the use of a cliché, Boniface, the landlord, in Farquhar's play *The Beaux' Stratagem* (1707) says it all the time. Nowadays, we are probably more inclined to use 'as the saying goes'.

—— **as we know it** a simple – and somewhat redundant – intensifier which has long been with us, however. From *Grove's Dictionary of Music* (1883): 'The Song as we know it in his [Schubert's] hands...such songs were his and his alone.' 'Politics as we know it will never be the same again' – *Private Eye* (4 December 1981). *See also* **end of civilization as we know it.**

as we say in the trade slightly self-conscious (even camp) tag after the speaker has uttered a piece of jargon or something unusually grandiloquent. First noticed in the 1960s and probably of American origin. From the record album *Snagglepuss Tells the Story of the Wizard of Oz* (1966): ' "Once upon a time", as we say in the trade...'.

ask a silly question... with 'get a silly answer' to follow or inferred. One's response to an answer that is less than helpful or amounts to a put-down. Probably since the late nineteenth century.

astonish me! a cultured variant of the more popular **amaze me!** or **surprise me!** inserted into conversation for example when the

15

other speaker has just said something like, 'I don't know whether you will approve of what I've done...' Almost certainly an allusion to the remark made by Sergei Diaghilev, the Russian ballet impresario, to Jean Cocteau, the French writer and designer, in Paris in 1912. Cocteau had complained to Diaghilev that he was not getting enough encouragement and the Russian exhorted him with the words, '*Étonne-moi!* I'll wait for you to astound me' (recorded in Cocteau's *Journals*, published 1956).

au reservoir! A jokey valediction (based on *au revoir*) and popularized by E.F. Benson in his *Lucia* novels of the 1920s. It may have existed before this, possibly dating from a *Punch* joke of the 1890s.

avoid like the plague a well-established cliché by the mid-twentieth century, meaning 'to avoid completely, to shun'. The poet Thomas Moore wrote in 1835, 'Saint Augustine...avoided the school as the plague'. The fourth-century St Jerome is also said to have quipped, 'Avoid as you would the plague, a clergyman who is also a man of business.'

aye, aye, that's yer lot! catchphrase of Jimmy Wheeler (1910–73), the British Cockney comedian. He would appear in a bookmaker's suit, complete with spiv moustache and hat, and play the violin. At the end of his final violin piece, he would break off his act and intone these words. On its own, **(and) that's yer lot!**, meaning 'that's all you are going to receive' probably predates this by a couple of decades.

aye, well – ye ken noo! 'well, you know better now, don't you!' – said after someone has admitted ignorance or has retold an experience which taught them a lesson. The punchline from an old Scottish story about a Presbyterian minister preaching a hellfire sermon whose peroration went something like this: 'And in the last days ye'll look up from the bottomless pit and ye'll cry, "Lord, Lord, we did na ken", and the Guid Lord in his infinite mercy will reply..."Aye, well – ye ken noo!"'

B
b

back to square one! meaning 'back to the beginning', this phrase is sometimes said to have gained currency in the 1930s through its use by British radio football commentators. *Radio Times* used to print a map of the football field divided into numbered squares, to which commentators would refer. Against this proposition is the fact that square 'one' was nowhere near the beginning. The game began at the centre spot, which was at the meeting point of squares 3, 4, 5 and 6. Possibly, therefore, the phrase may have had an earlier origin in the children's game of hopscotch or in the board game Snakes and Ladders.

back to the drawing board! meaning 'we've got to start again from scratch', this is usually said after a plan has been aborted. The phrase may have begun life in the caption to a cartoon by Peter Arno which appeared in the *New Yorker* during the early 1940s. An official, with a rolled-up engineering plan under his arm, is walking away from a recently crashed plane, and saying: 'Well, back to the old drawing board'.

backs to the wall, with our meaning 'up against it', this expression dates back to the 1530s at least, but it was memorably used when the Germans launched their last great offensive of the First World War. In April 1918 Sir Douglas Haig, the British Commander-in-Chief on the Western Front, issued an order for his troops to stand firm: 'With our backs to the wall, and believing in the justice of our cause, each one of us must fight on to the end.'

band played on, the *see* **and the band played on. . .**

bang, bang, you're dead! a child's apt summary of the manner of TV Westerns, probably dating from the 1950s. Compare the slightly later 'kiss, kiss, bang, bang', as an adult summary of the plot of James Bond movies.

bang to rights as in 'you've got me bang to rights!' said by a criminal to an arresting policeman, this is an alternative to **it's a fair cop!** Known in Britain by the 1930s and in the US by the early 1900s. Compare the somewhat rare American noun 'bang' for a criminal charge or arrest, as in **it's a bum bang**, which may have some connection with the banging of a cell door.

bangs like a shithouse door, she she copulates regularly and noisily. Australian, 1930s. A variation is **bangs like a shithouse rat**.

be good – and if you can't be good be careful! a nudging farewell, possibly originating with the American song 'Be Good! If You Can't Be Good, Be Careful!' (1907). It is the same sort of farewell remark as **don't do anything I wouldn't do!** which probably dates from the same period.

be like that! as also **be that way!**, a joshing remark made to someone who has said something or is doing something of which you disapprove. American and British use by the mid-twentieth century.

be my guest! go right ahead; do as you wish. An American expression by the 1950s. *Be My Guest* was the title of a book (1957) by the hotelier Conrad Hilton.

be soon! *see* **she knows, you know!**

beam me up, Scotty! transpose my body into matter, or some such thing – a nice piece of hokum from the US TV science-fiction series *Star Trek* (1966–9). According to enthusiasts for the show, known as Trekkies, Capt. Kirk (William Shatner) never actually said the phrase to Lt. Commander 'Scotty' Scott, the chief engineer on the Starship *Enterprise*. In the fourth episode, however, he may have said, 'Scotty, beam me up!' The more usual form of the injunction was '*Enterprise*, beam us up' or 'Beam us up, Mr Scott'.

This was the series whose spoken introduction proposed **to boldly go where no man has gone before!** The split infinitive endured but in the 1988 feature film that spun off from the TV series, political correctness decreed a change to 'where no *one* has gone before'.

be your age! *see* **act your age!**

beanz meanz Heinz!   a slogan from an advertising jingle for Heinz Baked Beans in the UK (from 1967), it is the type of line that drives teachers into a frenzy because it appears to condone wrong spelling.

beautiful downtown Burbank, this is   intoned by Gary Owens as the announcer on *Rowan and Martin's Laugh-In* (1960s). An ironic compliment to the area of Los Angeles in which the NBC TV studios are situated.

because it's there…   a flippant justification for doing almost anything, this is a phrase chiefly associated with the British mountaineer, George Leigh Mallory (1886–1924). In 1923, during a lecture tour in the US, he had frequently been asked why he wanted to be the first man to climb Mount Everest. He replied, 'Because it is there'. There have been many variations (and misattributions). Sir Edmund Hillary repeated it regarding his own successful attempt on Everest in 1953.

because the higher the fewer   nonsense answer to the nonsense riddle 'why is a mouse when it spins?' Remembered from the 1920s/30s. Other phrases from nonsensical riddles include: 'Q. **How is a man when he's out?**/A. The sooner he does, the much.' 'Q. **What is the difference between a chicken/duck?**/A. One of its legs is both the same.' 'Q. **Which would you rather, or go fishing?**/A. One man rode a horse and the other rhododendron.' 'Q. **Which would you rather be – or a wasp?**'

bee's knees, the   meaning, 'the very best around; absolutely top hole'. From the 1920s, American. At about the same time, there were also the **kipper's knickers**, the **cat's whiskers** and the **cat's pyjamas**.

been there, done that!   a motto known by the 1980s and reproducing the attitude of the tourist who is more interested in ticking off a list of sights seen than in enjoying them. It can refer to any form of human activity, not least experimentation with sex. About 1989 there were T-shirts available for jaded travellers bearing the words: 'Been there, done that, **got the T-shirt.**'

before you can say Jack Robinson   immediately; straightaway. An expression established by the second half of the eighteenth century, though no one is quite sure who Jack Robinson was – if anyone. Fanny Burney has 'I'll do it as soon as say Jack Robinson' in her novel *Evelina* (1778).

behind you!   *see* **oh no, there isn't!**

believe it or not!   an exclamation which may have originated with – and most certainly was popularized by – the long-running American syndicated newspaper feature, and radio and TV series, *Ripley's Believe It or Not* (from 1923). Robert Leroy Ripley (1893–1949) created and illustrated a comic strip dealing in curious and interesting facts.

bells and whistles on, put the   make an elaborate (and sometimes unnecessary) fuss about something. In computing, 'bells and whistles' are additional but not essential features put on hardware and software to make them commercially attractive (and so used by 1984). The origin of the phrase in both senses appears to lie in the bells and whistles fixed to fairground organs.

bells of hell go ting-a-ling-a-ling for you but not for me!, the catchphrase of smug self-satisfaction derived from a song popular during the First World War:

> O, Death where is thy sting-a-ling-a-ling,
> O, grave, thy victoree?
> The Bells of Hell go ting-a-ling-a-ling
> For you but not for me.

Brendan Behan made notable use of this song in his play *The Hostage* (1958). Even before the First World War, though, it was sung – just like this – as a Sunday School chorus. It may have been in a Sankey and Moody hymnal. The basic element is from 1 Corinthians 15:55: 'O death, where is thy sting? O grave, where is thy victory?'

Bernie, the bolt!   standard command to a technician in the British TV quiz show *The Golden Shot*, introduced by Bob Monkhouse in the late 1960s, early 1970s. It was an instruction to load the dangerous crossbows that were used in the game.

best things in life are free, the modern proverb which appears to have originated with the song of the same title (1927) by De Sylva, Brown and Henderson.

better out than in! what the perpetrator of a loud fart might say. Mid-twentieth century.

better Red than dead slogan used by some (mainly British) nuclear disarmers, from the 1950s onwards. Bertrand Russell wrote in 1958: 'If no alternative remains except communist domination or the extinction of the human race, the former alternative is the lesser of two evils.'

between a rock and a hard place in a position impossible to get out of, literally or metaphorically. Popular in the 1970s and almost certainly of North American origin, the phrase has been around since the 1920s. An early appearance occurs in John Buchan, *The Courts of the Morning* (1929) but the phrase was being discussed in *Dialect Notes*, No. 5 (1921) where it was defined as 'to be bankrupt...Common in Arizona in recent panics; sporadic in California'.

Beulah, peel me a grape! catchphrase expressing dismissive unconcern, first uttered by Mae West to a black maid in the film *I'm No Angel* (1933) after a male admirer has stormed out on her. It has had some wider currency since then but is nearly always used as a quotation.

B.F.N. – bye for now! catchphrase of Jimmy Young, the British former singer turned radio presenter in the late 1960s. The phrase **goodbye for now!** was known before this, especially as a way of ending phone conversations. The initialese version may hark back to **T.T.F.N.** ('Ta-ta for now') in the 1940s BBC radio show *ITMA*.

Big Brother is watching you! a fictional slogan from George Orwell's novel *Nineteen Eighty-Four* (1948). In a dictatorial state, every citizen is regimented and observed by a spying TV set in the home. The line became a popular catchphrase following a sensational BBC TV dramatization of the novel in 1954 and was used to warn, amusingly, of the dangers of any all-seeing authority.

big conk, big cock! phrase expressing the age-old superstition that there is a correlation between the size of a man's nose and his penis. Erasmus (1466–1536), of all people, is supposed to have included the aphorism (in Latin) in one of his works.

big deal! a deflating exclamation of American origin. Popular with a number of radio comedians in the 1940s/50s. Leo Rosten in *Hooray for Yiddish!* (1982) emphasizes its similarity with sarcastic, derisive, Jewish phrases and notes how the phrase 'is uttered with emphasis on the "big", in a dry disenchanted tone'.

big 'ead! said of a conceited person, and achieving catchphrase status when spoken by Max Bygraves in the BBC radio show *Educating Archie* (mid-1950s). He ran into trouble with educationists for not pronouncing the 'h' but he persisted and also recorded a song with the refrain 'Why does everybody call me "Big 'ead"?'

big-hearted Arthur (that's me)! catchphrase of the British comedian Arthur Askey and included in the BBC radio show *Band Waggon* (late 1930s). Askey commented in 1979: 'I have always used this expression, even when I was at school. When playing cricket, you know, if the ball was hit to the boundary and nobody would go to fetch it, I would, saying "Big-hearted Arthur, that's me!"'

bigger they come, the harder they fall, the proverbial phrase often attributed to Bob Fitzsimmons (1862–1917), a British-born boxer in the US, referring to an opponent of larger build (James L. Jeffries) by 1900. Also attributed to boxer John L. Sullivan but probably of earlier proverbial origin in any case.

bit missing *see* **few vouchers short...**

black mark, Bentley! reprimand given by Jimmy Edwards to Dick Bentley in the BBC radio show *Take It From Here* (late 1940s onwards). Frank Muir (who co-wrote the scripts with Denis Norden) has noted that the phrase arose from the use of 'black mark' by James Robertson Justice in Peter Ustinov's film of *Vice Versa*.

black over Bill's mother's, it's a bit (also **over Will's mother's way, it's dark/black**) this way of referring to the weather, when rain threatens, was being asked about in 1930, in the journal *Notes & Queries*. The Rev. P.W. Gallup of Winchester wrote in 1994 that he had traced use of the saying to eleven English counties and commented on its age: 'I have friends in their late eighties who as children knew it well from their parents and say that it was then widely known and used. This suggests that the saying has been used at least by several generations.'

bless his/her little cotton socks! a pleasant remark to make about a child, meaning , 'Isn't he/she sweet, such a dear little thing'. As 'bless your little cotton socks', it just means 'thank you'. Mostly English middle-class usage, dating from about 1900.

blind Freddie could see that, even an Australianism for what is blindingly obvious. From the 1930s.

blondes have more fun from the slogan, 'Is it true . . . blondes have more fun?', used to promote the American hair dye Lady Clairol from 1957. The phrase entered the language and had great persuasive effect. The British artist David Hockney once told how he came to bleach his hair in response to seeing the advertisement on TV in New York City. 'Blondes have more fun,' it said. 'You've only one life. Live it as a Blonde!' He immediately jumped up, left the apartment, found an all-night hairdresser and followed the advice of the advertiser.

Bob's your uncle!, (and) a way of saying 'there you are; there you have it; simple as that', but fairly meaningless with it. Current in Britain by the 1880s. Some believe that the origin lies with Arthur Balfour's appointment as Chief Secretary for Ireland by his uncle, *Robert* Arthur Talbot Gascoyne-Cecil, 3rd Marquis of Salisbury, the Prime Minister. That was in 1886.

boom, boom! a verbal underlining to the punchline of a joke. British music-hall star Billy Bennett (1887–1942) may have been the first to use this device to emphasize his comic couplets. It was rather like the drum-thud or trumpet-sting used, particularly by American entertainers, to point a joke. British entertainers Morecambe and Wise, Basil Brush, and many others, took it up later.

boy done well!, the   exclamation of support or congratulation, especially in British sporting contexts, though not exclusively so. It sounds like the kind of thing a boxer's manager might say – 'All right, he got K.O.'d in the first round – but my boy done well. . .'. From the 1980s on.

break a leg!   traditional theatrical greeting given before a performance, especially a first night, and employed because it is considered bad luck in the theatre to wish anyone 'good luck' directly. Another version is **snap a wrist!** Compare the German good luck expression, *Hals und Beinbruch* [May you break your neck and your leg]. Perhaps this entered theatrical speech (like several other expressions) via Yiddish.

bright-eyed and bushy-tailed   awake and alert, like a squirrel. This expression appears to have been used especially in connection with US astronauts in the 1960s. The great popularizing agent must have been B. Merrill's American song with the phrase as title in 1953:

> If the fox in the bush and the squirr'l in the tree be
> Why in the world can't you and me be
> Bright eyed and bushy tailed and sparkelly as we can be?

bring on the dancing girls!   let's move on to something more entertaining. What any host might say to cheer up his guests, but probably originating in a literal suggestion from some bored American impresario as to what was needed to pep up a show in the 1920s.

brute force and ignorance   what is needed to get, say, a recalcitrant machine working again. Sometimes pronounced 'hignorance'; sometimes abbreviated to 'B.F. & I.'. Known by 1930.

buck stops here, the   this is where ultimate responsibility lies. Harry S Truman (US President 1945–53) had a sign on his desk bearing these words, indicating that the Oval Office was where the passing of the buck had to cease. It appears to be a saying of his own invention. 'Passing the buck' is a poker player's expression. It refers to a marker that can be passed on by someone who does not wish to deal.

bully for you! congratulatory phrase, latterly perhaps used a touch resentfully and ironically. 'I've just won the football pools and married the woman of my dreams...' 'Bully for you!' Established by the mid-nineteenth century. A *Punch* cartoon (5 March 1881) drawn by Gerald du Maurier has the caption, 'Bully for little Timpkins!'

bum bang, it's a *see* **bang to rights.**

business as usual! standard declaration posted when a shop has suffered some misfortune like a fire or is undergoing alterations. In the First World War the phrase was adopted as a slogan in a more general sense. In a speech in London on 9 November 1914, Winston Churchill said: 'The maxim of the British people is "Business as usual".' The phrase was used until it was shown to be manifestly untrue and hopelessly inappropriate.

but I'm all right now! catchphrase of 'Sophie Tuckshop' (Hattie Jacques) who was forever eating things and feeling queasy on the BBC radio show *ITMA* (1940s).

but Miss ——, you're beautiful! cliché of the cinema, uttered by the boss when his hitherto bespectacled secretary reveals her natural charms. From the Hollywood of the 1930s/40s.

but that's another story! phrase with which (amusingly) to break off a narrative on the grounds of assumed irrelevance. The popularity of this catchphrase around 1900 derived from Rudyard Kipling's use of it in *Plain Tales from the Hills* (1888), but it had appeared earlier elsewhere. In Laurence Sterne's *Tristram Shandy* (1760), it is intended to prevent one of the many digressions of which that novel is full.

butler did it!, the a suggested solution (often ironic) to a mystery, this expression would seem to derive from detective stories of the 1920s and 30s, though there is no evidence of the phrase actually being used in that context. Oddly, but perhaps relevantly, one of the conventions of whodunnit writing of this period is that the butler or any other servant seldom, if ever, does 'do it'. In 1956, Robert Robinson made an allusion to it in his Oxford thriller *Landscape With Dead Dons*: ' "Well, well," said the Inspector, handing his coffee cup to Dimbleby, who was passing with a tray, "it always turns out to be the butler in the end." '

by gum, she's a hot 'un!   referring to an attractive girl – a phrase used by Frank Randle, the North of England variety star of the 1930s and 40s. It occurred in a sketch in which he played an 82-year-old hiker.

by jingo!   a mild and meaningless oath, this phrase derived its popularity from G.W. Hunt's notable anti-Russian music-hall song 'We Don't Want to Fight (But By Jingo If We Do...)' (1877). The song gave the words 'jingo' and 'jingoism' their modern meaning (excessive patriotism), but the oath had existed long before. Motteux in his translation of Rabelais in 1694 put 'by jingo' for *'par dieu'* and there is some evidence to show that 'jingo' was conjuror's gibberish dating from a decade or two before that.

by Jove, I needed that!   an exclamation, as though after long-awaited alcoholic refreshment, used by several comedians. British comedian Ken Dodd would say it (in the 1960s/70s) after apparently playing a quick burst on the banjo. Also employed in the BBC Radio *Goon Show* (1950s).

C
c

calling all cars! what the police controller says on the radio to patrolmen in American cops and robbers films and TV series of the 1950s, and thus used to evoke the genre and the period. However, the formula had obviously been known before this if the British film titles *Calling All Stars* (1937), *Calling All Ma's* (1937) and *Calling All Cars* (1954) are anything to go by.

came/comes the dawn! a stock phrase from romantic fiction in the early twentieth century – also, probably, a subtitle or intertitle from the early days of cinema. 'Came the Dawn' was the title of a P.G. Wodehouse short story reprinted in *Mulliner Omnibus* (1927). The phrase is also used to mean 'at last you understand', the realization has dawned.

camp as a row of tents extremely affected, outrageous, over the top. A pun on the word 'camp', which came into general use in the 1960s to describe the manner and behaviour of (especially) a type of homosexual male. As it happens, one of the suggested origins for the word 'camp' in this sense is that it derives from 'camp followers', the female prostitutes who would accompany an army on its journeyings to service the troops.

can a bloody duck swim! (sometimes **does/will a fish swim!**) meaning, 'You bet!', 'Of course I will'. British use since 1840s, at least. Lady Violet Bonham-Carter used the phrase to Winston Churchill when he asked her to serve as a Governor of the BBC in 1941. Thereafter he proceeded to refer to her as his 'Bloody Duck' and she had to sign her letters to him, 'Your B.D.'. Compare **is the Pope (a) Catholic?**

can dish it out but can't take it in said of people who are unable to accept the kind of criticism they dispense to others. A reader's letter to *Time* (4 January 1988) remarked of comedienne Joan Rivers's action in suing a magazine for misquoting her about her late husband: 'For years she has made big money at the expense of others with her caustic remarks. Obviously Rivers can dish it out but can't take it in.' The contrast was established by the 1930s.

can do! a sort of Pidgin English way of saying, 'Yes, I can do it', popular in the Royal Navy before the First World War. The negative **no can do** was established by the time of the Second World War.

can I do you now, sir? one of the great radio catchphrases – from the BBC's 1940s comedy hit *ITMA*. It was said by 'Mrs Mopp' (Dorothy Summers), the hoarse-voiced charlady or 'Corporation Cleanser', when entering the office of Tommy Handley, as the Mayor. Curiously, the first time Mrs Mopp used the phrase, on 10 October 1940, she said, 'Can I do *for* you now, sir?' This was soon replaced by the familiar emphases of 'Can I *do* you *now*, sir?' that people could still be heard using thirty years later.

can snakes do push-ups? *see* **is the Pope (a) Catholic?**

can you hear me, mother? catchphrase of the British comedian Sandy Powell (1900–82). As he recalled it, in about 1932/3, he was taking part in a live BBC radio show from Broadcasting House in London and doing his sketch 'Sandy at the North Pole': 'I was supposed to be broadcasting home and wanting to speak to my mother. When I got to the line, "Can you hear me, mother?" I dropped my script on the studio floor. While I was picking up the sheets all I could do was repeat the phrase over and over...I'm not saying it was the first radio catchphrase – they were all trying them out – but it was the first to catch on.'

can't be bad! a response to good news, popular in Britain in the 1970s. 'I've made a date with that well-stacked blonde in the typing pool' – 'Can't be bad!' Possibly derived from the Beatles' song 'She Loves You' (1963): 'Because she loves you/And you know that can't be bad...'.

can't pay, won't pay! a political catchphrase in the UK. In 1990, it was adopted as a slogan by those objecting to the British

Government's Community Charge or 'poll tax' and by other similar protest groups. It was taken from the English title (1981) of Dario Fo's play *Non Si Paga! Non Si Paga!* (1974), as translated by Lino Pertile in 1978.

carry on, ——! originally a military command: 'carry on, sergeant' is what an officer would say, having addressed some homily to the ranks, before walking off and leaving the sergeant to get on with his drill, or whatever. The actual services origin of the phrase is, however, nautical. From the *Daily Chronicle* (24 July 1909): ' "Carry on!" is a word they have in the Navy. It is the "great word" of the service. . .To-morrow the workaday life of the Fleet begins again and the word will be, "Carry on!" '

Hence, at the end of the BBC radio programme *In Town Tonight* (1933–60), a stentorian voice would bellow, **'Carry on, London!'** In 1936, when President F.D. Roosevelt was seeking re-election, a Democratic slogan was **Carry on, Roosevelt!** When Sub-Lieut. Eric Barker (1912–90) starred in the Royal Navy version of the BBC radio show *Merry Go Round* (c 1945), his favourite command to others was, **carry on smokin'!** A cable from the Caribbean was received in Whitehall during the summer of 1940: '**Carry on, Britain!** Barbados is behind you!'

Then, the injunction to 'carry on', was immortalized in the thirty-odd titles of the British film comedies in the *Carry On* series. The very first of these films showed the origin: *Carry On, Sergeant* (1958) was about a sergeant attempting to discipline a platoon of extremely raw recruits.

cat got your tongue?, (has the) question put to a person (usually young) who is not saying anything, presumably through guilt. Since the mid-nineteenth century and a prime example of nanny-speak.

cat's pyjamas/whiskers *see* **bee's knees.**

chalk it up to experience (or **put it down. . .**) what you are advised to do when a mistake has been made which cannot be rectified and a situation has been created which cannot be redeemed. Possibly since the nineteenth century and deriving from the slate in a public house upon which a drinker's credit or debit was displayed.

chance would be a fine thing! self-consolatory (or -deceiving) remark made when people are examining the prospect of enjoying an opportunity that is unlikely to come their way. Certainly in use by the 1900s and probably much older, especially in the sexual sense. Also used as a put-down. A woman might say disapprovingly of a man that she wouldn't sleep with him even if he asked. Another might respond, 'Chance'd be a fine thing!' – that is, 'You can say that, given that you won't ever get the opportunity.'

chase me, Charley/Charlie! provocative phrase spoken by a man and thus with a slight homosexual overtone. As used in 'Chase me, Charlie', the title of a song from Noël Coward's *Ace of Clubs* (1950), the phrase was not original. It had also been the title of a popular song current in 1900. 'Chase me' (on its own) has been the catchphrase of the camp British comedian, Duncan Norvelle, since before 1986.

cheap and cheerful self-deprecatingly compensatory phrase in middle-class British use since the 1950s. Used when showing clothes or furniture or home when these are not of the high standards that one would like. 'Do you like me new flat? It's cheap and cheerful – and it's *home*!'

cheap at half the price, it would be cheap, very reasonable. Not a totally sensible phrase, dating probably from the nineteenth century. Presumably what it means is that the purchase in question would still be cheap and a bargain if it was *double* the price that was being asked. In his *Memoirs* (1991), Kingsley Amis comments on phrases like this which perform semantic somersaults and manage to convey meanings quite the reverse of their literal ones. He cites from a soldier: 'I'd rather sleep with her with no clothes on than you in your best suit.'

cheeky monkey! (and **right, monkey!**) two Lancashire expressions that were made, for a while, very much his own by Al Read (1909–87), the Northern English comedian popular on BBC radio in the 1950s. The first is simply a way of calling someone cheeky – as in 'cheeky little monkey!' The second accuses the person addressed of being mischievous, like a monkey. For example: 'She said, "Did he say anything about the check suit?" and I thought, "Right, monkey!"'

chiefly yourselves! *see* **your own, your very own!**

chips are down, when the at a crucial stage in a situation, alluding to the chips used in betting games. When they are down, the bets are placed but the outcome is still unknown. Hence, a fateful moment when matters are at 'make or break'. American, mid-twentieth century.

chips with everything phrase descriptive of British working-class life and used as the title of a play (1962) by Arnold Wesker about class attitudes in the RAF during National Service. It alludes to the belief that the working classes tend to have chips (fried potatoes) as the accompaniment to almost every dish. Indeed, the play contains the line: 'You breed babies and you eat chips with everything.' Earlier, in an essay published as part of *Declaration* (1957), the film director Lindsay Anderson had written: 'Coming back to Britain is always something of an ordeal. It ought not to be, but it is. And you don't have to be a snob to feel it. It isn't just the food, the sauce bottles on the cafe tables, and the chips with everything. It isn't just saying goodbye to wine, goodbye to sunshine...'.

'Christmas comes but once a year' – thank God! the quotation is from a sixteenth-century rhyme ('and when it comes it brings good cheer') and the sour comment – presumably from someone objecting to the commercialization of the season – was known by the 1940s.

Christmas Day in the workhouse, 'twas comment on an unexpected gesture of generosity from one not known for such things – whether at Christmas or any other time of the year. The line is a quotation from the Victorian ballad or recitation, beginning (more correctly) 'It is Christmas Day in the Workhouse', and written by George R. Sims (1847–1922).

clap hands, here comes Charley! this apparently nonsensical catchphrase was made popular in Britain when Charlie Kunz, a pianist popular on radio in the 1930s/40s, took for his signature tune the song 'Clap hands, here comes Charley...here comes Charley now'. With lyrics by Billy Rose and Ballard MacDonald, and music by Joseph Meyer, this had first been recorded in the US in 1925. According to *The Book of Sex Lists*, the song was written 'in honour of a local chorine, first-named Charline, who had given many of the music publishers' contact men (song pluggers) cases of gonorrhoea – a venereal disease commonly known as "the clap"'.

In the 1940s, 'to do a clap hands Charlie' was RAF slang for flying an aircraft in such a way as to make the wings seem to meet overhead.

cleanliness is next to godliness a nannyish, proverbial phrase which is quoted in a sermon 'On Dress' by John Wesley, the Methodist evangelist (1703–91). It has been suggested that it is to be found in the writings of Phinehas ben Yair, a rabbi. In the 1880s, Thomas J. Barratt, one of the fathers of modern advertising, seized upon it as a slogan to promote Pears' Soap, chiefly in the UK.

clear as mud, it's as i.e. it's not clear at all. Current since the early nineteenth century.

close your eyes and think of England traditional advice given to women when confronted with the inevitability of sexual intercourse, or jocular encouragement to either sex about doing anything unpalatable. The source given for this phrase – Lady Hillingdon's (or Hillingham's) *Journal* (1912) is suspect and has not been verified: 'I am happy now that Charles calls on my bedchamber less frequently than of old. As it is, I now endure but two calls a week and when I hear his steps outside my door I lie down on my bed, close my eyes, open my legs and think of England.' *Salome Dear, Not With a Porcupine* (ed. Arthur Marshall, 1982) has it instead that the newly-wedded Mrs Stanley Baldwin was supposed to have declared subsequently: 'I shut my eyes tight and thought of the Empire.' In 1977, there was play by John Chapman and Anthony Marriott at the Apollo Theatre, London, with the title *Shut Your Eyes and Think of England*.

Sometimes the phrase occurs in the form **lie back and think of**

England but this probably comes from confusion with **she should lie back and enjoy it.**

collapse of stout party! catchphrase that might be used as the tag-line to a story about the humbling of a pompous person. It has long been associated with *Punch* and was thought to have occurred in the wordy captions once given to that magazine's cartoons. But as Ronald Pearsall explains in his book with the title *Collapse of Stout Party* (1975): 'To many people Victorian wit and humour is summed up by *Punch* when every joke is supposed to end with "Collapse of Stout Party", though this phrase tends to be as elusive as "Elementary, my dear Watson" in the Sherlock Holmes sagas.' There is, however, a reference to a 'Stout Party' in the caption to a cartoon in the edition of *Punch* dated 25 August 1855.

come again? 'repeat what you have just said, please!' Usually uttered, not when the speaker has failed to hear the foregoing but cannot believe or understand it. British and American use by the 1930s, at least.

come back/home —— all is forgiven! *see* ——, **where are you now?**

come hell and high water meaning, 'come what may'. Not found before the twentieth century, though it sounds like a venerable phrase. *Come Hell or High Water* was used as the title of a book by the yachtswoman Clare Francis in 1977. She followed it in 1978 with *Come Wind or Weather*. *Hell and High Water* was the title of a US film in 1954.

come in, number ——, your time is up! mimicking the kind of thing the owners of pleasure boats say, this is sometimes applied in other contexts to people who are overstaying their welcome. Mid-twentieth century.

come on down! in the American TV consumer game *The Price is Right* (1957–), the host (Bill Cullen was the first) would appear to summon contestants from the studio audience by saying '[name], come on down!' This procedure was reproduced when the quiz was broadcast on British ITV in 1984–8, with Leslie Crowther uttering the words.

come the revolution...   introductory phrase to some prediction (often ironic) of what life would hold when (usually Communist) revolution swept the world. Second half of the twentieth century. Possibly derived from the joke ascribed to the American vaude-ville comedian, Willis Howard: 'Come the revolution, everyone will eat strawberries and cream' – 'But, Comrade, I don't *like* strawberries and cream' – 'Come the revolution, *everyone* will eat strawberries and cream!'

come up and see me sometime?, why don't you   nudging invita-tion in parody of Mae West (1892–1980) who had a notable stage hit on Broadway with her play *Diamond Lil* (first performed 9 April 1928). When she appeared in the 1933 film version entitled *She Done Him Wrong*, what she said to a very young Cary Grant (playing a coy undercover policeman) was: 'You know I always did like a man in uniform. And that one fits you grand. Why don't you come up some time and see me? I'm home every evening.' As a catchphrase, the words have been re-arranged to make them easier to say. Mae West herself took to saying them in the re-arranged version.

come up and see my etchings   nudging invitation from a man to a woman, as though he were an artist plotting to seduce her. By the 1920s, at least.

come with me to the Casbah!   nudging invitation invariably deliv-ered in a foreign accent (French or Arab) – a line forever associ-ated with the film *Algiers* (1938) and its star, Charles Boyer. He is supposed to have said it to Hedy Lamarr. Boyer impersonators used it, the film was laughed at because of it, but nowhere is it said in the film. It was simply a Hollywood legend that grew up. Boyer himself denied he had ever said it and thought it had been invented by a press agent. In *Daddy, We Hardly Knew You* (1989), Germaine Greer writes of the early 1940s: 'Frightened and revolted the Australians fled for the nearest watering-hole [in the Middle East]. "Kem wiz me to ze Casbah", Daddy used to say, in his Charles Boyer imitation. Poor Daddy. He was too frightened ever to go there.'

comes the dawn   *see* **came the dawn.**

comes with the territory *see* **goes with the territory.**

cometh the hour cometh the man proverbial expression to announce the arrival of the right man at the right moment to accomplish some special task. The origin is not too clear. At the climax of Sir Walter Scott's novel *Guy Mannering* (1815), Meg Merrilies says, 'Because the Hour's come, and the Man'. In 1818, Scott used 'The hour's come, but not [*sic*] the man' as an epigraph in *The Heart of Midlothian*. Harriet Martineau entitled her biography of Toussaint L'Ouverture (1840), *The Hour and the Man*. An American, William Yancey, said about Jefferson Davis, President-elect of the Confederacy in 1861: 'The man and the hour have met', which says the same thing in a different way.

Now, the phrase is regularly used in British sports reporting. From *The Times* (13 August 1991): ' "[Cricketer] Graham [Gooch] is a very special guy", [Ted] Dexter said. "It has been a case of 'Cometh the hour, cometh the man.' I do not know anyone who would have taken the tough times in Australia harder than he did." '

comin' in on a wing and a pray'r *see* **we got back on a wing and a prayer.**

condemned man ate a hearty breakfast, the evocation of a tradition that seems to have been established in Britain and/or the American West that a condemned man could have anything he desired to eat for his last meal. In 1914, a book of short stories about the Royal Navy called *Naval Occasions and Some Traits of the Sailor* by 'Bartimeus' had: 'The Indiarubber Man opposite feigned breathless interest in his actions, and murmured something into his cup about condemned men partaking of hearty breakfasts.' The tone of this suggests that it was, indeed, getting on for a cliché even then. *The Prisoner Ate a Hearty Breakfast* was the title of a novel (1940) written by Jerome Ellison. In the film *Kind Hearts and Coronets* (1949), Louis Mazzini, on the morning of his supposed execution, disavows his intention of eating 'the traditional hearty breakfast'.

coughin' well tonight! the British comedian, George Formby Snr (1877–1921), used to make this tragically true remark about himself. He had a convulsive cough, the result of a tubercular condition, and it eventually killed him. He was ironically known as 'The Wigan Nightingale'.

couldn't knock the skin off a rice pudding!, you an expression of contempt for an incompetent or cowardly person. In use by the time of the First World War. From the *Sunday Express* (24 July 1983): 'There seems to be some dispute as to what Mr Roy Hattersley [British Labour MP] actually said to Mr Michael Foot about the quality of Mr Foot's leadership [of the Labour Party]. No dispute as to how Mr Michael Foot replied. He wagged a finger at Mr Hattersley: "Don't you ever talk like that to me again. I'll have your head off your shoulders, the skin off your back".' According to the *Observer* (31 July 1983), Mr Hattersley then went on to say. 'You could not knock the skin off a rice pudding.'

couldn't run a whelk-stall!, you an expression of contempt for an incompetent or organizationally inept person. It may have originated with John Burns, a British Labour MP: 'From whom am I to take my marching orders? From men who fancy they are Admirable Crichtons...but who have not got sufficient brains and ability to run a whelk-stall?' (reported in the *South-Western Star*, 13 January 1894). The phrases **couldn't organize a piss-up in a brewery** or **couldn't fight his/her way out of a paper bag** are more likely to be employed nowadays.

couple of bales shy of a full trailer load *see* **few vouchers short...**

cowabunga! this cry was re-popularized by the Teenage Mutant Ninja Turtles phenomenon of the early 1990s, but had been around since the 1950s when, in the American cartoon series *The Howdy Doody Show*, it was used as an expression of anger – 'kowa-bunga' or 'Kawabonga' – by Chief Thunderthud. In the 1960s it transferred to *Gidget*, the American TV series about a surfer, as a cry of exhilaration when cresting a wave and was taken into surfing slang. In the 1970s the phrase graduated to TV's *Sesame Street*.

crazy, man, crazy! a phrase of encouragement originally shouted at jazz musicians in the 1940s. Then it took on wider use.

cricket!, it's not   *see* it's not cricket!

cry all the way to the bank, to   meaning, to be in a position to ignore criticism because of your financial position, this expression was certainly popularized, if not actually invented, by the flamboyant pianist, Liberace. In his autobiography (1973), Liberace writes: 'When the reviews are bad I tell my staff that they can join me as I cry all the way to the bank.' (A less pointed version is, 'to *laugh* all the way to the bank'.)

curate's egg, like the   *see* good in parts – like...

customer is always right, the   Gordon Selfridge (*c* 1856–1947) was an American who, after a spell with Marshall Field & Co came to Britain and introduced the idea of the monster department store. It appears that he was the first to say 'the customer is always right' and many other phrases now generally associated with the business of selling through stores. However, the hotelier César Ritz was being credited with the saying, 'the customer is never wrong' by 1908.

cut 'em off at the pass, to   phrase from Western films where the cry would be uttered, meaning 'to intercept, ambush' (sometimes in the form head 'em off at the pass). It resurfaced as one of the milder sayings in the transcripts of the Watergate tapes (published as *The White House Transcripts*, 1974). As used by President Nixon it meant simply 'we will use certain tactics to stop them'. The phrase occurred in a crucial exchange in the White House Oval Office on 21 March 1973 between the President and his Special Counsel, John Dean.

cut the mustard, to   meaning, to succeed, to have the ability to do what's necessary – one might say of someone, 'He didn't cut much mustard'. An American phrase dating from about 1900 when 'mustard' was slang for the 'real thing' or the 'genuine article', and this may have contributed to the coinage. From the Tennessee Williams play *Sweet Bird of Youth* (1959): 'Boss Finley's too old to cut the mustard' [i.e. perform sexually].

D
d

daddy, what did you do in the Great War?   *see* **what did you do in the Great War, Daddy?**

daft as a brush   meaning 'stupid', dates from the 1920s and is, in full, 'daft as a brush without bristles', probably from North of England slang, as is also **soft as a brush**, meaning the same. The comedian Ken Platt commented in 1979: 'I started saying "daft as a brush" when I was doing shows in the Army in the 1940s. People used to write and tell me I'd got it wrong!'

damn(ed) clever these Chinese! (or **dead clever chaps/devils these Chinese!**)   referring to their reputation for wiliness rather than their intellectual skills. A Second World War phrase taken up from time to time by the BBC radio *Goon Show* in the 1950s. Compare the line 'Damn clever, these *Armenians*' uttered by Claudette Colbert in the film *It Happened One Night* (US, 1934).

damn fine cup of coffee – and hot!   the American TV series *Twin Peaks* was first aired in 1990 and introduced a seriously weird FBI Special Agent called Dale Cooper (Kyle Maclachlan). '[He is] one of TV's true originals. His much-loved and oft-repeated catchphrase "Damn fine cup of coffee, and hot!" has indeed caught on and Maclachlan himself parodies it crisply in a TV commercial' (*Radio Times*, 15–21 June 1991).

damn the torpedoes – full speed ahead!   meaning, 'never mind the risks [torpedoes = mines], we'll go ahead any way'. A historical quotation. David Glasgow Farragut, the American admiral, said it on 5 August 1864 at the Battle of Mobile Bay during the Civil War.

day war broke out . . ., the   catchphrase from the Second World War radio monologues of the British comedian Robb Wilton

(1881–1957): 'The day war broke out...my missus said to me, "It's up to you...you've got to stop it." I said, "Stop what?" She said, "The war."' Later, when circumstances changed, the phrase became 'the day *peace* broke out'.

dead – and never called me 'Mother'!   a line recalled as typical of the three-volume sentimental Victorian novel, yet nowhere does it appear in the English writer Mrs Henry Wood's *East Lynne* (1861) where it supposedly occurred. Nevertheless, it was inserted in one of the numerous *stage* versions of the novel (that by T.A. Palmer in 1874) which were made between the publication of the novel and the end of the century. Act III has, 'Dead, dead, dead! and he never knew me, never called me mother!' Mrs Wood's obituary writer noted in 1887: 'At present, there are three dramatic versions of *East Lynne* nightly presented in various parts of the world. Had the author been granted even a small percentage on the returns she would have been a rich woman...The adapters of *East Lynne* grew rich and Mrs Henry Wood was kept out of their calculations.' Thus did *East Lynne* become 'a synonym for bad theatrical melodrama' (Colin Shindler, *The Listener*, 23–30 December 1982). The line occurs in a scene when an errant but penitent mother who has returned to East Lynne, her former home, in the guise of a governess, has to watch the slow death of her eight-year-old son ('Little Willie') unable to reveal her true identity. Whether the line was carried through to any of the various film versions of the tale, I do not know, but expect so.

Sometimes **dead, dead – and she never called me 'Mother'!** (despite the sex of the child in the original).

dead clever chaps/devils these Chinese!   *see* **damn(ed) clever these Chinese!**

dead in the water   completely helpless, lacking support, finished. In other words, one is saying that an opponent or antagonist is like a dead fish. He is still in the water and not swimming anywhere. Suddenly popular in the late 1980s and undoubtedly of North American origin. From the *Guardian* (2 March 1987): 'Mr John Leese, editor of both the *Standard* and the *Evening News*, replied: "This obviously means that Mr Maxwell's [news]paper is dead in the water."'

dead parrot meaning, 'something that is quite incapable of resuscitation', this expression derives from the most famous of all the sketches in the BBC TV comedy show *Monty Python's Flying Circus* (edition of 7 December 1969). A man who has just bought a parrot that turns out to be dead, registers a complaint with the pet shop owner. In 1988, there were signs of the phrase becoming an established idiom. The *Observer* commented (8 May): 'Mr Steel [the Liberal leader]'s future – like his document – was widely regarded as a "dead parrot". Surely this was the end of his 12-year reign as Liberal leader?' In October 1990, Margaret Thatcher belatedly came round to the phrase (fed by a speech-writer, no doubt) and called the Liberal Democrats a 'dead parrot' at the Tory Party Conference.

decisions, decisions! what a harried person might exclaim over having to make some choice, however trivial (perhaps merely deciding which chocolate to take from a box). Well established by the 1980s, though perhaps making its first appearance a good deal earlier.

deficiency in the marbles department *see* **few vouchers short...**

did I ever tell you about the time I was in Sidi Barrani? said by Kenneth Horne to Richard Murdoch in the BBC radio series *Much Binding in the Marsh* (1947–53). It was usually by way of introduction to a boring anecdote and therefore warned the hearer to take avoiding action.

did she fall or was she pushed? the original form of this enquiry is said to date from the 1890s when it had to do with loss of virginity. It supposedly originated in newspaper reports (*c* 1908) of a woman's death on cliffs near Beachy Head. Now applied to men and women, the formula usually raises the question of whether they have departed from jobs of their own volition or whether they were eased out by others. (Hence, the 1970s graffito, 'Humpty Dumpty was pushed...by the CIA'.)

did the earth move for you? a remark addressed to one's partner (usually male to female) after sexual intercourse (now only jokingly). It appears to have originated as 'Did thee feel the earth move?' in Ernest Hemingway's novel *For Whom the Bell Tolls* (1940).

did you spot this week's deliberate mistake? as a way of covering up a mistake that was *not* deliberate, this expression arose from the BBC radio series *Monday Night at Seven* (later *Eight*) in *c* 1938. Ronnie Waldman had taken over as deviser of the 'Puzzle Corner' part of the programme and through an oversight had allowed a mistake to creep into one of the questions. When Broadcasting House was besieged by telephone callers putting him right, the producer concluded that such listener participation was worth exploiting as a regular thing. And so, from then on, there was always a 'deliberate mistake'. 'This week's deliberate mistake' has continued to be used jokingly as a cover for ineptitude.

didn't he do well? as host of BBC TV's *The Generation Game* (from 1971), the British entertainer Bruce Forsyth had to encourage members of participating families in the little games that comprised the show. 'Didn't he do well?' apparently first arose when a contestant recalled almost all the items that had passed before him on a conveyor belt (in a version of Kim's Game). However, it is also said to have originated *c* 1973 with what a studio attendant used to shout down from the lighting grid during rehearsals.

different drummer, (marching to/hearing a) acting in a way expressive of one's own individualism. The concept comes from Henry David Thoreau in *Walden* (1854): 'If a man does not keep pace with his companions, perhaps it is because he hears a different drummer. Let him step to the music which he hears, however measured or far away.' Re-popularized from about 1970.

difficult we do at once – the impossible will take a little longer, the a motto popular in the 1960s/70s and used as such by the US Army Service Forces. The idea has, however, been traced back to Charles Alexandre de Calonne (*d* 1802), who said: '*Madame, si c'est possible, c'est fait; impossible, impossible? cela se fera*' [Madame, if it is possible, it is done; if it is impossible, it will be done]. Henry Kissinger once joked: 'The illegal we do immediately, the unconstitutional takes a little longer' (quoted in William Shawcross, *Sideshow*, 1979).

different strokes for different folks   meaning, 'different people have different requirements, each to his own taste' (a possible sexual connotation here). The proverb is repeated several times in the song 'Everyday People' (1968) sung by Sly and the Family Stone. *Diff'rent Strokes* was the title of a US TV series (from 1978 onwards) about a widowed millionaire who adopts two black boys.

dipstick!   *see* **yer plonker!**

dirt/dust before the broom!   *see* **age before beauty!**

dirty work at the crossroads   meaning 'despicable behaviour; foul play' (in any location), this is mostly American idiom, but not quite a cliché. P.G. Wodehouse had it in the book *Man Upstairs* in 1914 and Walter Melville, a nineteenth-century melodramatist, in *The Girl Who Took the Wrong Turning, or, No Wedding Bells for Him*. One suggestion is that it might have something to do with the old custom of burying suicides at crossroads.

discussing Ugandan affairs (or **talking about Uganda**)   having sexual intercourse. A coinage from the British satirical magazine *Private Eye* (9 March 1973), in which there appeared a gossip item about a former cabinet colleague of President Obote of Uganda. Upstairs at a party, he was said to have been found in a compromising position with a well-known female journalist and this was described as 'talking about Uganda'. The expression caught on – at least among the readers of *Private Eye* – and references to 'Ugandan practices' or 'Ugandan discussions' came to be used in certain circles. It later transpired that the gentleman in question was one-legged.

do chickens have lips?   *see* **is the Pope (a) Catholic?**

do frogs have water-tight ass-holes?   *see* **is the Pope (a) Catholic?**

do not pass go   a phrase from the board game Monopoly, invented by the American Charles Darrow in 1929. It may be taken to mean, 'You won't even get started on doing something'. A *Sunday Mirror* editorial (3 May 1981) stated: 'The laws of contempt are the ones under which editors and other media folk can be sent straight to jail without passing Go.' A businessman said to a woman who had paid for her husband to be beaten up (report of trial, *The Times*, 30 November 1982): 'If the police find out you are paying, you will go to jail, directly to jail, you will not pass "go" or collect £200.'

do that (small) thing!   how nice of you to offer to do that! or please go ahead! or thanks, yes! Current in the UK 1950s/60s.

do the right thing   do the appropriate thing/what has to be done. American usage, particularly in the 1980s. *Do the Right Thing* was the title of a film (US, 1989) about blacks in a Brooklyn slum. The British equivalent would be **do the decent thing** (known by 1914), although 'do the right thing' seems almost as well established (known by the 1880s).

do you come here often? – only in the mating season   response in the BBC radio *Goon Show* (1950s) to the traditional chatting up line, 'Do you come here often?' – common by the 1920s/30s.

do you know ——?/no, but if you hum it...   comic exchange, current in the US and the UK by the 1960s. From BBC radio *Round The Horne* (29 May 1966): 'Do you know Limehouse?'/'No, but if you hum a few bars, I'll soon pick it up.'

do you mind?   catchphrase spoken by Kenneth Connor as 'Sidney Mincing' in the BBC radio show *Ray's a Laugh* somewhere in the years 1949–60. Appearing in a different situation each week, Mincing was usually some sort of unhelpful, downbeat shop assistant and was introduced, for example, thus, by Ray in a furniture store: 'It looks like a contemptuous lamp-standard with a weird-looking shade.' Mincing: '*Do you mind!* My name is Sidney Mincing and I happen to be the proprietor of this dish pans, frying pans and Peter Pans (as it's all on the Never-Never) emporium. What can I do for you?'

do you see who I see?   *see* **look who it isn't!**

do your own thing   a 1960s expression meaning, 'establish your own identity'/'follow your own star', which is said to have been anticipated by Ralph Waldo Emerson (1803–82), the American poet and essayist. The passage from his 'Essay on Self Reliance' actually states: 'If you maintain a dead church, contribute to a dead Bible-society, vote with a great party either for the government or against it ... under all these screens, I have difficulty to detect the precise man you are ... But do your [. . .] thing, and I shall know you.'

Doctor Livingstone, I presume? catchphrase used on meeting someone unexpectedly for the first time or perhaps with some attendant difficulty. Originally, the greeting was given by Sir Henry Morton Stanley, the British explorer and journalist (1841–1904) to the explorer and missionary Dr David Livingstone at Ujiji, Lake Tanganyika, on 10 November 1871. Stanley had been sent by the *New York Herald* to look for Livingstone who was missing on a journey in central Africa. In *How I Found Livingstone* (1872), Stanley described the moment: 'I would have run to him, only I was a coward in the presence of such a mob – would have embraced him, only, he being an Englishman, I did not know how he would receive me; so I did what cowardice and false pride suggested was the best thing – walked deliberately to him, took off my hat and said: "Dr Livingstone, I presume?" "YES", said he, with a kind smile, lifting his cap slightly.'

One unhelpful suggestion is that Stanley was making a tongue-in-cheek reference to a moment in Sheridan's *School for Scandal* (1777) in which, after much mutual confusion, two of the main characters finally get to meet with the line, 'Mr Stanley, I presume.' But, really, it was not such a remarkable salutation after all. In the American Civil War, General Robert E. Lee, when he entered Maryland at Williamsport on 25 June 1863, was greeted by the spokesman of a women's committee of welcome with the words, 'This is General Lee, I presume?'

In the 1960s, when Robert F. Kennedy was campaigning south of Atlanta, in the US, he said to one of the rare white men he met: 'Dr Livingstone, I presume.'

dodgy! rather as the British upper classes tend to rely almost exclusively on two adjectives – 'fascinating' and 'boring' – so, too, did the comedian Norman Vaughan in the 1960s. Accompanied by an upward gesture of the thumb, his **swinging!** was the equivalent of upper-class 'fascinating' and his 'dodgy!' (with a downward gesture of the thumb), the equivalent of their 'boring'. Vaughan said in 1979: 'The words "swinging" and "dodgy" came originally from my association with jazz musicians and just seemed to creep into everyday conversation. Then when I got the big break [introducing ITV's *Sunday Night at the London Palladium* in 1962] they were the first catchphrases that the papers and then the public seized upon.'

does a bear shit in the woods?   *see* **is the Pope (a) Catholic?**

does a dog have fleas?   *see* **is the Pope (a) Catholic?**

does/will a fish swim?   *see* **can a bloody duck swim?**

does a wooden horse have a hickory dick?   *see* **is the Pope (a) Catholic?**

does he dance at the other end of the ball-room?   *see* **is she a friend of Dorothy?**

does Muhammad Ali own a mirror?   *see* **is the Pope (a) Catholic?**

does she or doesn't she?   a slogan for Clairol hair-colouring in the US, from 1955 – i.e. does she dye her hair or doesn't she? Initially, the possible double meaning meant that some publications refused to carry the advertisement. But subsequent research at *Life* Magazine failed to turn up a single female staff member who admitted detecting any innuendo and the phrases were locked into the form they kept for the next eighteen years. 'J' did find a double meaning, as shown by this comment from *The Sensuous Woman* (1969): 'Our world has changed. It's no longer a question of "Does she or doesn't she?" We all know she wants to, is about to, or does.'

The accompanying line (in answer) **only her hairdresser knows for sure** also caught on. A New York graffito, quoted in 1974, stated: 'Only *his* hairdresser knows for sure.'

does your mother know you're out?   *see* **mother know you're out?, does your.**

doesn't it make you want to spit?   catchphrase used by the British comedian Arthur Askey in the BBC radio comedy show *Band Waggon* (from 1938). Askey was rapped over the knuckles for introducing this 'unpleasant expression'. In 1979, he recalled: '[Sir John] Reith [the BBC Director-General] thought it a bit vulgar but I was in the driving seat. The show was so popular, he couldn't fire me. I suppose I said it all the more!'

doesn't know his ass from a hole in the ground   one of numerous 'doesn't know' phrases designed to describe another person's ignorance or stupidity. Mostly American, dating perhaps from the early 1900s and mostly featuring the word arse/ass.

doesn't time fly when you're having fun?   an expression, now mostly used ironically, when work is hard or boredom is rife. Since the 1880s, at least. Of course, 'Doesn't time fly?', on its own, is a version of the ancient *tempus fugit* [time flies].

dog follows its master!/dogs follow their master!   *see* **age before beauty!**

don't be filthy!   don't use bad language or make obscene suggestions – but usually applied following a *double entendre* or something quite innocent. Used by Arthur Askey in the BBC radio show *Band Waggon* (from 1938).

don't call/ring us, we'll call you   what theatre producers and directors are supposed to say to actors at auditions, the implication being that 'we' will never actually get round to calling 'you'. Now more widely applied to anyone unwelcome seen to be asking a favour. A *Punch* cartoon on 11 October 1961 showed the European Council of Ministers saying to a British diplomat: 'Thank you. Don't call us: we'll call you.' Also used in this situation: **we'll let you know.**

don't come the raw prawn (with me)!   don't try to put one over on me, delude or deceive me – the archetypal Australianism, dating from around the time of the Second World War. A raw prawn is presumably held to be less palatable than a cooked one, but lurking in the background is the abusive Australian use of 'you prawn!' to signify that someone is sexless.

don't do anything I wouldn't do! a farewell piece of advice to someone who is perhaps about to have a meeting with a friend where a sexual liaison is not out of the question. Jocular but fairly meaningless, by the early 1900s.

don't fire until you see the whites of their eyes a suggestion that you should not use up your ammunition (metaphorically speaking) before it can be effective. Or, wait until you are right up close to a problem before you begin to deal with it. In origin, a historical quotation: at the Battle of Bunker Hill (17 June 1775) in the American War of Independence, the instruction given by either US General Israel Pitman or, more likely, Colonel William Prescott, was: 'Men, you are all marksmen – don't one of you fire until you see the whites of their eyes.' However, Frederick the Great had earlier said something very similar at Prague on 6 May 1757.

don't force it, Phoebe! catchphrase of British comedian Charlie Chester in the BBC radio show *Stand Easy* (1946–50). Another triumph of alliteration.

don't forget the diver! catchphrase from the BBC radio comedy show *ITMA* (1940s), spoken by Horace Percival as 'the Diver'. This was derived from memories that the star of the show, Tommy Handley, had of an actual man who used to dive off the pier at New Brighton in the 1920s/30s. 'Don't forget the diver, sir, don't forget the diver', the man would say, collecting money. 'Every penny makes the water warmer, sir.'

The radio character first appeared in 1940 and no lift/elevator went down for the next few years without somebody using the Diver's main catchphrase or his other one, **I'm going down now, sir!** – which bomber pilots in the Second World War would use when about to make a descent.

don't forget the fruit gums, mum! an advertising slogan for Rowntree's fruit gums, promoted heavily on TV in the UK, late 1950s. It was based on research that showed most fruit gums were bought by women but eaten by children. However, later 'mum' was changed to 'chum', to save parents from nagging.

don't get mad, get even! one of several axioms said to come from the Boston-Irish political jungle or, more precisely, from Joseph P. Kennedy (1888–1969), father of President Kennedy. *Don't Get Mad Get Even* is the title of a book (1983) – 'a manual for retaliation' – by Alan Abel.

don't get your knickers in a twist! don't make a drama out of a crisis, don't get excited or you'll make the problem worse. British use, mid-twentieth century.

don't go down the mine, Daddy! phrase used when warning anyone against doing anything. Winston Churchill was visiting Berlin in 1945 and preparing to enter Hitler's bunker, when his daughter Mary said to him, 'Don't go down the mine, Daddy.' It comes from a tear-jerking ballad popular with soldiers during the First World War and written by Will Geddes and Robert Donnelly in 1910. The correct title is, 'Don't Go Down *In* the Mine, *Dad*.'

don't hold your breath! don't expect results too soon – perhaps related to the child's threat 'I'll hold my breath until you. . .' Not noted before the 1970s. 'I think the recession's over, you know' – 'I'm not holding my breath.'

don't just stand there: do something! an amusing exhortation dating from the 1940s. Now sometimes reversed: 'don't do anything – just stand there!'

don't panic! a usually ineffectual exhortation. In the BBC TV comedy series *Dad's Army* (1968–77), the elderly Lance-Corporal Jones (Clive Dunn) would shout it at the Home Guard platoon. These are also the words written on the cover of the eponymous fictional guide featured in *The Hitch Hiker's Guide to the Galaxy*, the BBC radio series (1978) and book by Douglas Adams.

don't shoot the pianist! Oscar Wilde reported having seen the notice 'Please do not shoot the pianist. He is doing his best' in a bar or dancing saloon in the Rocky Mountains ('Leadville' from *Impressions of America*, *c* 1882–3). Hence, the film *Tirez Sur Le Pianiste* (France, 1960), translated as 'Shoot the Pianist/Piano-Player' and Elton John's 1972 record album, *Don't Shoot Me, I'm Only the Piano-Player*.

don't some mothers have 'em?   an old Lancashire – and possibly general North Country – saying, used to describe the stupidity of the person indicated. The British comedian Jimmy Clitheroe (1916–73) was a person of restricted growth and with a high-pitched voice who played the part of a naughty schoolboy especially on the BBC radio comedy programme *The Clitheroe Kid* which ran from 1957 to 1972. In the form, 'Some mothers do 'ave 'em', the phrase was used in the very first edition of TV's *Coronation Street* in 1960 and later as the title of a Michael Crawford series on BBC TV (1974–9).

don't worry, be happy   Bobby McFerrin's song with this title became George Bush's unofficial campaign theme in the presidential election of 1988 and won the Grammy award for the year's best song. *The Times* (8 March 1989) noted: 'The song has spawned a whole "happy" industry and re-launched the Smiley face emblem that emerged in America in the late 1960s and was taken up in Britain by the acid-house scene last year. Bloomingdales, the Manhattan department store, now features a "Don't worry, be happy shop".'

'Be happy, don't worry' was earlier a saying of Meher Baba (1894–1969), the so-called Indian God-Man.

don't you just love being in control?   originally a slogan from TV advertising for British Gas from 1991, this soon acquired catchphrase status in the UK, not least because of its scope for sexual innuendo. From the *Daily Telegraph* (5 April 1993): 'Most annoying of all is the circle of fire [in a National Theatre production of *Macbeth*], like a giant gas ring, which whooshes into jets of flame at certain key moments. It is ludicrously obtrusive and sometimes it doesn't seem to be working properly, adding to the viewer's sense of fretful alienation. As Alan Howard stands in the middle of it, looking haggard, you suddenly wonder if the whole dire production is actually an advertisement for British Gas. Will he suddenly flick his thumb and say "Don't you just love being in control?"'

Originally, the control element came from the selling point that a gas appliance responds more quickly to its operator's demands than does an electrical one.

don't you know there's a war on? a response to complaints used by (Will) Hatton and (Ethel) Manners portraying a Cockney chappie and a Lancashire lass in their British variety act of the 1940s. Fairly widely taken up, ironically *after* the Second World War, somehow or other the phrase found its way into the script of the US film *It's A Wonderful Life* (1946), where it is exclaimed by James Stewart. The similar 'Remember there's a war on' dates from the First World War.

doomed I am, doomed! catchphrase uttered by Spasm the butler (played by Kenneth Williams) in the BBC radio comedy series *Round the Horne* (1965–9). Or **we be doomed, we all be doomed!**

down in the forest something stirred gently mocking suggestion merely that something has happened (perhaps after prolonged inactivity) – and not without possible innuendo. The line comes from the song 'Down in the Forest' (1915) with words by H. Simpson and music by Sir Landon Ronald. And what was it that stirred? 'It was only the note of a bird.'

down memory lane once a pleasant phrase, now a journalistic cliché. It seems to have developed from 'Memory Lane', the title of a popular waltz (1924) written by Buddy De Sylva, Larry Spier, and Con Conrad – not to be confused with 'Down Forget-Me-Not Lane' by Horatio Nicholls, Charlie Chester and Reg Morgan (1941). *Down Memory Lane* was the title of a compilation of Mack Sennett comedy shorts (US, 1949). The *Oxford English Dictionary* (2nd edition) gives 'Down Memory Lane' as a 'title by Dannet and Rachel' (1954).

down the hatch! Drinker's phrase before pouring the liquid down the mouth. Possibly ex-Navy. Recorded by 1931.

dream on, baby, dream on meaning, 'if you really believe that, then carry on kidding yourself'. From the *Independent on Sunday* (24 November 1991), here is the Country and Western singer Tammy Wynette talking about an embarrassing encounter with an ex-husband who came up and asked her to autograph a photo for him: 'I thought, "Now what do I say here?" and then it hit me like a light and I wrote – "Dream on, baby, dream on!"'. . .Sweet revenge at last.' Could this have a black American blues origin, if not in fact a Country and Western one?

dreaming oh my darling love. . .   *see* **I'm dreaming. . .**

drop dead!, (why don't you)   said by (mostly) young persons in almost any situation to someone with whom they are in disagreement. American, 1930s. Leo Rosten in *Hooray for Yiddish* (1982) draws attention to the Yiddish equivalent *Ver derharget!*, meaning 'get yourself killed'. As he also suggests, this is a vigorous version of 'Fuck you!' and the more useful because its component words are perfectly respectable. He points to the enormously effective use of the phrase as the Act Two curtain line of Garson Kanin's play *Born Yesterday* (1946). Judy Holliday said 'Du-rop du-ead!' – and 'the slow, sweet, studied rendition was stupendous. Waspish ladies have been tossing "Drop dead!" into their phones (to obscene callers) and as retorts (to abusive cabbies) ever since.'

drop the gun, Louis!   a line used by Humphrey Bogart impersonators – but what he actually says to Claude Rains playing 'Captain Louis Renault' in *Casablanca* (1942) is: 'Not so fast, Louis!'

E
e

easy as juggling with soot, as *see* **as busy as a...**

easy as pie! *see* **piece of cake.**

eat my shorts! became a threatening imperative when used by Bart Simpson in *The Simpsons*, the American TV cartoon series (from 1990), having previously been popular in the 1980s with US high school and college kids. (Shorts = underpants.)

eat your heart out! as something said to another person, and meaning 'doesn't that make you jealous?', this expression acquired popularity in the mid-twentieth century largely through American show-business use. Originally, 'to eat one's (own) heart out', simply meaning 'to pine', was current in English by the sixteenth century.

ee bah gum! a mild Lancastrian/North of England oath – though probably more often attributed mockingly by outsiders – and based on the older 'by gum' (which is possibly a contraction of 'by God Almighty' and was known by 1806). The Yorkshire comedian Dick Henderson used it in a monologue about first meeting his wife (probably 1920s): 'Apart from that she has one very good point – ee, by gum, she can cook.'

elementary, my dear Watson! the answer is obvious to anyone of the smallest intelligence. The Sherlock Holmes phrase appears nowhere in the writings of Sir Arthur Conan Doyle (1859–1930), though the great detective does exclaim 'Elementary' to Dr Watson in *The Memoirs of Sherlock Holmes* ('The Crooked Man') (1894) and 'Ho! (*Sneer.*) Elementary! The child's play of deduction!' in the play *Sherlock Holmes* written with William Gillette in 1901 (1922 revision).

In the 1929 film *The Return of Sherlock Holmes* – the first with sound – the final lines of dialogue are: *Watson:* 'Amazing, Holmes!' *Holmes:* 'Elementary, my dear Watson, elementary.'

eleven pence half-penny *see* **few vouchers short…**

end of civilization as we know it, the an alleged Hollywood cliché – the kind of thing said when people are under threat from invaders from Mars, or wherever: 'This could mean the end of civilization as we know it…'. It is uttered when dismissing the threat of a war 'which could mean the end…' by Orson Welles in *Citizen Kane* (1941).

engage brain before speaking! admonition, current in the UK by 1980.

English as she is spoke catchphrase capturing how the language might be spoken by foreigners or the illiterate. Its origin lies in an English edition of a book of selections (1883) from the notorious French-Portuguese phrasebook *O Novo Guia da Conversação em frances e portuguez* by José da Fonseca, which had been published in Paris in 1836. The original text was in parallel columns; then, in 1865, a third column, carrying English translations, was added by one Pedro Carolino. Field and Tuer's English book *English As She Is Spoke* took its title from a phrase in the chapter on 'Familiar Dialogues'. In 1883, Mark Twain also introduced an edition of the complete work in the US.

enough of this ——, let's ——! format catchphrase used particularly regarding sex. 'Enough of this bourgeois love-making, let's fuck!' is said to be the punchline of a joke about a female Russian soldier in the Second World War who makes an innocuous remark to a male Russian soldier. A milder version from the 1980s: '**Enough with the small talk, off with the clothes!**'

enough said! agreement has been reached, let us not prolong discussion of these matters. Also in the form abbreviation **nuff said!** (or 'nuff ced' or 'N.C.' or 'N.S.' – especially in the US where these variations date from the 1840s).

even your best friends won't tell you a line which originated in the famous Listerine mouthwash advertisement headed **often a**

bridesmaid but never a bride (US, 1920s), warning of the likely effect of halitosis on your social life. In fact, the line in the Listerine copy was 'and even your closest friends won't tell you'.

evenin' all! accompanied by a shaky salute to the helmet, PC George Dixon (Jack Warner) would bid viewers welcome with this phrase through several decades of *Dixon of Dock Green* on BBC TV (1955–76). There seems to be an assumption that all British policemen used to talk like this. BBC radio's *PC 49* used to say 'Good morning all!' and probably 'evening all!', too.

every day and in every way I am getting better and better (and variants) a self-improvement slogan devised by the French psychologist Emile Coué, originator of a system of 'Self-Mastery Through Conscious Auto-Suggestion' which had a brief vogue in the 1920s. His patients had to repeat the phrase over and over and it became a popular catchphrase of the time, though physical improvement did not necessarily follow. The French original was: '*Tous les jours, à tous les points de vue, je vais de mieux en mieux*'. Couéism died with its inventor in 1926, though there have been attempted revivals. John Lennon alludes to the slogan in his song 'Beautiful Boy' (1980).

every home should have one! an all-purpose advertising slogan, probably from the US in the 1920s/30s. Used as the title of a British film about an advertising man in 1970. Against the American origin, one might mention that *Punch* (18 October 1905) had a cartoon in which the caption contained the interesting variation: 'The Portable Gramophone...no country house should be without it.'

every little helps as the old lady said when she pissed into the sea a pretty common saying of the 'Wellerism' type. British use, since the 1910s/20s?, often when contributing a small sum of money to some fund or charity. It is probably derived from the seventeenth-century proverbial '...as the wren said when she pissed in the sea'.

everybody out! the traditional cry of the strike-happy trade union official, raised to catchphrase status by the BBC TV series *The Rag*

Trade (1961–5). Miriam Karlin in her best flame-thrower voice as Paddy, the Cockney shop steward, would shout the phrase at every opportunity.

everything in the garden's lovely   all is well, no cause for complaint. In this proverbial sense, the saying comes from the title of a song made popular by Marie Lloyd (*d* 1922). *Everything in the Garden* was the title of a stage play (1962) by Giles Cooper, about suburban housewives turning to prostitution.

everything you always wanted to know about —— but were afraid to ask   a format phrase catchphrase inspired by the title *Everything You Always Wanted To Know About Sex But Were Afraid to Ask*, a book (published in 1970) by David Reuben MD. The use was popularized even further when Woody Allen entitled a film *Everything You Always Wanted To Know About Sex, But Were Afraid To Ask* (US, 1972) – though, in fact, he simply bought the title of the book and none of its contents. Almost any subject you can think of has been inserted into the sentence. Just some of the book titles there have been: *Everything That Linguists Have Always Wanted to Know About Logic But Were Ashamed To Ask*; *Everything You Always Wanted to Know About Drinking Problems And Then a Few Things You Didn't Want to Know*; *Everything You Always Wanted to Know About Elementary Statistics But Were Afraid to Ask*; *Everything You Always Wanted to Know About Mergers, Acquisitions and Divestitures But Didn't Know Whom to Ask*; *Everything You Wanted to Know About Stars But Didn't Know Where to Ask*; *Everything You Wanted to Know About the Catholic Church But Were Too Pious to Ask*; *Everything You Wanted to Know About the Catholic Church But Were Too Weak to Ask. . .*

everything's coming up roses   all is well, prospects are good, everything's blooming. This is the title of a song with words by Stephen Sondheim in the musical *Gypsy* (1959). But did the expression exist before this? It is possibly adapted from the expression, 'to come out of something smelling of roses', but there do not even seem to be any examples of *that* in use before the date of the Sondheim song.

excuse my French!   *see* **pardon my French!**

exit stage left!   a catchphrase of the cartoon lion called Snaggle-puss, created by the Hannah-Barbera studios in the 1960s – a self-imposed stage direction.

exterminate, exterminate!   deadly, mobile machines looking like pepperpots and called Daleks barked out this chilling phrase in the science fiction TV series *Dr Who* (BBC TV from 1964). It caught on hugely with children.

F
f

fair crack of the whip, a a fair chance, an equal opportunity to do something. Known by the 1920s. The origin is obvious: in the days of horse-drawn transport, whoever had the whip was also holding the reins and was therefore in charge of the vehicle's going forward.

fairies, off/away with the in a dazed state of mind. Known in Australia and Britain by the 1980s.

fame at last! ironic exclamation on finding one's name in print – especially in an unflattering context, say in a list of chores. From the 1940s.

family hold back! (also **F.H.B.**) social instruction, chiefly middle-class, for the family to moderate its food and drink intake lest there not be enough to go round for any guests at a meal. Since the mid-twentieth century?

famous last words! response given to someone who has just made a rash statement of the type: 'I always think I drive better when I've got a few drinks inside me.' From the 1930s.

faster than a speeding bullet! one of the attributes of the cartoon hero *Superman* as famously described in the introduction to the 1940s American radio adaptation: '*The Adventures of Superman!* Faster than a speeding bullet! More powerful than a locomotive! Able to leap tall buildings at a single bound! Look! Up in the sky!...'

fat lady sings *see* **opera ain't over...**

fate worse than death, a now used jokingly of any situation one might wish to avoid, this has latterly and most usually described

57

an unwanted pregnancy. It originally referred to rape or the loss of virginity. In John Cleland's *Memoirs of a Woman of Pleasure* (1748–9), Fanny Hill talks of a 'dread of worse than death'.

feeding time at the zoo, (it's just like) a meal or any event where there is no discipline, especially when involving young children. Since the 1950s/60s?

fell off the back of a lorry, it the traditional response of a man suspected of stealing something and who is challenged to say where he obtained it. British use since the 1950s? Now also used as an example of a weak excuse about anything.

few vouchers short of a pop-up toaster, a one of numerous phrases used to describe mental shortcomings, or **a deficiency in the marbles department** of someone who is **not all there** and has either **a screw loose** or **a bit missing**. Mostly mid-twentieth century and of chiefly American origin. Just a few others: **Not quite enough coupons for the coffee percolator and matching set of cups; eleven pence half-penny** [i.e. not the full twelve pence of a shilling]; **not the full shilling; tuppence short of a shilling; ninepence to the shilling; one apple short of a full load; one grape short of a bunch; rowing with one oar in the water; not playing with a full deck; one brick/a few bricks short of a (full) load; a couple of bales shy of a full trailer load; two sticks short of a bundle; one pork pie/two sandwiches short of a picnic; one card short of a full deck; got off two stops short of Cincinnati; the stairs do not reach all the way to the attic; the lift/elevator doesn't go to the top floor/all the way up; and the light's on, but no one's in.**

fifty million Frenchmen can't be wrong as a slightly grudging expression this appears to have originated with American servicemen during the First World War, justifying support for their French allies. The precise number of millions was variable. On the other hand, the phrase has been understood to extol the 'supreme virtue of copulation'. There was later a song with the title (by Rose, Raskin and Fisher), recorded by Sophie Tucker in 1927. Cole Porter's musical *Fifty Million Frenchmen* opened in New York on 27 November 1929. An unrelated US film with this three-word title was released in 1931.

The American nightclub hostess Texas Guinan said, contrariwise, 'It goes to show that fifty million Frenchmen *can* be wrong' when she and her showgirls were refused entry to France in 1931. Bernard Shaw also held out against the phrase. He insisted: 'Fifty million Frenchmen can't be right.'

fight his way out of a paper bag *see* **couldn't run a whelk-stall.**

fine/lovely/nice weather for ducks! what you say when it is raining. 'Fine ——' may be the predominant form of what is probably a very old construction. G.L. Apperson in his *English Proverbs and Proverbial Phrases* (1929) finds 'another fine week for the ducks' in Charles Dickens, *The Old Curiosity Shop* (1840). 'Lovely ——' and 'nice ——' may be a good deal more recent.

finger of suspicion points at you!, the a humorous way of making an accusation. The notion of a 'finger of suspicion' in more serious vein probably dates back to crime writing in the nineteenth century. The British singer Dickie Valentine recorded a song 'Finger of Suspicion' in 1954, referring to matters amatory.

fings ain't wot they used t'be *see* **things ain't what they used to be.**

first catch your hare a proverb similar to 'Catch your bear before you sell its skin', 'Never spend your money before you have it' and 'Don't count your chickens before they are hatched'. That is, you should not begin to do something until you have acquired a certain necessary element (which may be difficult to acquire). This idea has been expressed in proverbial form since the fourteenth century. For a long time, the saying was taken to be a piece of practical, blunt good sense to be found in Mrs Beeton's *Book of Household Management* (1851), but it does not in fact appear there. However, in Mrs Hannah Glasse's earlier *The Art of Cookery made plain and easy* (1747), there is the similar: 'Take your hare when it is cased [skinned].' It was known in the familar form by 1855 when it appeared in Thackeray's *The Rose and the Ring*.

first —— years are the hardest, the mock encouragement/discouragement when talking about marriage or a job, and suggesting, in an ironical way, that the initial stages of anything are the most difficult. It probably derives from the army saying, 'Cheer up – the first seven years are the worst!' from around the First World War, referring to the term of a regular soldier's service.

flavour of the month   originally a generic advertising phrase aimed at persuading people to try new varieties of ice cream and not just stick to their customary choice (in the US, by the 1940s). Latterly, it has become an idiom for any fad, craze or person that is quickly discarded after a period of being in the news or in demand.

Fleet's lit up!, the   drunk's remark, taken from the most famous British broadcasting gaffe. Lt. Commander Tommy Woodrooffe (1899–1978), a leading BBC radio commentator of the 1930s, was due to give a fifteen-minute description of the 'illumination' of the Fleet after the Coronation Naval Review at Spithead in 1937. What he said, in a commentary that was faded out after less than four minutes, began: 'At the present moment, the whole Fleet's lit up. When I say "lit up", I mean lit up by fairy lamps...'. Many listeners concluded that Woodrooffe himself had been 'lit up' as the result of enjoying too much hospitality but he denied this, saying he had had a kind of blackout. The phrase was used as the title of a 'musical frolic' at the London Hippodrome in 1938 and Bud Flanagan recorded a song written by Vivian Ellis called 'The Fleet's Lit Up'. The use of 'lit up' to mean 'tipsy' dates back to the 1910s, at least.

flippin' kids!   catchphrase of the British comedian Tony Hancock when appearing on BBC radio's *Educating Archie* (early 1950s). For a while, he was billed as 'Tony (Flippin' Kids) Hancock' before moving on to his own shows which more or less eschewed the use of catchphrases.

follow that cab/van/taxi!   a cliché of the cinema, spoken to a taxi driver by the hero/policeman in pursuit of a villain. Few people can ever have said it in real life. In *Let's Dance* (US, 1950), Fred Astaire says 'follow that cab' in order to chase Betty Hutton.

for my next trick...!, (and)   catchphrase 'excuse' for any minor mishap, derived from the patter of stage magicians. By the 1950s, if not long before.

for the man who has everything   slogan for promoting some odd luxury gift item, inessential and over-priced. A salesman at the eponymous jewellery store in *Breakfast at Tiffany's* (film US, 1961) produces something, 'For the lady and gentleman who has everything'. From America in the 1920s/30s?

for this relief, much thanks!   after lavatorial relief. A quotation from Shakespeare's *Hamlet*. Spoken at the very beginning of the play (I.i.8) by Francisco, a sentinel on guard duty, to Bernardo who comes to relieve him; 'relief' is used here in the sense of relieving another person of guard duty.

for you, Tommy, the war is over!   said by an enemy capturing a British soldier ('Tommy Atkins' being the traditional nickname for such), presumably in fiction. Apparently a catchphrase in the Second World War, spoken by either German or Italian captors, and with or without the 'Tommy'.

frankly, my dear, I don't give a damn!   all-purpose dismissal phrase. A quotation from the last scene of the film *Gone With the Wind* (1939) in which Scarlett O'Hara is finally abandoned by her husband Rhett Butler. Rhett replies with these words to her entreaty: 'Where shall I go? What shall I do?' The words were only allowed on to the soundtrack after months of negotiation with the Hays Office which controlled film censorship. In those days, the word 'damn' was forbidden, even if it was what Margaret Mitchell had written in her novel (though she had not included the 'frankly'). Accordingly, Clark Gable, as Rhett, had to put the emphasis unnaturally on 'give' rather than on 'damn'.

free, gratis and for nothing   curiously repetitive phrase emphasizing that something is free. 'Free, gratis' was known by the 1680s and the longer version occurs in Charles Dickens, *The Pickwick Papers* (1836–7) where Sam Weller's father says 'free gratis for nothin''.

free, white and twenty-one   phrase indicating that one has reached the age of consent and is in charge of one's own life, especially sex life. Known in the US and UK, an early example occurs in John Buchan, *The Courts of the Morning* (1929). A minor American gangster states that someone is 'free, white, twenty-one and hairy-chested.'

——**from Hell** ghastly, hellish and – when, as usually, applied to a person, to be avoided at all costs. Exaggeratedly characteristic of the type and strongly emphasizing the negative qualities. Suddenly popular in the early 1990s. Hence, from the *New York Times* (9 May 1993): 'Lisa Samalin's painting of grandma from hell' and (13 June 1993), a mention of Hillary Clinton, 'alternately deified and vilified as nun or Lady Macbeth, Florence Nightingale or Yuppie From Hell'. Seemingly derived from the titles of horror movies and rock albums: *Mutant Hollywood Chainsaw Hookers From Hell!*, 'Cowboys from Hell', 'Bitches from Hell', and so on.

fuck this/that for a lark! expression of disgust at some chore or duty imposed. Mostly British use since the 1940s. Also the obscurer **sod/fuck this for a game of soldiers!**

fuck/damn you, Jack, I'm all right! *see* **I'm all right, Jack!**

fucked by the fickle finger of fate laid low by a blow of fate. An alliterative North American armed forces' expression of the 1930s. Revived on NBC TV's *Rowan and Martin's Laugh-In* (1967–73) as the 'Flying Fickle Finger of Fate Award', the name of the prize in a mock talent contest segment of the show ('who knows when the Fickle Finger of Fate may beckon *you* to stardom?').

full monty, the the full amount, everything included – a phrase suddenly popular in British English from the late 1980s. Possibly a corruption of the 'full amount'? The somewhat Cockney comedian Jim Davidson entitled his autobiography *The Full Monty* in 1993.

full of Eastern promise slogan for Fry's Turkish Delight, current on British TV in the late 1950s.

fully paid-up member of the human race, a complimentary of a human being who is a rounded personality. Of the British Conservative politician Kenneth Clarke, the *Observer* wrote (31 July 1988): 'He is always well-informed (or anyway well-briefed), always reasonable and equable. He seems to be a fully paid-up member of the human race.'

funny as Dick's hatband   *see* **queer as Dick's hatband.**

funny peculiar or funny ha-ha?   phrase used in response to the statement 'that's funny'. From the basic distinction made clear by Ian Hay in his play *Housemaster* (1936): 'What do you mean, funny? Funny-peculiar, or funny ha-ha?' *Funny Peculiar* was the title of a play (1976) by Mike Stott, and also of an (unrelated) series of compilations of newspaper clangers and oddities by Denys Parsons beginning with *Funny Ha Ha and Funny Peculiar* (1965).

funny thing happened to me on the way to the theatre (tonight), a   comedian's remark preliminary to telling a joke, and dating presumably from music-hall/vaudeville days. Hence the titles of a book by Nancy Spain – *A Funny Thing Happened on the Way* (1964) – and of the comedy musical *A Funny Thing Happened on the Way to the Forum* (filmed 1966).

G
g

gag me with a spoon! yuk!, that makes me want to throw up, it disgusts me. A choice example of 'Val-speak', the language of pubescent teenage Valley Girls from California's San Fernando Valley. They were identified and their language first explored in the early 1980s. Also **grody to the max!** – vile, grotty to the maximum degree.

game for anything *see* **anything for a laugh!**

game/it isn't over till it's over, the a proverbial saying usually attributed to 'Yogi' Berra, the American baseball player and coach (1925–). In the form **it ain't over till it's over** this was his reported comment on a National League pennant race (1973) when he was managing the New York Mets. In other words, it is a warning comparable to **the opera ain't over till the fat lady sings** and of American origin also. From the *Independent* (27 February 1991): 'Brigadier General Richard Neal, the US spokesman in Riyadh, warned "let there be no mistake the [Gulf] war is over. Parts of the Iraqi army are still in Kuwait City". . .He added: "It's not over until it's over." '

game's not over till the fat lady sings *see* **opera ain't over. . .**

garbage in, garbage out what you get out of something depends very much on what you put into it. A term from computing, known by the 1960s (and sometimes abbreviated to **GIGO**, pronounced 'guy-go'). Basically, it means that if you put bad data into a computer, you can come up with anything you want but what comes out will be useless and meaningless.

George don't do that! quotation from Joyce Grenfell's 'Nursery School Sketches' (1953) that trembles on the brink of being a proper catchphrase. This line came from a sketch in which she played a slightly harassed but unflappable teacher. Part of its charm lay in the audience's never knowing precisely what it was that George was being asked not to do.

Geronimo!   a popular exclamation, used loosely to mean anything from 'Let's go!' to 'I've found it!'. It was apparently during the North African campaign of November 1942 that US paratroopers first shouted 'Geronimo!' as they jumped out of planes. The exclamation was derived from an expression reputed to have been used by the actual Apache Geronimo who died in 1909. It is said that when he was being pursued by the army, he made a leap on horseback over a sheer cliff into water. As the troops did not dare follow him, he cried 'Geronimo!' as he leapt. From Christy Brown, *Down All the Days* (1970): 'He heard his brothers cry out in unison: "The dirty lousy bastards – hitting a cripple! Geronimo!. . ." And off they flew in maddened pursuit of the ungentlemanly enemy.'

ger(t)cha!   expression of disbelief – 'get along with you!' The word had a burst of popularity in about 1980 when it was used in TV advertisements for Courage Best Bitter in the UK, but it was known by the 1930s.

get a life!   a suggestion that the person addressed should find him/herself a worthwhile, focused role to play in life. Suddenly popular in the early 1990s, probably from the US. Sometimes in the form **get yourself a life!** From a speech by Edwin J. Feulner Jr given at Grove City College, Pennsylvania (14 May 1994): 'During one of the 1992 presidential debates. . .a young man asked the candidates. . . "We are your children. . .what will you do to take care of us, to take care of our needs?". . .My friend Bill Bennett commented: "Wouldn't it have been refreshing," he said, "wouldn't it have been great if any one of them had said, 'Just a minute. Get a life. . .Satisfy your own needs. . .Take care of yourself, man; get a hold of yourself." '

get back on your jamjar!   said dismissively to someone who is behaving objectionably. This appears to be rhyming slang for 'get back on your tram-car' (i.e. go away) and so it is not in origin a racist slur alluding to the golliwog figure who appears on jars of Robertson's jam (although such a use was reported in 1985).

get off my cloud!   leave me alone! Presumably, the image evoked is of someone sitting peacefully on a tuft of cloud in heaven. The phrase was popularized by the song 'Get Off My Cloud', recorded by the Rolling Stones in 1965.

get out of that!   what one might say to anyone in a tricky situation but used as part of a 'visual catchphrase' by the British co-medians Morecambe and Wise on TV shows starting in the early 1960s. Eric Morecambe would put his hand under Ernie Wise's chin, as in a judo hold, and say the line. The pair's other 'visual catchphrases' included: the 'throttling' of Eric which appeared to happen as he went through the gap in the theatre curtain but was, of course, self-administered; the imaginary stone which thuds into a paper bag held out to catch it; Eric's spectacles hooked over one ear but under the other; the rapid self-slap on the back of the neck; Eric's two-handed slap of Ernie's cheeks; the shoulder hug; and the characteristic dance with hands alter-nately behind head and bottom while the pair hop in deliberate emulation of Groucho Marx.

get there fustest with the mostest (or **git there firstest with the mostest**)   get there first with the most men – proverbial expres-sion advising speed and strength in any operation, especially military. Derived from a reputed saying of the US Confederate General, Nathan B. Forrest (*d* 1877). He could hardly read or write but he managed to say that the way to win battles was to be 'firstest with the mostest', or that you needed to 'git thar fustest with the mostest'.

ghost walks on Friday, the   'it's pay day' (for actors). Current by the 1830s, this expression is said to derive from events surround-ing a touring company's production of *Hamlet*. The cast had been unpaid for many weeks and when Hamlet came to speak the line (of his father's ghost), 'Perchance 'twill walk again', the ghost replied; 'Nay, 'twill walk no more until its salary is paid.' Consequently, a theatrical manager who hands out the pay has sometimes been called a 'ghost'.

GIGO   see **garbage in, garbage out**

git there firstest with the mostest   *see* **get there fustest...**

gi'us a job, I can do that! (or **gizza job...**)   in fact, there are *two* catchphrases in this sentence, sometimes used independently, but both from a TV drama series. Alan Bleasdale's *The Boys from the Blackstuff* (about unemployment in Liverpool) was first shown on BBC TV in 1982 and introduced the character of Yosser Hughes. His plea became a nationally repeated catchphrase, not least because of the political ramifications at a time of widespread unemployment. But also, from the *Observer* (30 January 1983): 'At Anfield nowadays whenever the Liverpool goalkeeper makes a save, the Kop affectionately chants at him the catch-phrase of Yosser Hughes: "We could do that." It's a slogan which might usefully rise to the lips of the chairbound viewer just as often.'

give 'im/'er the money, Barney!   yes, he's right, well done! Catchphrase from the folksy BBC radio general knowledge quiz *Have A Go* (1946–67). Winners took away humble prizes of pots of jam and the odd shilling or two. The host Wilfred Pickles would use this expression when a winner had been established. The 'Barney' in question was Barney Colehan, a BBC producer. Later, Mrs Pickles supervised the prizes – hence the alternative **give 'im/'er the money, Mabel!**

give it your best shot   do your best, give it all you've got. 1980s expression, especially in the US. Presumably it comes from the sporting sense of 'shot' (as in golf) rather than the gun sense. The US film *Hoosiers* (1986), about a basketball team, was also known as *Best Shot*. From the *Washington Post* (13 February 1984): ' "We're not able to adequately counsel the farmer with the present plan", he said. "With this, we'll be able to give him our best shot." '

give over!   stop what you're doing or saying – it's annoying me! From Northern English dialect. By 1900.

go ahead, make my day! invitation to offend the speaker thus giving him the right to retaliate. A line originally spoken by Clint Eastwood, himself brandishing a .44 Magnum, to a gunman he was holding at bay in the film *Sudden Impact* (1983). At the end of the film he says (to another villain, similarly armed), 'Come on, make my day'. In neither case does he add 'punk', as is sometimes supposed.

go (and) boil your head! go away, don't be silly! Probably by 1900, especially in Scots use.

go for gold! slogan meaning, literally, 'aim for a gold medal' and first used by the US Olympic team at the Lake Placid Winter Olympics in 1980. (*Going for Gold* became the title of an Emma Lathen thriller set in Lake Placid, published in 1983, and there was a TV movie *Going for the Gold* in 1985.) Other teams, including the British, had taken it up by the time of the 1984 Olympics. A BBC TV quiz called *Going for Gold* began in 1987. (In 1832, 'To Stop the Duke, Go for Gold' aimed at preventing the Duke of Wellington from forming a government in the run up to the Reform Bill.)

go for it! do your utmost! A popular slogan from the early 1980s, mostly in America – though any number of Sales Managers have encouraged their teams to strive this way in the UK, too. Lisa Bernbach in *The Official Preppie Handbook* (1980) pointed to a possible US campus origin, giving the phrase as a general exhortation meaning, 'Let's get carried away and act stupid'. At about the same time, the phrase was used in aerobics. Jane Fonda in a work-out book (1981) and video (*c* 1983), cried, 'Go for it, go for the burn!' (where the burn was a sensation felt during exercise). There was also a US beer slogan (current 1981), 'Go for it! Schlitz makes it great'. Media mogul Ted Turner was later called a 'go-for-it guy', and so on.

go jump in the lake! go away, get lost, to hell with you. From the 1910s. Mainly North American.

go, man, go! phrase of encouragement originally shouted at jazz musicians in the 1940s, which later took on a wider use. TV newscaster Walter Cronkite reverted famously to 'Go, baby, go!' when describing the launch of Apollo XI in 1969 and this form became a fairly standard cry at rocket and missile departures thereafter.

go to it! an exhortation famously used by Herbert Morrison, the English Labour politician (1888–1965), during the Second World War. On 22 May 1940 Morrison, as the Minister of Supply, concluded a radio broadcast calling for a voluntary labour force with these words. They echoed the public mood after Dunkirk and were subsequently used as a wall-poster slogan – in vivid letters. 'Go to it', meaning 'to act vigorously, set to with a will', dates from the early nineteenth century at least.

go West, young man! a phrase of encouragement – not to be taken literally; an exhortation to seek opportunity where it is most likely to be found. Originally in the US and a quotation – but an example of a misattribution that refuses to be corrected. Its originator was John Babsone Lane Soule, who first wrote it in the Terre Haute, Indiana, *Express* in 1851 when, indeed, the thing to do in the United States was to head westwards, where gold and much else beckoned. However, Horace Greeley repeated it in *his* New York newspaper, the *Tribune*, and, being rather more famous, a candidate for the Presidency, and all, it stuck with him. Greeley reprinted Soule's article to show where he had taken it from, but to no avail. The original sentence was, 'Go west, young man, and grow up with the country'.

God bless 'im/'er originally the wording of a toast to Royalty, this gradually turned into a more general, genial way of referring to such people and others. From George Eliot, *Felix Holt* (1866): 'You'll rally round the throne – and the King, God bless him, and the usual toasts.' From *Punch*, Vol. CXX (1902): 'The Queen God Bless 'Er.' Robert Lacey revived the custom in 1990 with a book entitled *The Queen Mother, God Bless Her*. The American cartoonist Helen Hokinson entitled one of her collections *The Ladies, God Bless 'Em* (1950), which takes the toast out into a broader field.

goes with the territory, that (or **comes with…**) reply to someone who is complaining about something, pointing out that the problem is only to be expected as it is all part of the job. Late twentieth century. Since at least 1900, 'territory' has been the American term for the area a salesman covers and it seems quite likely that the origin of the 'goes with' lies in the 'Requiem' scene at the end of Arthur Miller's play *Death of a Salesman* (1948): 'For a salesman, there is no rock bottom to the life. . .He's a man way out there in the blue, riding on a smile and a shoeshine. . .A salesman is got to dream, boy. It comes with the territory.'

gone for a Burton   dead. Early in the Second World War, an RAF expression was coined to describe what had happened to a missing flyer: he had 'gone for a Burton', meaning that he had gone for a drink (*in* the drink = the sea) or, as another phrase put it, 'he'd bought it'. Several explanations have been given for this coinage. Most likely is that during the 1930s 'Gone for a Burton' was used in advertisements to promote a Bass beer known in the trade as 'a Burton' (though, in fact, several ales are produced at Burton-on-Trent).

good for a laugh   *see* **anything for a laugh!**

good game. . .good game!   encouragement to contestants in BBC TV's popular *Generation Game* show in the 1970s from the host, Bruce Forsyth.

good idea, son!, a   phrase of approval spoken in a leaden Cockney accent. Popularized by Max Bygraves during his period as 'tutor' in the BBC radio show *Educating Archie* (early 1950s) and in a song. From the same show: **I've arrived – and to prove it, I'm here!** (which formed part of his bill matter when he appeared at the London Palladium in 1952).

good in parts – like the curate's egg (or **excellent in parts. . .**) meaning 'patchy, of uneven quality', this phrase comes from the caption to a *Punch* cartoon (1895) in which a Bishop is saying: 'I'm afraid you've got a bad egg, Mr Jones.' The nervous young curate, keen not to say anything critical, flannels: 'Oh no, my Lord, I assure you! Parts of it are excellent.'

good man is hard to find, a   version of the seventeenth-century proverb 'Good men are scarce'. In the present form, it was the title of a song by Eddie Green (1919). Nowadays, it is most frequently encountered in reverse. 'A hard man is good to find' was used, nudgingly, as the slogan for Soloflex body-building equipment in the US (1985). In this form the saying is sometimes attributed to Mae West.

good night, Vienna! all over, or 'curtains' for the lot of us, but capable of any sort of suggestive, space-filling use. 'I got her on me knee, gave her a kiss and then "Good night, Vienna"!' From the title of a musical *Goodnight, Vienna* (1932).

good old Charlie-ee! fairly meaningless interjection by Richard Murdoch in the BBC radio show *Much Binding in the Marsh* (late 1940s). The phrase was an old one, however – used for example in *Punch* (2 February 1910).

good time was had by all, a phrase invariably used at the end of reports in parish magazines when church picnics or social evenings are written up. Stevie Smith entitled a collection of her poems *A Good Time Was Had By All* (1937).

good. . .to the last drop! when visiting Joel Cheek, the perfector of the Maxwell House coffee blend, in 1907, President Theodore Roosevelt drank a cup and passed this comment. The slogan has been in use ever since, despite those who have enquired, 'What's wrong with the last drop then?' Professors of English have considered the problem and ruled that 'to' can be inclusive and need not mean 'up to but not including'.

goodbye for now! *see* B.F.N. – bye for now!

goodness gracious me! exclamation of surprise or amazement, known since the early nineteenth century but the key phrase in Peter Sellers's Indian impersonation to which all citizens of the subcontinent subsequently conformed. It occurred in a song called 'Goodness Gracious Me' recorded by Sellers and Sophia Loren in 1960 and based on their characters in the film of Shaw's *The Millionairess*.

goody, goody gumdrops! childish phrase of enthusiasm. Used by Humphrey Lestocq, host of the BBC TV's children's show *Whirli-*

gig in the early 1950s. Harold Acton in his book *Nancy Mitford: a Memoir* (1975) quotes 'goody-goody gum-*trees*' as being a favourite of Noël Coward in the late 1920s.

Gordon Bennett! euphemistic exclamation which had a resurgence in Britain in the early 1980s. Understandably, people shrink from blaspheming. 'Oh Gawd!' is felt to be less offensive than 'Oh God!' At the turn of the century it was natural for people facetiously to water down the exclamation 'God!' by saying 'Gordon!' The name Gordon Bennett was to hand – from James Gordon Bennett II (1841–1918), the eccentrically wealthy editor-in-chief of the *New York Herald* who lived in Europe. The initial letters of the name also had the explosive quality found in 'Gorblimey!' [God blind me!].

got off two stops short of Cincinnati *see* **few vouchers short. . .**

gotcha! form of 'got you', in the US by the 1930s. The headline 'GOTCHA!' was how the London *Sun* newspaper 'celebrated' the sinking of the Argentine cruiser *General Belgrano* during the Falklands War (front page, 4 May 1982).

gottle o' geer 'bottle of beer', said with teeth tightly clenched, mocking the inadequacies of many ventriloquist acts. Known by the 1960s, at least.

grass is always greener on the other side of the fence, the a borderline catchphrase but a venerable proverb. A sixteenth-century translation of a Latin proverb shows the original form: 'The corn in another man's ground seemeth ever more fertile than doth our own.' By 1956, the time of the Hugh and Margaret Williams play *The Grass is Greener* – 'on the other side of the hedge' – the modern form was well established. Wolfgang Mieder in *Proverbium* (1993) questions whether the two proverbs are in fact related but finds an earlier citation of the modern one: an American song with words by Raymond B. Egan and music by Richard A. Whiting entitled 'The Grass is Always Greener (In the Other Fellow's Yard)', published in 1924.

great balls of fire! exclamation of wonderment. It occurs several times in the script of the film *Gone With the Wind* (1939), suggest-

ing southern US origins. Used as the title of a hit song recorded by
Jerry Lee Lewis in 1957.

great Scott! a watered-down expletive, like **Gordon Bennett!**
'Great Scott!' clearly sounds like 'Great God!' and yet is not blas-
phemous. It may have become popular when US General Win-
field Scott was the hero of the Mexican War (1847) and its origin
is almost certainly American.

greatest thing since sliced bread, the a really hot property, brilliant idea or the most wonderful person. Quite when the idea that
pre-sliced bread was one of the landmark inventions arose, is not
clear. Sliced bread had first appeared on the market by the 1920s.

Greeks had a word for it, the phrase used when one wishes to
express disapproval, as in the similar, 'There's a name for that
sort of behaviour'. From the title of a play (1929) by Zoë Akins.

grody to the max! *see* **gag me with a spoon!**

guns before butter political catchphrase associated with Joseph
Goebbels, the German Nazi leader. 'We can do without butter,
but, despite all our love of peace, not without arms. One cannot
shoot with butter, but with guns' – from a translation of a speech,
given in Berlin (17 January 1936). When a nation is under
pressure to choose between material comforts and some kind of
war effort, the choice has to be made between 'guns *and* butter'.
Some will urge 'guns *before* butter'. Later that same year, Her-
mann Goering said in a broadcast, 'Guns will make us powerful;
butter will only make us fat', so he may also be credited with the
'guns or butter' slogan. But there is a third candidate. Airey
Neave in his book *Nuremberg* (1978) stated of Rudolf Hess: 'It was
he who urged the German people to make sacrifices and coined
the phrase: "Guns before butter".'

H
h

ha bloody ha!　sarcastic response to a silly remark or a deed that the speaker does not find funny. From the 1950s?

had one (of those) but the wheel fell off, we　response to pretentious use of language or anything unintelligible. By the late nineteenth century. More recently: **we had one (of those) but it died.**

hang the Kaiser!　said originally to be a dismissive phrase among British soldiers in the First World War who would say, 'Oh, hang the Kaiser!' when bored with all the talk about Kaiser Wilhelm II (1859–1941). However, in due course it became an unofficial British political slogan. During the Versailles Peace Conference and for some time afterwards, Britain's Northcliffe newspapers and others kept up the cry in its literal sense. Candidates at the 1918 General Election are said to have lost votes if they did not subscribe to the policy. The Allies committed themselves to try the ex-Kaiser in the Treaty of Versailles (28 June 1919), but the Government of the Netherlands refused to hand him over for trial in June 1920. The ex-Kaiser died, unhanged, in 1941.

happy as a sandboy　very contented with one's lot. Presumably arising from the expectation that the boys who used to deliver sand (for domestic purposes) from door to door had a useful, undemanding job and could afford to be contented. In use by the 1820s. Charles Dickens in *The Old Curiosity Shop* (1840–1) has 'The Jolly Sandboys' as the name of a pub, with a sign, 'representing three Sandboys increasing their jollity with as many jugs of ale and bags of gold'.

happy as Larry　extremely happy. Probably an Australian expression and supposedly referring to the boxer Larry Foley (1847–1917). In use by the early 1900s.

hard act to follow, that's a   meaning, 'my predecessor has been very good and I may not be able to equal him'. Clearly derived from show business, say in the early 1900s, where an act appearing after a particularly successful one might have its work cut out to attract the audience's support.

hard cheese!   tough luck! Known since the late nineteenth century and possibly linked to the meaning of 'cheese' as 'the best thing'. Hard cheese is not the best.

have a banana!   meaningless cry, popularly interpolated at the end of the first line of the song 'Let's All Go Down the Strand' (1904). At that time, Britain was becoming 'banana conscious' as a result of the promotional activities of Elders & Fyffes, banana importers. As ever with bananas, there may be a hint of sexual innuendo.

have a nice day!   notorious American farewell wish, current since the 1940s and superseding 'have a good day'. In 1992, it emerged that, as a valediction, 'have a nice day' was being coupled with **missing you already!**

have gun, will travel   ready and available to do what is required. Best known as the title of a Western TV series (made in the US, 1957–64): the hired-gun hero had written on his business card, 'Have gun. Will travel. Wire Paladin. San Francisco'. Then it became a format phrase capable of much variation: 'Have pill, will'; 'Have wife, must travel', and so on.

have I got news for you!   be prepared to receive some startling information (with a slight hint of 'where have you *been?*'). Mostly US from the 1950s? *Have I Got News for You* was the title of a BBC TV news quiz (from 1990).

having a wonderful time – wish you were here!   cliché of holiday correspondence presumably since the heyday of the picture postcard in Edwardian times. There are really two catchphrases: 'Wish You Were Here' has been used as the title of songs (reaching the charts in 1953 and 1984) and of an ITV travel series (from 1973 onwards). *Wish You Were Here* was also used in 1987 as the title of a British film about sexual awakenings in a seaside resort.

Having Wonderful Time, a play about a holiday hotel in the Catskills, by Arthur Kober (1937) became, in an exchange of phrases, the musical *Wish You Were Here* in 1952.

hawae the lads!   cry of encouragement (like 'come on!') from the North-East of England, also in the forms 'Haway' (or 'Howay') and 'Away' (or 'A-wee'). According to the Frank Graham's *New Geordie Dictionary* (1979), it is a corruption of 'hadaway' as in 'hadaway wi'ye', which actually means the opposite, 'begone!'

he ain't heavy, he's my brother!   King George VI reflected on the benefits of mutual co-operation in his 1942 Christmas radio broadcast: 'A former President of the United States of America used to tell of a boy who was carrying an even smaller child up a hill. Asked whether the heavy burden was not too much for him, the boy answered: "It's not a burden, it's my brother!" So let us welcome the future in a spirit of brotherhood.' It has been suggested that the American President referred to must have been Abraham Lincoln.

However, the King's quotation may have been no more than a dignification of a charity slogan and motto. As a headline, 'He ain't heavy...he's my brother' was used in a 1936 American advertisement for the 'Community Chest' campaign ('35 appeals in 1'). Before that, a similar slogan had been used to promote the Nebraska orphanage and poor boys' home known as 'Boys Town'. It is said that in the early 1920s, the Rev. Edward J. Flanagan – played by Spencer Tracy in the film *Boys' Town* (1938) – admitted to the home a boy named Howard Loomis who could not walk without the aid of crutches. The larger boys often took turns carrying him about on their backs. One day, Father Flanagan is said to have seen a boy carrying Loomis and asked whether this was not a heavy load. The reply was: 'He ain't heavy, Father . . . he's m'brother.' Boys Town still uses the motto (in the 'Father/m'brother' form). Other applications have included the song 'He ain't heavy, he's my brother' popularized by the Hollies in 1969.

he can put his shoes/boots under my bed anytime   'I find him sexually attractive.' Possibly American in origin, but definitely known by 1970.

he can run, but he can't hide   *see* **you can run but you can't hide**

he knows whereof he speaks/spoke   conscious archaism used in place of 'he knows what he's talking about/he has a particular reason for saying that'. From Hendrik Van Loon, *The Story of Mankind* (1922): '[Erasmus] had travelled a great deal and knew whereof he wrote.'

he's fallen in the wa-ter!   spoken in a sing-song high voice by 'Little Jim' (Spike Milligan) in the BBC radio *Goon Show* (1950s).

he's lovely, Mrs Hoskin, he's lovely!   catchphrase spoken by Ted Ray as 'Ivy' to Bob Pearson as 'Mrs Hoskin' in the BBC radio show *Ray's A Laugh* (1950s). Ray recalled in his book *Raising the Laughs* (1952): 'George Inns [the producer] agreed that the climax of their original conversation should be the mention of a mystical "Dr Hardcastle" whom Ivy secretly adored. We had absolutely no inkling of how warmly the listening millions were to take our new voices to their hearts; but from the moment Bob, in his new role, had spoken the words, "I sent for young Dr Hardcastle", and we heard Ivy's excited little intake of breath, followed by, "He's loo-vely, Mrs Hoskin...he's loo-oo-vely!" a new phrase had come into being.'

he's very good, you know!   patronizing, double-edged compliment spoken by various characters in the BBC radio *Goon Show* (1950s).

head 'em off at the pass   *see* **cut 'em off at the pass.**

heavens to Murgatroyd!   catchphrase of the rather camp cartoon lion called Snagglepuss, created by the Hannah-Barbera studios in the 1960s. He made his first appearance in *The Yogi Bear Show*, but his catchphrase was apparently not original. An American correspondent noted (1993): 'It was a favorite expression of a favorite uncle of mine in the 1940s, and my wife also remembers it from her growing-up years in the '40s.'

'Hell!' said the Duchess (when she caught her teats in the mangle!)   expletive turned into a Wellerism, probably by the 1890s. But there are other uses. The opening lines of Agatha

Christie's *The Murder on the Links* (1923): 'I believe that a well-known anecdote exists to the effect that a young writer, determined to make the commencement of his story forcible and original enough to catch the attention of the most blasé of editors, penned the first sentence: "Hell!' said the Duchess".' Note also *Hell! Said the Duchess. A Bed-time Story* by Michael Arlen (1934).

hello birds, hello trees, hello clouds, hello sky! an expression of joy in nature, as though spoken by a poet, aesthete or other fey character. Of uncertain origin, though used in a Warner Bros. cartoon film dating from 1941. The most prominent British use has been in the schoolboy 'Nigel Molesworth' books by Geoffrey Willans and Ronald Searle. For example, from *Back in the Jug Agane* (1959): 'And who is this who skip weedily up to me, eh? "Hullo clouds, hullo sky," he sa. "Hullo birds, hullo poetry books, hullo skool sossages, hullo molesworth 1." You hav guessed it is dere little basil fotherington-tomas.'

hello, folks! another early coinage of the British comedian Arthur Askey (1900–82) was **hello, playmates!** though, as Askey pointed out (1979), this was originally 'hello, folks!' When he used this phrase in the first broadcast of *Band Waggon* (BBC radio, 1938), he received a call from Tommy Handley telling him to lay off as Handley himself considered it to be *his* catchphrase (and used it throughout the 1940s on *ITMA*). So Askey changed his greeting to 'Hello, playmates!' (with *Hello, Playmates!* becoming the title of another of his radio shows in the mid-1950s).

hello, folks, and what about the workers?, a touch of following on from the above, the Goons on BBC radio in the 1950s took up the cry 'hello, folks!' and gave it a high-pitched, strangulated delivery. Harry Secombe combined this with another catchphrase to form 'hello, folks, and what about the workers?' Finally, Eric Morecambe in the 1970s gave it a sexual connotation as 'a touch of hello folks, and what about the workers!' (a similar process involved the phrase **how's your father?**).

hello, good evening, and welcome! TV greeting – rather redoubling itself – from the British broadcaster, David Frost. It originated in the period when he was commuting back and forth to host TV chat shows in London and New York, and in particular was presenting ITV's *The Frost Programme* (1966). The phrase was used as the title of a BBC TV 'Wednesday Play' on 16 October 1968.

hello, hello, hello!   *see* **'ullo, 'ullo, 'ullo!**

hello, John, got a new motor?   the use of 'John' as a mode of address to any man (in England) was taken up by the British comedian Alexei Sayle in about 1980. Compare the use of 'Jimmy' in Scotland and 'Boyo' in Wales. ''Ullo, John, got a new motor?' was the full catchphrase, echoing East End of London and Essex use, and, in this form, was the title of a record by Sayle, released in 1984.

hello, me old pal, me old beauty!   greeting of the rustic yokel character Walter Gabriel in BBC radio's agricultural soap opera *The Archers* since 1951. Uttered more as 'oooo arr, me ol' pal, me ol' beauty!' by the late Chriss Gittins (*d* 1988) and, no doubt, adopted from traditional yokel-ese. The phrase was already established by June 1961 when Tony Hancock as 'Joshua' in a TV parody called *The Bowmans* had the line, 'Me old pal, me old beauty'.

hello, playmates!   *see* **hello, folks!**

hello, sailor!   a camp catchphrase in early 1970s Britain, reaching a peak in 1975/6, and promoted by various branches of the media. A greeting as between one gay character – especially male – and another of the same, though originally it must have been something that a female prostitute would have called out to a heterosexual customer.

An early appearance occurs in a reminiscence of Graham Payn singing the song 'Matelot' in Noël Coward's *Sigh No More* in 1945. The chorus is said to have muttered 'Hello, sailor!' whenever Payn appeared. In Spike Milligan's script for 'Tales of Men's Shirts' in the BBC radio *Goon Show* (31 December 1959), 'Hello, sailor!' is spoken, for no very good reason, by Minnie Bannister. The cast of radio's *I'm Sorry I'll Read That Again* promoted it heavily in the early 1970s, perhaps influenced by there being a number of newsworthy sailors about at that time, including Prince Philip, Prince Charles and the Prime Minister, Edward Heath.

here am I, slaving over a hot stove all day (while all you do is...) the housewife's lament, since the early 1900s. A catchphrase when used ironically or as a joke. Compare the caption to a drawing (*c* 1912) by Art Young: 'Here am I, standin' over a hot stove all day, and you workin' in a nice, cool sewer!'

here come de judge! an old vaudeville catchphrase revived when Dewey 'Pigmeat' Markham, a black vaudeville veteran, was brought back to take part in a series of blackout sketches on NBC TV's *Rowan and Martin's Laugh-In* in the late 1960s. The build-up to the sketches was the chant, 'Here comes de judge!' In July 1968, Markham and an American vocalist called Shorty Long both had records of a song called 'Here Come(s) the Judge' in the US and UK charts.

here we are again! Joseph Grimaldi (1779–1837) used this catchphrase as Joey the Clown in pantomime and it has subsequently been used by almost all clowns on entering the circus ring. Now used as much outside the circus ring in everyday conversation as a greeting.

here we go, here we go, here we go! chant, sung to the tune of Sousa's 'Stars and Stripes for Ever', beloved of British football supporters, though it does have other applications. It suddenly became very noticeable at the time of the Mexico World Cup in June 1986. The previous year, the Everton football team had made a record of the chant, arranged and adapted by Tony Hiller and Harold Spiro. This version included an excursion into Offenbach's famous Can-Can tune.

here's another nice mess you've gotten me into Oliver Hardy's exasperated cry to his partner Stan Laurel after yet another example of the latter's ineptitude had come to light was spoken in several of the comedians' American films. Latterly, it has often been remembered as **another fine mess**, possibly on account of one of the duo's thirty-minute features (released in 1930) being entitled *Another Fine Mess*.

here's Johnny!   Said with a drawn-out, rising inflection on the first word, this was Ed McMahon's introduction to Johnny Carson on NBC TV's *Tonight* show from its inception in 1961: '[*Drum roll*] 'And now...heeeeere's Johnny!' Jack Nicholson playing a psychopath chopped through a door with an axe and cried 'Here's Johnny!' in the film *The Shining* (1981).

here's looking at you, kid!   drinker's toast made popular by the film *Casablanca* (1942) in which Humphrey Bogart said it to Ingrid Bergman.

here's one I made earlier (or **prepared earlier ...**)   curiously popular catchphrase in Britain that originated with 'live' TV cookery demonstrations in the 1950s in which it was important that the showing of the finished product was not left to chance. The phrase was also borrowed by presenters of BBC TV's children's programme *Blue Peter* (from 1963 onwards) who had to explain how to make models of the Taj Mahal out of milk-bottle tops, for example, but would not actually be seen doing so there and then. In fact, the one prepared earlier might well have been made by someone else...

here's to our next merrie meeting   saying or toast. As a catchphrase, it occurs in Henry Hall's signature theme for the BBC Dance Orchestra (which Hall took over in March 1932):

> Here's to the next time and a merry meeting,
> Here's to the next time, we send you all our greeting,
> Set it to music, sing it in rhyme,
> Now, all together, Here's to the next time!

Then it was remembered that BBC Radio's popular organist, Robin Richmond, was for many years (until the 1980s) presenter of *The Organist Entertains* and the phrase was his weekly signing off. But the alliterative lure of 'merry meetings' has been around a good deal longer. King Richard III has 'Our stern alarums chang'd to merry meetings' in the famous opening speech to Shakespeare's play. *Punch* for 27 July 1904 has in the caption to a cartoon accompanying 'Operatic Notes' 'TO OUR NEXT MERRY MEETING!'

Even more significantly, the *Punch Almanack* for 1902 has a cartoon of two foxes drinking in a club, celebrating the fact that all the best hunting horses are away in the Boer War. One fox is saying, 'To our next merry meeting!' Does this indicate that this was an established toast? Does it also suggest that the original 'meeting' referred to in the phrase was the kind you have in fox-hunting?

hey! – Mambo!   an irritating call dating from the late 1950s. Walking quietly along the street ('minding your own business') you would be hailed by someone shouting 'Hey!' When you turned round, they added 'Mambo!', alluding to the hit record 'Mambo Italiano' recorded by Dean Martin in 1955.

hey – your back wheel's going round!   'helpful' comment volunteered by a juvenile pedestrian to a cyclist or motorist with the purpose of distracting or annoying him. Since the early 1900s. Possibly addressed earlier to users of any form of wheeled transport.

hi-de-hi!   chant from dance-band vocals of the 1920s/30s, in particular, Cab Calloway's song 'Minnie the Moocher' (1931) containing the refrain, 'Ho-de-ho, hi-de-hi.' The phrase also occurs in George Gershwin's song 'Lorelei' (1933). In addition, according to Denis Gifford's *The Golden Age of Radio*, 'Hi-de-hi! Ho-de-ho!' was the catchphrase of Christopher Stone, the BBC's first 'disc-jockey', when he went off and presented *Post Toasties Radio Corner*, a children's programme for Radio Normandy in 1937. For several years from 1980 onwards, BBC TV had a comedy series set in a 1950s holiday camp called *Hi-de-hi*.

hi-tiddly-i-ti   snappy ending from children's singing games, vocalizing the familiar musical phrase 'om-tiddly-om-pom, pom pom', which is said first to have occurred in Fischler's 'Hot Scotch Rag' of 1911. The phrase 'Hi-tidli-i-ti/-i-ti-hi' had already occurred, however, in *Punch* in 1900. Other versions: 'Tripe and bananas, fried fish!'; 'Guard to the guard-room, dismiss!'; 'Shave and a haircut, five bob/two bits!'

hi-yo, Silver!   cry of the Lone Ranger to his horse in the various American radio, cinema and TV accounts of their exploits (from 1933 onwards).

hint! hint!   a rather obvious way of emphasizing, say, that you have a birthday coming up and that the person you are addressing might take the hint and buy you something you are both looking at, as a present. Mid-twentieth century.

ho ho, *very* satirical!   ironical appreciation of a satirical joke. Probably a reaction to the British 'satire boom' of the early 1960s. The phrase originated on the cover of one of the very first issues of *Private Eye* (7 February 1962). It is a comment on a piece of artwork showing the Albert Memorial as 'Britain's first man in space'.

hokey pokey penny a lump (or **okey-pokey...**)   cry of vendors of a type of imitation ice cream made from shaved ice mixed with syrup, current by 1900. Perhaps it was thought that the imitation was a form of hocus-pocus or trickery, or else it could have been a corruption of '*ecce, ecce!*', the cry with which Italian street vendors would have called attention to their wares.

hold it gently but firmly (like a schoolgirl holding her first cock)   instruction to embryo pilot as to how to handle a joystick, since the early 1930s.

hold the fort (for I am coming)   the phrase 'hold the fort' has two meanings: 'look after this place while I'm away' and 'hang on, relief is at hand'. In the second sense, there is a specific origin. In the American Civil War, General William T. Sherman signalled words to this effect to General John M. Corse at the Battle of Allatoona, Georgia (5 October 1864). What he *actually* semaphored from Keneshaw Mountain was either 'Sherman says hold fast. We are coming' or 'Hold out. Relief is coming'.

The catchphrase became popular in its present form as the first line of a hymn or gospel song written by Philip Paul Bliss in *c* 1870 ('Ho, My Comrades, See the Signal!' in *The Charm*). This was introduced to Britain by Moody and Sankey during their evangelical tour of the British Isles in 1873 (and not written by them, as is sometimes supposed):

> 'Hold the fort, for I am coming,'
> Jesus signals still;
> Wave the answer back to heaven,
> 'By thy grace we will.'

hold your horses! hold everything, don't jump to conclusions! Known in the US and Australia by the 1940s.

holy ——— ! the use of this prefix in exclamations was a hallmark of the *Batman* series. Batman and Robin were characters created by Bob Kane in 1939 and featured in comic books before being portrayed by Adam West and Burt Ward in a filmed series for TV (1966–8). Hence, 'Holy flypaper!'/'Holy cow!'/'Holy schizo-phrenia!', etc.

home, James, and don't spare the horses! catchphrase used jocu-larly, as if talking to a driver, telling someone to proceed or get a move on. From the title of a song (1934) by the American song-writer Fred Hillebrand and recorded by Elsie Carlisle in that year and by Hillebrand himself in 1935. The component 'Home, James!' had existed long before – in the works of W.M. Thackeray in the 1840s, for example.

honest Injun! honestly, you can take my word for it! In the US and UK by the 1880s/90s.

honey, I (just) forgot to duck! explanation or excuse derived from a remark made by the US boxer Jack Dempsey to his wife, on losing his World Heavyweight title to Gene Tunney during a fight in Philadelphia in 1926. The line was recalled by ex-sports com-mentator Ronald Reagan when explaining to *his* wife what had happened during an assassination attempt in 1981.

hope your rabbit dies!, I from a child's threat to another child, known by the 1930s.

horses sweat, men perspire, and ladies only glow saying used to reprove someone who talks of 'sweating'. It is listed as a nanny's reprimand in *Nanny Says* (1972) in the form: 'Horses sweat, gentlemen perspire, but ladies only gently glow.' J.M. Cohen includes it in one of his *Comic and Curious Verse* volumes

(1956–9) as merely by Anon, in the form: 'Here's a little proverb that you surely ought to know:/ Horses sweat and men perspire, but ladies only glow.'

how about that then? an expression (probably of American origin) of surprise or wonderment dating from the 1930s.

how goes the enemy? what time is it? Slightly facetious catchphrase apparently derived from a line in the play *The Dramatist* (1789) by Frederick Reynolds.

how is a man when he's out? *see* **because the higher the fewer!**

how now, brown cow? phrase long used as an elocution exercise in the UK. It made an early appearance in a song with the title 'How Now Brown Cow?' (words by Rowland Leigh and music by Richard Addinsell) in the revue *RSVP* at the Vaudeville Theatre, London (1926).

how to win friends and influence people title of a book (1936) by Dale Carnegie. Carnegie's courses incorporating his self-improvement plan had already been aimed at business people for a quarter of a century before the book came out.

how'm I doing? self-serving inquiry used, for example, by Ed Koch who was Mayor of New York City in 1977–89. He would call it out as he ranged around New York. 'You're doing fine, Ed' the people were supposed to shout back. An earlier song with the title was disinterred in due course.

how's your father? catchphrase associated with the British music-hall comedian Harry Tate (1872–1940). Apparently, he would exclaim it as a way of changing the subject and in order to get out of a difficult situation. The phrase either subsequently or simultaneously took on a life of its own meaning the same as a 'thingummy' or anything the speaker did not wish to name. From that, in phrases like 'indulging in a spot of how's-your-father', it became a euphemism for sexual activity.

how's your poor (old) feet? jocular inquiry dating from the nineteenth century. A version without the 'old' dates from *c* 1851, allegedly referring to the fatigue resulting from visiting the Great Exhibition [in London].

hubba! hubba! (or **hubba! bubba!**)   said like a wolf-whistle to a pretty girl. Popular in the US military, 1940s, and used by Bob Hope in radio shows of that period. Said to be based on the Chinese cry *how-pu-how*.

hurts me more than it's hurting you, this   traditional sentiment expressed by teacher or parent administering corporal punishment to a child. An early occurrence is in Harry Graham's *Ruthless Rhymes* (1899): 'Father, chancing to chastise/His indignant daughter Sue,/Said: "I hope you realize/That this hurts me more than you." ' A *Punch* cartoon (11 April 1905) has the politician Augustine Birrell saying to a boy representing 'the Education Act 1902" ' (which Birrell was reforming): 'My boy, this can't hurt you more than it's going to hurt me.'

hush, keep it dark!   elaboration of the basic Second World War security slogan (in the UK), 'Keep it dark'. *Shush, Keep It Dark* was the title of a variety show running in London during September 1940. Later, the naval version of the BBC radio show *Merry Go Round* (1943–8) featured a character called Commander High-Price (Jon Pertwee) whose catchphrase was, 'Hush, keep it dark!'

I
i

I am the greatest!   Muhammad Ali, formerly Cassius Clay, who became world heavyweight boxing champion in 1964, admitted that he copied his 'I am the greatest. . .I am the prettiest' routine from a wrestler called Gorgeous George he had once seen in Las Vegas: 'I noticed they all paid to get in – and I said, this is a good idea!' In a moment of unusual modesty, Ali added: 'I'm not really the greatest. I only say I'm the greatest because it sells tickets.'

I believe you, (but) thousands wouldn't   reassuring statement to a friend or colleague but possibly implying that the thousands are quite right in their unbelief. Mostly British use, by the 1920s.

I bet you say that to all the girls!   said by a woman to a man in response to flattery. British use, by the 1930s.

I counted them all out and I counted them all back   a catchphrase alluding to the deceptive conveying of information. 'I'm not allowed to say how many planes [Harrier jets from HMS *Hermes*] joined the raid, but I counted them all out and I counted them all back,' said Brian Hanrahan, a British journalist (1949–), in a report broadcast by BBC Television on 1 May 1982. Hanrahan was attempting to convey the success of a British attack on Port Stanley airport during the Falklands War. As the BBC's then Director-General Alasdair Milne commented in *DG: The Memoirs of a British Broadcaster* (1988), it was, 'An elegant way of telling the truth without compromising the exigencies of military censorship'.

I didn't get where I am today. . .   characteristic phrase of the pompous, popularized by its frequent use by 'C.J.', the boss (John Barron), in BBC TV's comedy *The Fall and Rise of Reginald Perrin* (1976–80).

I didn't know you cared!   said after an unexpected gesture or compliment but, often ironically, when the compliment is double-edged or outright critical. By the 1940s. *I Didn't Know You Cared* was taken as the title of a BBC TV comedy series (1975) set in a dour North Country family.

I didn't oughter 'ave et it!   the British actor and entertainer Jack Warner recounts in his book *Jack of All Trades* (1975) the occasion when this catchphrase was born. He was leaving Broadcasting House in London with Richard Murdoch: 'I had to step over the legs of a couple of fellows who were sitting in the sunshine with their backs against the wall eating their lunches from paper bags. As we passed, I heard one say to the other, "I don't know what my old woman has given me for dinner today but I didn't oughter 'ave et it." I remarked to Dickie, "If that isn't a cue for a song, I don't know what is!" It provided me with my first catchphrase to be picked out by members of the public.'

I do not like this game!   catchphrase of 'Bluebottle' (Peter Sellers) in the BBC radio *Goon Show* (1950s): *Seagoon:* 'Now, Bluebottle, take this stick of dynamite.' *Bluebottle:* 'No, I do not like this game!'

I don't know much about ——, but I know what I like!   the philistine's slogan, as it is usually applied to music, art or literature. Gelett Burgess identified it as a platitude in *Are You a Bromide?* (1906). From Max Beerbohm's novel *Zuleika Dobson* (1911): 'She was one of the people who say "I don't know anything about music really, but I know what I like".'

I don't mean maybe   *see* **and I don't mean maybe!**

I don't mind if I do!   acceptance of anything sounding remotely like the offer of a drink. Popularized by 'Colonel Chinstrap' (Jack Train), a character in the BBC radio comedy show *ITMA* (1940s). *Punch* carried a cartoon in 1880 with the caption: *Porter:* 'Virginia Water!' *Bibulous old gentleman (seated in railway carriage):* 'Gin and water!' I don't mind if I do!'

——, I don't think!   a catchphrase reversing the statement that precedes it (compare **—— not!**). Charles Dickens in *Pickwick*

Papers, (1837) has: '"Amiably disposed...I don't think",
resumed Mr Weller in a tone of moral reproof.' *Punch* (7 April
1909) refers to it as a 'popular slang phrase'.

I don't want to hear about it!   *see* **I don't wish to know that!**

I don't wish to know that (kindly leave the stage!)   traditional
response to a corny joke in music hall, variety and vaudeville.
Usually said by a person who has been interrupted while engaged
in some other activity on stage (and part of the **I say! I say! I say!**
routine). In the 1930s, the phrase was associated in the UK with
Murray and Mooney (later, Mooney and King), but may have
been used earlier by Dave and Joe O'Gorman. In similar circumstances, Dan Rowan used to say to Dick Martin on *Laugh-In*
(1960s), **I don't want to hear about it**. Martin was endlessly on
the look-out for 'action' and Rowan could hardly keep his partner's mind off sex: *Rowan* (fretting about Martin's frail appearance): 'For your own good, you should pick up some weight.'
Martin: 'Shoulda been with me last night. I picked up 118
pounds.' *Rowan*: 'I don't want to hear about it. . .' *Martin*: 'It was
for my own good, too!'

I feel like a million dollars   *see* **looks like a million dollars.**

I forgot the question!   repetition phrase from Goldie Hawn, originally the blonde dum-dum in *Rowan and Martin's Laugh-In* (NBC
TV, 1960s). In the middle of a quick exchange, she would giggle
and then miaow 'I forgot the question!' At first her fluffs were a
case of misreading cue cards, then they became part of her act.

I haven't (got) a thing to wear...!   the wives' catchphrase
designed to reduce husbands to helpless silence. Meaning, 'I
haven't got a dress suitable for this occasion we're going to and
which I haven't worn several times before.' By 1900, probably.

**I haven't laughed so much since Auntie caught her tit in the
mangle!** (or **mother/aunt** and **tit/tits**)   probably British services
origin, and known by the early 1950s. See also under **'Hell!' said
the Duchess. . .** for a much earlier version.

I hear what you say. . .   phrase of argument, meaning 'I can see what you are getting at but it is not going to make me alter my opinions.' By the 1970s.

I hear you meaning, 'I understand you, but I am not necessarily going to take any notice of what you say.' Compare the previous entry. Lord Reith, who used it in a TV conversation with Malcolm Muggeridge in 1967, glossed it as a Scots phrase meaning 'the remark is not worth answering or...the remark you made was untrue'.

I just don't care any more! *see* **shut that door!**

I kid you not! don't mistake what I say – I mean it. Probably American in origin, from about the 1940s. The phrase occurs in the film of Herman Wouk's *The Caine Mutiny* (1954).

I love my wife but, oh, you kid! what the married man says on seeing an attractive girl – possibly amounting to a not very serious 'pass', but indicating that despite the tug of marital fidelity it is still possible for a married man to dream a little. Very popular in the US in the 1910s–1940s, though never in the UK. '**Oh you kid!**' has also existed on its own as a rather meaningless exclamation.

I married him for better or worse but not for lunch said to be an Australian catchphrase used by a woman whose husband has retired, works at home or comes home for his midday meal – dating from the 1940s and known in Britain since the 1960s. This rather pleasing play on words from the Anglican marriage service has also been ascribed to the Duchess of Windsor in *The Windsor Story* (1979) by J. Bryan III and Charles J.V. Murphy, in the context: '[The Duke of Windsor] usually lunched alone on a salad while the duchess went out ("I married the Duke for better or worse but not for lunch").'

I must love you and leave you semi-jocular farewell remark since the nineteenth century. During the Vietnam War, one of the few memorable US patriotic slogans, current from the late 1960s, was 'America, Love It or Leave It'. This was perhaps inspired by the old phrase and/or by the song 'Love Me or Leave Me' (1928, hit version 1955). *Love 'Em and Leave 'Em* was the title of a Louise Brooks film (US, 1927), foreshadowing a later macho attitude to women.

I nearly bought my own beer   *see* **laugh?...**

I nearly fell off the wife   *see* **laugh?...**

I need that like a hole in the head   'that's the last thing I need' – apparently the last part of the phrase is a direct translation from the Yiddish *lock in kop*. In the US by the early 1950s. A play called *A Hole in the Head* by Arnold Schulman was produced in 1957 and a Frank Sinatra movie in 1959.

I never promised you a rose garden   'it was never going to be roses, roses all the way between us – or a bed of roses – but I never suggested that it would be otherwise.' Used by Joanne Greenberg ('Hannah Green') as the title of a best-selling novel in 1964 (film US, 1977): and as a line in the song 'Rose Garden' in 1968.

I only asked (pronounced **arsked**)   defensive reaction to a put down. Bernard Bresslaw played a large, gormless army private – 'Popeye' Popplewell – in Granada TV's *The Army Game* from 1957 to 1962. A feature film for the cinema called *I Only Arsked* was made in 1958.

I only work here, (don't blame/ask me)   defensive response to any criticism of how an organization is run. British, from the late 1940s.

I say! I say! I say!   comedian's introductory patter. It is hard to know whether Murray and Mooney, the British variety duo, invented this interruption, but they perfected the routine in their act during the 1930s. Mooney would interrupt with 'I say, I say, I say!' To whatever he had to impart, Murray would reply with the traditional **I don't wish to know that – kindly leave the stage!**

I say, what a smasher!   referring to an attractive woman, from Charlie Chester's BBC radio show *Calling All Forces* (1946–50), though the phrase already existed, possibly from the Scots 'a wee smasher'. Iona and Peter Opie in *The Lore and Language of School-children* (1959) show how the phrase penetrated, firstly, to 'Girls,

13, Swansea, 1952' who recited: 'I say, what a smasher,/Betty Grable's getting fatter,/Pick a brick and throw it at her./If you wish to steal a kiss,/I say, what a smasher.' And, secondly, to 'Boy, 11, Birmingham': 'I say what a smasher/Pick it up and slosh it at her./If you miss/Give her a kiss/I say what a smasher.'

I say, you fellows! defensive cry of Billy Bunter, the famous fat schoolboy creation of Frank Richards in numerous stories written between 1900 and 1960. When Bunter came to be re-created for BBC TV (1952–62), he was played memorably by Gerald Campion who gave a distinctive metallic ring to this phrase.

I shall forget my own name in a minute the nameless man from the ministry (Horace Percival) in BBC radio *ITMA* (1940s) resurrected this old phrase to show the limits of his forgetfulness. It occurs in Charles Dickens, *The Chimes* (First Quarter) (1844) as 'I'll forget my own name next'. Even earlier, in the Motteux translation of Cervantes, *Don Quixote* (1605) there is: 'My memory is so bad that many times I forget my own name!'

I should cocoa! perhaps rhyming slang for 'I should hope so!'? But certainly a slightly dated British English exclamation meaning 'certainly not!' Current in the 1930s.

I should of stood in bed! *see* **we wuz robbed!**

I spy (with my little eye)! 'I've seen/spotted something'. The origin of the phrase probably lies in the simple children's game of 'I spy' or 'Hy-spy' (known in the eighteenth century), a form of hide and seek. Then there is also the children's game of 'I spy with my little eye...something beginning with...', in which the guessers have to work out what object this initial letter refers to. Known by 1910.

In the 1950s, there was a British craze for 'I Spy' which extended the game of train-spotting to other fields. According to the subject of the little book being used, the spotter would score points for having observed different breeds of animal, types of building, and so on. The craze was presided over by 'Big Chief I Spy' in the *Daily Express*.

As for 'with my little eye', this might be an allusion to the nursery rhyme 'Who Killed Cock Robin?' (1740s) in which the question 'Who saw him die?' is answered with, 'I, said the fly,/ With my little eye'.

I think the answer lies in the soil! view on every subject volunteered by 'Arthur Fallowfield' (Kenneth Williams) in the BBC radio show *Beyond Our Ken* (early 1950s). The character was that of a ruminative countryman (perhaps based on the real-life Ralph Wightman or A.G. Street) answering questions in a take-off of the *Any Questions* programme.

I think we should be told! the public should be given the answer to this important question – a would-be campaigning journalist's line. In the mid-1980s, *Private Eye* ran a regular parody of the opinion column written by John Junor for the *Sunday Express*. In 1985, Sir John – as he was by then – insisted that he had never once used the phrase in his actual column. He did, however, admit to having used the *Eye* parody's other stock phrase – **pass the sick-bag, Alice!** (registering disgust) – though only once.

I took my harp to a party but nobody asked me to play meaning, 'I went prepared to do something, but wasn't given the opportunity.' From a song by Desmond Carter and Noel Gay, popularized by Gracie Fields and Phyllis Robins in the mid-1930s.

I wanna tell you a sto-ry! it is possible that the British entertainer Max Bygraves may once have said of his own accord, 'I wanna tell you a story' (with the appropriate hand-gestures – as if shaking water off them) but it was the impressionist Mike Yarwood who capitalized on it in the early 1970s. Bygraves then used the phrase himself in self-parody and chose it as the title of his autobiography (1976).

I want to be alone! the Swedish-born film star Greta Garbo (1905–90) claimed that what she said was 'I want to be *let* alone' and, indeed, nowhere in all the film publicity surrounding her in the 1930s has the precise phrase been found. What complicates the issue is that Garbo *did* use the line several times on the screen. For example, in the 1929 silent film *The Single Standard* she gives the brush-off to a stranger and the subtitle declares: 'I am walking alone because I want to be alone.' And, as the ageing ballerina who loses her nerve and flees back to her suite in *Grand Hotel* (1932), she actually *speaks* it. Frequently uttered in parody, as by Groucho Marx in *A Night at the Opera* (1935).

I was a seven stone weakling   *see* **you, too, can have a body like mine!**

I was only obeying orders!   much parodied self-excusal from responsibility for one's actions. The Charter of the International Military Tribunal at Nuremberg (1945–6) specifically excluded the traditional German defence of 'superior orders'. But the plea was, nevertheless, much advanced. Rex Harrison says in the film *Night Train to Munich* (UK; as early as 1940): 'Captain Marsen was only obeying orders.' Kenneth Mars as a mad, Nazi-fixated playwright in *The Producers* (US, 1967) says, 'I only followed orders!'

I washed my hair last night – and now I can't do a thing with it   commonplace excuse for one's less than good appearance. By the 1960s. The second part is sometimes given as a chorused response as though anticipating the cliché involved.

I would like to spend more time with my family   cliché of British political resignations (and not accepted as the real reason for the move). In March 1990, when two of Prime Minister Thatcher's ministers – Norman Fowler and Peter Walker – had withdrawn from the Cabinet, both giving as their reason for going that they wished to 'spend more time with their families', Gordon Brown, the Labour MP, suggested in the House of Commons that Nicholas Ridley might care to follow suit. But the Secretary of State for Industry was having none of it. 'The last thing I want to do,' he said, 'is spend more time with my family.'

I wouldn't kick her out of bed!   male's remark about an attractive woman, since the 1920s? US and UK.

I wouldn't like to meet him in the dark/on a dark night/up a dark alley   said of any formidably hefty or ugly man. 1960s/70s.

I wouldn't piss on him if he was on fire   an expression of extreme dislike, said to be of Australian origin, 1970s. Compare what Rodney Bickerstaffe, the British trade union leader, said at the Labour Party Conference in Blackpool (1992): 'John Major. Norman Lamont. I wouldn't spit in their mouths if their teeth were on fire.' The figure of speech was undoubtedly not original. 'I wasn't going to say "spit" but Willis [TUC General Secretary] made me change it.'

I wouldn't trust him as far as I could throw him   I wouldn't trust him very far at all. British use mostly, by the 1870s.

I'd like to get you on a slow boat to China   I would like to get you on your own (for amatory purposes) – a quotation from the song 'On a Slow Boat to China' (1948) by Frank Loesser, which continues '. . .all to myself alone'.

I'll be back!   menacing phrase that caught on when used by Arnold Schwarzenegger in *The Terminator* (1984), in which he plays a time-travelling robot who terminates his opponents with extreme prejudice (ripping their hearts out, etc.). Coincidentally, the last words of the film *Pimpernel Smith* (UK, 1941) are: 'I'll be back. . .we'll all be back.' These are spoken by Leslie Howard as a professor of archaeology who goes into war-torn Europe to rescue refugees.

I'll drink to that!   'I agree with what you say or the course of action you propose' – but only in light-hearted situations. American origin, by the 1950s. Had something of a revival when Dick Martin took to saying it to Dan Rowan in *Rowan and Martin's Laugh-In* (NBC TV, 1960s).

I'll give it five!   Janice Nicholls, a sixteen-year-old clerk/ telephonist from Birmingham was conscripted on to ABC TV's pop show *Thank Your Lucky Stars* (*c* 1963) as a member of the 'Spin-a-Disc' panel. Awarding points to newly released records, her delivery of 'I'll give it five' in a Black Country accent came out as 'Oi'll give it foyve' and the phrase caught on – also her mitigating remark for some awful performance, '. . .but **I like the backing. . .**'.

I'll take a rain-check (or **let's take a...**) phrase for proposing that you call off an arrangement and postpone it till another time. Originally, in the US, a rain-check (or -cheque) was a ticket for re-admission to a sporting event when the event had had to be postponed because of rain. The person to whom it was given would be able to produce it at a later date and claim free admission. Used since the 1940s in the US, since the 1960s in the UK.

I'll try anything once! meaning, '**there's always a first time**, so I'll do it' – and often said somewhat fatalistically. H.L. Mencken noted 'I am always glad to try anything once' as an 'American saying not recorded before the nineteenth century'. Certainly current by 1921.

I'm a stranger here myself, (no, I'm sorry) excuse given for inability or unwillingness to be of assistance to someone who comes up to you in the street asking, say, for directions. Since the 1950s? *I'm a Stranger Here Myself* is the title of a book (1938) by Ogden Nash and also of a song with lyrics by Ogden Nash and music by Kurt Weill from the show *One Touch of Venus* (1943). It is also a line spoken in Nicholas Ray's camp Western *Johnny Guitar* (1953) and the title of two books, one by John Seymour (1978), 'the story of a Welsh farm', and one by Deric Longden (1994) described as a view of 'Huddersfield seen as a foreign country'.

I'm all behind like the cow's tail! what people say when they are behind with their tasks, and have done since the nineteenth century.

I'm all right, Jack! (or **fuck/damn you, Jack, I'm all right!**) in the mid-twentieth century, this catchphrase had come to represent the selfish, uncaring attitude of any person or group of people. *I'm All Right Jack* was the title of a British film (1959) satirizing labour relations, bosses and the trade unions. The unbowdlerized versions may well have arisen in the Royal Navy in the late nineteenth century, hence the use of 'Jack', the traditional name for a sailor since *c* 1700. Hence also the example included in Sir David Bone's naval novel *The Brassbounder* (1910): 'It's "Damn you, Jack – I'm all right!" with you chaps.'

I'm as mad as hell and I'm not taking any more   political slogan adopted in 1978 by Howard Jarvis (1902–86), the California social activist, when campaigning to have property taxes reduced. Jarvis entitled a book *I'm Mad as Hell* but duly credited Paddy Chayevsky with the coinage. Chayevsky wrote the film *Network* (1976) in which Peter Finch played a TV pundit-cum-evangelist who exhorted his viewers to get mad: 'I want you to get up right now and go to the window, open it and stick your head out and yell: "I'm as mad as hell, and I'm not going to take this any more!"'

I'm dreaming, oh my darling love, of thee!   refrain from Edgar Wallace's poem 'Dreaming of Thee'/'The Lovesick Tommy's Dream of Home' quoted in mockery of such maudlin sentiment. Became popular in 1938 when the British comedy performer Cyril Fletcher recited it in caricature Cockney voice in a BBC broadcast.

Fletcher's customary cry when embarking on one of his 'Odd Odes' was **pin back your lugholes!** (i.e. 'listen here, lend me your ears') and it was known by the late 1930s. Other Fletcherisms have included **thanking you!** (genteelly pronounced 'thenking yew', and as *Thanking Yew* used as the title of a BBC radio series, 1940) and **ours is a nice 'ouse ours is** – from the possibly Cockney and ironic description which may date back to the 1920s – the sort of argument a respectable matron might advance to prevent any behaviour in the home of which she might disapprove.

I'm ——, fly me!   slogan for National Airlines in the US, current in the early 1970s – e.g. 'I'm Margie, fly me', referring to (supposedly actual) air hostesses whose pictures appeared in the advertisements. The campaign aroused the ire of feminist groups. Another suggestive line used was, 'I'm going to fly you like you've never been flown before'. The group 10 CC had a hit with 'I'm Mandy Fly Me', obviously inspired by the slogan, in 1976. Wall's Sausages later parodied it in Britain with, 'I'm meaty, fry me' (also 1976).

I'm free!   lilting cry of 'Mr Humphries' (John Inman), the extremely camp salesman of menswear at Grace Bros store in the BBC TV comedy series *Are You Being Served?* (1974–84).

I'm from Missouri (you'll have to show me)   a way of showing scepticism and demanding proof. From something said by Willard D. Vandiver, a Congressman from Columbia, Missouri, 1897 to 1905: 'I come from a state that raises corn and cotton and cockleburs and Democrats, and frothy eloquence neither convinces nor satisfies me. I am from Missouri. You have got to show me.' Inspecting the Navy Yard at Philadelphia in 1899 as a member of the House Naval Committee, Vandiver good-humouredly made the above statement when speaking at a dinner. Missouri, accordingly, became known as the 'Show Me' state.

I'm going down now, sir!   *see* **don't forget the diver!**

I'm going to make him an offer he can't refuse   tough-talking businessman's catchphrase from Mario Puzo's novel about the Mafia, *The Godfather* (1969). Johnny Fontane, a singer, desperately wants a part in a movie and goes to see his 'godfather', Don Corleone, for help. All the contracts have been signed and there is no chance of the studio chief changing his mind. Still, the godfather promises Fontane he will get him the part. As he says of the studio chief, 'He's a businessman. I'll make him an offer he can't refuse.'

In the 1971 film, this became, 'I'm going to make him an offer he can't refuse' and, in 1973, Jimmy Helms had a hit with the song 'Gonna Make You An Offer You Can't Refuse'.

I'm in charge!   mock-bossy catchphrase of the British entertainer Bruce Forsyth when hosting the ATV show *Sunday Night at the London Palladium* (from 1958). One night he was surpervising 'Beat the Clock', a game involving members of the audience, when a young couple got into a muddle, throwing plates at a see-saw table. Bruce Forsyth recalled (1980): 'We had a particularly stroppy contestant. In the end I just turned round and told him, "Hold on a minute. . .I'm in charge!" It just happened, but the audience loved it and it caught on.'

I'm looking for someone to love!　the honest lament of 'Arthur Fallowfield' (Kenneth Williams), a loam-rich-voiced country-man in BBC radio's *Beyond Our Ken* (early 1960s).

I'm only here for the beer!　'I'm not here to help, show goodwill, or anything else, but just to get drunk and enjoy the free hospitality.' From a slogan for the British beer Double Diamond, in the early 1970s. It passed into the language as an inconsequential catchphrase, though – from the advertiser's point of view – hardly a good slogan because it became detached from the particular brand of beer.

I'm sorry I'll read that again　the BBC radio newsreader's traditional apology for a stumble. Registered as a catchphrase when it became the title of a long-running radio comedy show (1964–73) featuring ex-Cambridge Footlights performers.

I'm worried about Jim!　Ellis Powell played the eponymous heroine of BBC radio's *Mrs Dale's Diary*, which ran from 1948 to 1969, and this is what she always seemed to be confiding to that diary about her doctor husband. Although she may not have spoken the phrase very often, it was essential in parodies of the programme.

I've arrived – and to prove it, I'm here!　*see* **good idea, son!**

I've died and gone to heaven!　I'm in ecstasy, in a state of bliss (but also used ironically in situations where the opposite is the case). American, possibly of black origin, and in vogue by the 1980s.

I've failed!　In a Sherlock Holmes sketch (of the 1940s/50s), the Scots comedian Dave Willis would come on stage with a huge magnifying glass. Peering through it, he would go up to an imaginary flower and, without bending his knees, would balance and hover over it, examining it through the glass, getting closer and closer until he fell over. 'I've failed!' he would wail in a wee voice.

In a song about war-time air-raids he would sing: 'Then all run helter-skelter/But don't run after me,/You'll no get in my shelter/For it's far too wee!' Hence, he would declare of others, **'You're far too wee!'** From the same source came, 'An aeroplane, an aeroplane, away, way up 'a 'ky' – hence, **Way up 'a 'ky** (English: 'Way up in the sky').

I've given you the best years of my life! what one half of a fictional couple is apt to say when they are splitting up. Something like the line is spoken in the film *Mr and Mrs Smith* (US, 1941).

I've got the time if you've got the inclination chatting-up line also used in response to an expletive like 'fuck me!' or 'bugger me!' American origin, since the 1950s?

I've had more —— than you've had hot dinners originally perhaps 'I've had more women...', this is an experienced person's boast to one less so. Well-established by the mid-twentieth century.

I've seen the elephant an American expression meaning that the speaker does not consider himself to be a raw recruit – he has been bloodied by experience and has seen all there is to see. According to John D. Unruh Jr, *The Plains Across: The Overland Emigrants and the Trans-Mississippi West, 1840–60* (1979), this was a popular expression in nineteenth-century America, 'connoting, in the main, experiencing hardship and difficulty and somehow surviving'. Another version continues: '...**and I've heard the owl, and I've been to the other side of the mountain**'. Clearly, even in the early part of that century, an elephant was still the prime example of something remarkable and worth going out of one's way to see.

I've started so I'll finish... in BBC TV's *Mastermind* quiz (first broadcast in 1972), the chairman, Magnus Magnusson, would say this if one of his questions was interrupted when the time ran out. It became a figure of speech – sometimes also given a double meaning.

if anything can go wrong, it will observation commonly known as Murphy's Law (or Sod's Law or Spode's Law), this saying dates back to the 1940s. The Australian *Macquarie Dictionary* (1981) suggests that it was named after a character who always made mistakes, in a series of educational cartoons published by the US Navy. Its inventor has been named as George Nichols, a project manager for Northrop, the Californian aviation firm, in 1949. He developed the idea from a remark by a colleague, Captain Edward A. Murphy Jr of the Wright Field-Aircraft Laboratory, 'If there is a wrong way to do something, then someone will do it.'

if I said you had a beautiful body would you hold it against me? chatting-up line that became the title of a hit song by the American duo, the Bellamy Brothers, in 1979 (though they sang 'have' instead of 'had'). But it was known before. The BBC TV comedy show *Monty Python's Flying Circus* had it in 1970 but, not unexpectedly, the British comedian Max Miller (1895–1963), seems to have got there first. In a selection of his jokes once published by the *Sunday Dispatch* (in the 1950s?) we find: 'I saw a girl who was proud of her figure. Just to make conversation I asked her, "What would you do if a chap criticised your figure?" "Well," she said, "I wouldn't hold it against him." '

if in doubt, strike it out! journalist's lore, meaning, 'if you're not sure of a fact or about the wisdom of including an item of information or opinion, leave it out'. It may be that the advice was more specific, originally. Mark Twain in *Pudd'nhead Wilson* (1894) says: 'As to the adjective, when in doubt strike it out.' The precise phrase appears in the 'Green Book' issued *c* 1949 to guide BBC Light Entertainment producers as to which jokes were, or were not, then permissible on the radio: 'Material about which a producer has any doubts should, if it cannot be submitted to someone in higher authority, be deleted, and an artist's assurance that it has been previously broadcast is no justification for repeating it. "When in doubt, take it out" is the wisest maxim.'

if it ain't broken, why fix it? modern proverbial expression, meaning, 'don't interfere with what is working perfectly well as it is'. American in origin, it made an early appearance with Bert Lance, President Carter's Director of the Office of Management and Budget, speaking on the subject of governmental reorganization in 1977.

if it moves, salute it, if it don't, paint it! sardonic catchphrase summing up American and British military attitudes since the 1940s. A longer version is: 'If you can lift it, carry it; if you can't lift it, paint it; if it moves of its own accord, salute it.' Latterly there has been the more vulgar (from the US), 'If it moves, salute it; if it doesn't move, paint it; if you can't paint it, fuck it!' This links to a sentiment attributed to the well-known bachelor and hi-tech British journalist, Andrew Neil (in 1990): 'if you can't plug it into the mains or fuck it, the editor's not interested.'

if it was raining pea soup I'd only have a fork   one of a series of moans by the terminally miserable/unfortunate/ disaster-prone that seems to have its origins in Australia in the 1940s. Others: '**if it was raining palaces I'd end up with a toilet at the bottom of the garden**' – a British version of the Australian: '**if it was raining palaces, I'd be hit on the head with the handle of a dunny [privy] door**'; '**if it was raining virgins, I'd end up with a poofter**'.

if it's Tuesday, this must be Belgium   *If It's Tuesday, This Must be Belgium* was the title of a 1969 film about a group of American tourists rushing around Europe. It popularized (if not originated) a format phrase which people could use when they were in the midst of any kind of hectic activity, whilst also reflecting on the confused state of many tourists superficially 'doing' the sights without really knowing where they are.

if you can't be good, be careful!   *see* **be good...**

if you can't beat 'em, join 'em!   familiar proverb, probably American in origin in the alternative form, 'If you can't lick 'em, join 'em'. Meaning that, if a rival faction is more successful than one's own, it is better to go over to their side. Since the 1940s, possibly first used in a political context. Compare the Scottish proverb 'Better bend than break'.

if you can't stand the heat get out of the kitchen   if you can't stand the pace or the strain, don't get involved. Particularly referring to the burden of decision-making and hostile criticism that any politican has to endure. Usually attributed to US President Harry S Truman (in about 1952) who may actually have said something rather more down-to-earth: 'If you can't stand the stink, get out of the shit-house.'

if you knows of a better 'ole, go to it!, (well)   fatalistic acceptance of adverse circumstances, this expression comes from the caption to a cartoon (1915) by the British cartoonist, Bruce Bairnsfather. It depicted the soldier 'Old Bill' with a comrade, under bombardment and up to their waists in mud on the Somme during the First World War. Two films (UK, 1918; US, 1926), based on the strip, were called *The Better 'Ole* and followed a musical with the title staged in London and New York (1917–18).

if you want anything, just whistle! amatory but not exactly chatting-up phrase, derived from lines in the film *To Have and Have Not* (1945). What Lauren Bacall says to Humphrey Bogart (and not the other way round) is: 'You know you don't have to act with me, Steve. You don't have to say anything, and you don't have to do anything. Not a thing. Oh, maybe just whistle. You know how to whistle, don't you, Steve? You just put your lips together and blow.'

if you want me, Thingmy, ring me! catchphrase from the Scottish BBC radio show *It's All Yours* (early 1950s). Stanley Baxter as 'Bella Vague' (who called everyone 'Thingmy') would say as an exit line: 'Don't forget, I'm in the book – so if you want me, Thingmy, ring me!' Willie Joss would say '**Arrivederci!**' and Jimmy Logan's phrase was '**Sausages are the boys!**', meaning 'That's the best!'

if you want to get ahead, get a hat! slogan for the (British) Hat Council and remembered from the early 1950s, if not from much earlier.

if you'll excuse the pun! parenthetical filler phrase, of the kind used by the humourless, after having sunk to making one. Alternatives are **pardon the pun!** and **no pun intended!** Nothing new about it: in *Pictures from Italy* (1846), Charles Dickens wrote, 'The ten fingers, which are always – I intend no pun – at hand.'

illegal, immoral or fattening, (anything you like is either) originated in a view set forth by Alexander Woollcott in *The Knock at the Stage Door* (1933): 'All the things I really like to do are either illegal, immoral, or fattening.' Compare the song, 'It's Illegal, It's Immoral Or It Makes You Fat' by Griffin, Hecht, and Bruce, popularized in the UK by the Beverley Sisters (1950s).

illegitimi(s) non carborundum   a cod-Latin phrase supposed to mean 'don't let the bastards grind you down' and coming in various spellings and versions. Popular since the Second World War though something like the phrase has also been reported from 1929. During the war, it was used by US General 'Vinegar Joe' Stilwell as his motto. 'Carborundum' is the trade-name of a very hard substance composed of silicon carbide, used in grinding.

The same meaning is also conveyed by the phrase *nil carborundum...* (as in the title of a play by Henry Livings, 1962) – a pun upon the genuine Latin *nil desperandum* ('never say die' – lit.: 'there is nought to be despaired of') which comes from '*nil desperandum est Teucro duce et auspice Teucro*' [nothing is to be despaired of with Teucer as leader and protector] (Horace, *Odes*, I.vii.27).

in like Flynn   someone who is 'in like Flynn' is a quick seducer – at least, according to the Australian use of the phrase. Appropriately, it is derived from the name of Errol Flynn (1909–59), the Australian-born film actor. It alludes to his legendary bedroom prowess, though the phrase can also mean that a person simply seizes an offered opportunity (of any kind). From the 1940s onwards, and used in the US to mean someone who was into anything automatically or quickly.

in your shell-like (ear), (let me have a word)   phrase used when asking to have a 'quiet word' with someone. Mocking a poetic simile known since the nineteenth century; for example, Thomas Hood's *Bianca's Dream* (1827) has: 'Her small and shell-like ear'.

include me out!   leave me out of this discussion or plan – a famous and typical 'Goldwynism', that is a remark made by the Hollywood film producer Samuel Goldwyn (1882–1974). Goldwyn had a habit of massacring the English language in a way that nevertheless conveyed vividly what he wanted to say. This phrase apparently arose when Goldwyn and Jack L. Warner were in disagreement over a labour dispute. Busby Berkeley, who had made his first musical for Goldwyn, was discovered moonlighting for Warner Brothers. Goldwyn said to Warner: 'How can we sit together and deal with this industry if you're going to do things like this to me? If this is the way you do it, gentlemen, include me out!'

Many Goldwynisms are invented but Goldwyn himself might appear to have acknowledged this one when speaking at Balliol College, Oxford, on 1 March 1945: 'For years I have been known for saying "Include me out" but today I am giving it up for ever.'

inconspicuous as Liberace at a wharfies' picnic, as *see* **as busy as a...**

is Bismarck a herring? *see* **is the Pope (a) Catholic?**

is everybody happy? rallying call of several entertainers and the traditional cry of holiday camp hosts. The American comedian Harry Brown has been mentioned as using it in the early 1900s. Ian Whitcomb states in *After the Ball* (1972): 'Ted Lewis, ex-clarinettist of the Earl Fuller Jazz Band [post 1919], toured as the "Top-Hatted Tragedian of Jazz", the Hamlet of the Halls, posing the eternal question, "Is everybody happy?"' 'Is Everybody Happy Now?' was a popular song in the US (1927) and *Is Everybody Happy?* was the title of an early sound film (US, 1929; remade 1943) recounting the life of Ted Lewis and featuring him.

is he one of us? question posed concerning anyone being considered for membership of a select group, but specifically said to have been a frequent test of her colleagues' loyalty by Margaret Thatcher when British Prime Minister (in use by 1985).

is it bigger than a breadbox? *What's My Line?* has been a popular TV panel game in the US and the UK since 1950 with panellists attempting to work out what jobs the challengers do. In the US, while attempting to establish the size of an article made by one contestant, the comedian Steve Allen formulated the classic enquiry 'is it bigger than a breadbox?' From 'Tinseltown' in Armistead Maupin, *Further Tales of the City* (1982): ' Right...how big was his dick again?...Bigger than a breadbox?' "

is it true...blondes have more fun? *see* **blondes have more fun.**

is she a friend of Dorothy? inquiry as to whether a man [*sic*] is homosexual. Probably this originated among American homosexuals, and was current by 1984. 'Dorothy' was the put-upon heroine of *The Wizard of Oz* and was played in the 1939 film by

Judy Garland, a woman much revered in male homosexual circles.

A similar expression, current at much the same time, was **does he dance at the other end of the ball-room?**

is she. . .or isn't she? slogan for Harmony hair-spray, in the UK, current in 1980. Nothing to do with the slogan **does she. . .or doesn't she?**, but a deliberate echo – as, presumably, was the line 'Is she or isn't she a phoney?', spoken in the film *Breakfast at Tiffany's* (1961).

The advertisement went on: 'Harmony has a ultra-fine spray to leave hair softer and more natural. She *is* wearing a hairspray but with Harmony it's so fine you're the only one that knows for sure.' The slogan also had a nudging quality as thought it was questioning the woman's sexual nature or experience (as in '**is he or isn't he. . .a homosexual**').

—— **is the name of the game** meaning '. . .is what it's all about', a phrase from the US of the early 1960s. National Security Adviser McGeorge Bundy talking about foreign policy goals in Europe in 1966 said: 'Settlement is the name of the game.' In time, almost everything was, following the title of an American TV movie called *Fame Is the Name of the Game* (1966). Then followed several series of TV's *The Name of the Game* (1968–71). The expression was replaced for a while by —— **is where it's at**.

is the Pope (a) Catholic? one of several common American 'responses to stupid questions', along with: **do chickens have lips?**, **can snakes do push-ups?**, **do frogs have water-tight assholes?** and **does a bear shit in the woods?** Possibly dating from the 1950s. In the *Midwestern Journal of Language and Folklore* (1975), Charles Clay Doyle described these phrases as 'sarcastic interrogative affirmatives'. Robert L. Chapman in his *New Dictionary of American Slang* (1986) provides these further examples (in addition to the variations, 'is the Pope Polish/Italian?'): **does a wooden horse have a hickory dick?**, **does a dog have fleas?**, **is Bismarck a herring?**, **does Muhammad Ali own a mirror?**

is there a doctor in the house? traditional cry, usually in a theatre or at some other large gathering of people, when a member of the audience is taken ill. One suspects it dates from the nineteenth century, if not before. *Doctor in the House* (1952) was the title of a novel by Richard Gordon (but is also a play on the term 'house doctor').

is there a law against it? reply to a suggestion the speaker thinks is unreasonable, meaning 'why shouldn't I?' Since the 1950s? In the US: **is there some kind of law?**

is there —— after ——? a format phrase derived from the question of whether there is life after death, of which there have been numerous versions since the 1960s. Popular with journalists: 'Is there life after redundancy?' (1984), 'Can there be life after Wogan?' (1984). An American book by Don A. Aslett had the title *Is There Life After Housework?* (1981) and there have been films *Is There Sex After Death?* (1973) and *Is There Sex After Marriage?* (1976). 'Is there life *before* death?' had earlier been the epigraph to Chapter 9 of Stephen Vizinczey's novel *In Praise of Older Women* (1966), credited to 'Anon. Hungarian'.

is where it's at *see* **—— is the name of the game**.

is you is or is you ain't? are you or are you not. . .? From the song 'Is You Is Or Is You Ain't My Baby?' (1943) written by Louis Jordan and Billy Austin. It suffered a revival in *c* 1990 when commercials for a British credit card included the jingle, 'Does you does or does you don't take Access?'

is your journey really necessary? are you travelling just for the sake of it? A slogan first devised in 1939 to discourage evacuated British civil servants from going home for Christmas. From 1941, it was addressed to all civilians, to try and prevent a burden being put on the railway network during wartime.

it ain't over till it's over *see* **game isn't over till it's over**.

it all depends what you mean by... phrase used by arguers and debaters. *The Brains Trust* was a popular discussion programme first broadcast on BBC radio in 1941. A regular participant was 'Professor' C.E.M. Joad (1891–1953) who became something of a national figure. His discussion technique was to try and undermine arguments by using the phrase which made him famous. When the chairman once read out a question from a listener, Mr W.E. Jack of Keynsham – 'Are thoughts things or about things?' – Joad inevitably began his answer with 'It all depends what you mean by a "thing".'

it can't happen here! self-deluding catchphrase that appears to have arisen in the US in the 1930s. Sinclair Lewis's novel *It Can't Happen Here* was published in 1935 and adapted for the stage the following year. It warned against fascism in the United States.

it couldn't have happened to a nicer chap/guy he deserves it – whatever stroke of luck he has received. From the 1940s. Now increasingly used, ironically, when misfortune has struck.

it don't arf make you larf! favourite phrase of the British comedian Max Wall (1908–90), him of the incomparable voice and appearance. By the 1950s.

it looks like something out of *Quatermass* said of a peculiar-looking plant or growth – but especially of a rambling and leafy one. The allusion is to *The Quatermass Experiment* (BBC TV, 1953) – first in a series of science-fiction drama series by Nigel Kneale involving a certain Professor Quatermass. In this one, viewers were held enthralled by the tale of a British astronaut who returned from a space trip and started turning into a plant. Eventually, he holed up in Poets' Corner at Westminster Abbey, by which time he was a mass of waving fronds.

it must have been something he/she/I ate reason advanced for a person's mood or behaviour, as though it could only be accounted for in terms of food eaten that has had an unsettling effect. From the 1950s.

it seemed like a good idea at the time limp excuse for having started out on some project that has gone awry. It is spoken, for example, in a 1931 film called *The Last Flight*, the story of a group of American airmen who remain in Europe after the end of the First World War. One of them is gored to death when he leaps into the arena during a bullfight. Journalists outside the hospital ask his friend why the man should have done such a thing. The friend (played by Richard Barthelmess) replies: 'Because it seemed like a good idea at the time.' Compare **because it's there.**

it sends me!   the way for young people to describe the effect of popular music on their souls, especially in the 1950s, but it had been known since the 1930s.

it takes two to tango!   co-operation is what it's all about. A modern proverbial expression which appears to derive directly from the song 'Takes Two to Tango' (1952), written by Al Hoffman and Dick Manning, and popularized by Pearl Bailey. An obvious sexual application is implicit.

it was a dark and stormy night. . .   a story-teller's clichéd opening. As a scene-setting phrase, this appears to have been irresistible to more than one story-teller over the years and has now become a joke. It was used in all seriousness by the English novelist Edward Bulwer-Lytton at the start of *Paul Clifford* (1830). At some stage, the phrase also became part of a jokey children's 'circular' story-telling game, 'The tale without an end'. Iona and Peter Opie in *The Lore and Language of Schoolchildren* (1959) describe the workings thus: 'The tale usually begins: "It was a dark and stormy night, and the Captain said to the Bo'sun, 'Bo'sun, tell us a story', so the Bo'sun began. . ."' And such is any child's readiness to hear a good story that the tale may be told three times round before the listeners appreciate that they are being diddled.'

Used as the title of one of Charles Schultz's 'Snoopy' books (1960s), the line is also given to Snoopy in his doomed attempts to write the Great American Novel.

it was going to be a long night   'He was doing the crossword from *The Washington Star*. He had finished three clues; it was going to be a long night' – Jeffrey Archer, *Shall We Tell the President* (1977), but a cliché of earlier origin.

it went round twice and then didn't fit   *see* **queer as Dick's hatband.**

it'll all come out in the wash   truth will emerge in due course, a situation will be resolved. The English novelist Anthony Trollope was using the expression in the 1870s, though the phrase appears to have been put into common parlance by Rudyard Kipling via its use as a refrain in his 1903 poem 'Stellenbosch': 'And it all goes into the laundry,/But it never comes out in the wash...'.

it'll be all right on the night!   don't worry, everything will work/be OK when we actually come to doing it. A reassuring theatrical phrase dating from the late nineteenth century, at least. Curiously – when the phrase has to be invoked – things quite often *are* better on the subsequent (first) night. In the same way, a disastrous dress rehearsal often foreshadows a successful first night. The phrase was the title of a song by Alan Melville and Ivor Novello in the musical *Gay's the Word* (1950) and was also used as the title of a long-running series of TV 'blooper' programmes in the 1980s, though witlessly spelt 'alright'.

it'll play in Peoria   the policy will appeal to voters in 'Middle America', the middle ground, ordinary people away from the centres of the media. In about 1968, when Richard Nixon was standing for the American presidency, John Ehrlichman is credited with having devised this yardstick. Peoria is in Illinois and was earlier the hometown of one of Sgt Bilko's men in the 1950s TV series – so was picked on humorously even then.

it's a fair cop!   *see* **bang to rights.**

it's a hard life!   jocular or ironic exclamation, often when the 'hardness' is merely trivial – as when repeatedly having to answer the door or the phone. Early twentieth century, US and UK.

it's a wrap!   that's it, we've finished for the day. Film/TV slang, after the expression 'wrap it up', meaning to put an end to something, presumably because wrapping up is the last thing you do when a goods purchase has been completed. Since the 1960s/70s.

it's all done in the best possible taste, (but)   justification for, say, nudity being used in a stage production or film. From *The Kenny Everett Television Show* (BBC TV, 1980s), in which the line was spoken by Everett as a large-breasted Hollywood actress, 'Cupid Stunt', being interviewed about her latest role. Taken from the sort of thing actresses invariably do say in this situation.

it's all happening! a rather 1960s phrase intended to suggest that life is very exciting and swinging. A British film with the title came out in 1963. *Gadzooks It's All Happening* was the title of a BBC TV show a year or two later.

In the same period, Norman Vaughan used the stock phrase **it's all been happening this week!** to introduce topical gags when he was compèring TV's *Sunday Night at the London Palladium* (from 1962).

it's all part of life's rich pageant! phrase with which to dismiss a misfortune or disaster phlegmatically. In the film *A Shot in the Dark* (1964), Peter Sellers as 'Inspector Clouseau' has just fallen into a fountain when Elke Sommer commiserates with him: 'You'll catch your death of pneumonia.' Clouseau replies, 'It's all part of life's rich pageant.'

The origin of this phrase – sometimes **life's rich pattern** or **tapestry** is substituted for 'pageant' – may lie in a gramophone record monologue called 'The Games Mistress', written and performed by Arthur Marshall in the mid-1930s. It concludes, 'Never mind, dear – laugh it off, laugh it off. It's all part of life's rich pageant.' Consequently, Marshall called his autobiography, *Life's Rich Pageant* (1984).

it's all part of the service! response to an expression of gratitude from a customer. Spoken by a tradesman it suggests that thanks (or further payment) are not necessary as he has 'only been doing his job'. Elevated to a slogan by Austin Reed, the British menswear stores, in 1930 as: **it's just a part of the Austin Reed service.**

it's been a hard day's night catchphrase meaning that the speaker has had an exhausting time and derived from *A Hard Day's Night*, the title of the Beatles' first feature film (UK, 1964). The title was apparently chosen towards the end of filming when Ringo Starr used the phrase to describe a 'heavy' night out (according to Ray Coleman, *John Lennon*, 1984). What, in fact, Ringo must have done was to use the title of the Lennon and McCartney song (presumably already written if it was towards the end of filming) in a conversational way. Indeed, Hunter Davies in *The Beatles* (1968) noted: 'Ringo Starr came out with the phrase, though John had used it earlier in a poem.'

it's being so cheerful as keeps me going!   plucky statement given an ironic twist when used in the BBC radio comedy show *ITMA* (1940s). There it was said by the gloomy, down-in-the-mouth laundrywoman 'Mona Lott' (Joan Harben). When told to keep her pecker up by Tommy Handley, the show's star, she would reply, 'I always do, sir, it's being so cheerful as keeps me going.' Her family was always running into bad luck, so she had plenty upon which to exercise her particular form of fortitude. Something like the phrase had earlier appeared in a *Punch* cartoon of 27 September 1916: 'Wot a life. No rest, no beer, no nuffin. It's only us keeping so cheerful as pulls us through.'

it's fingerlickin' good!   it's so tasty that you even want to lick it off your fingers. A slogan for Kentucky Fried Chicken, current by the late 1950s. But the word 'fingerlickin'' may have been an established southern US/possibly black/musicians' phrase before being made famous by the slogan. 'Licking good', on its own, was a phrase current by the 1890s.

it's liberty hall!   *see* **anything goes!**

it's not cricket   it isn't fair or proper or the done thing. An expression suggesting that certain conduct is not worthy of an Englishman and a gentleman. Known by the 1850s in connection with the game of cricket itself, but then figuratively elsewhere. 'AS IT WERE NOT QUITE CRICKET' – *Punch* headline (15 January 1902). In *First Childhood*, (1934), Lord Berners quotes the remark, 'To kick your wife! And in public too! It's not cricket, is it?' and footnotes thus: ' "Not cricket", an expression which came into vogue in the 'nineties to denote actions considered unworthy of an Englishman and a gentleman.'

it's not fancy, but it's good!   slogan for Horn & Hardart, the American restaurant chain that dispenses meals through vending machines. Current in the 1960s.

it's not over till it's over!   warning phrase comparable to **the opera ain't over till the fat lady sings** and of American origin also. By the 1980s.

it's not the heat, it's the humidity!   expression explaining why you are uncomfortable in a certain type of climate. Popular with British forces in the Middle East and Far East during the Second World War, but apparently of American origin. The first paragraph of P.G. Wodehouse's novel *Sam the Sudden* (1925) describes the inhabitants of New York on a late August afternoon: '[One half] crawling about and asking those they met if this was hot enough for them, the other maintaining that what they minded was not so much the heat as the humidity.' In his book *What Is a Bromide?* (1906), the American author Gelett Burgess lists 'it's not the heat, it's the humidity' as the sort of thing a 'bromide' (someone addicted to clichés and platitudes) would say.

it's only rock'n'roll meaning, 'it doesn't matter; the importance should not be exaggerated'. From the title of a song by Mick Jagger and Keith Richard of the Rolling Stones (1974).

it's showtime, folks! exclamation used by theatrical people, sometimes to remind themselves that now is the time to get out there on the stage and shine, and sometimes used a touch sarcastically. Also used in other fields where an element of performance or presentational glitter is required. In the film *All That Jazz* (US, 1979), Roy Scheider (playing a choreographer) ritually says the line before getting on with whatever has to be done in his life.

it's that man again! BBC radio's hugely popular comedy show *ITMA* (1940s) took as its title an acronym based on a late 1930s expression, often used in newspaper headlines, referring to Adolf Hitler, who was always bursting into the news with some territorial claim or other.

it's the old army game! phrase summing up the attitude of those condemned to spend their lives in the ranks. Apparently of American origin, possibly by 1900, it refers to the military system as it works to the disadvantage of those in the lower ranks. From Theodore Fredenburgh's *Soldiers March* (1930): 'I get the idea. It's the old army game: first, pass the buck. . .'. *The Army Game* was the title of an immensely popular British TV comedy series (1957–62).

it's the thought that counts, (ah well) conventional response when a gift is considered to be of little value or inappropriate. By the 1960s?

it's turned out nice again! the British North Country entertainer George Formby (1904–61) disclaimed any credit for originating the phrase with which he always opened his act. 'It's
simply a familiar Lancashire expression', he once said. 'People
use it naturally up there. I used it as part of a gag and have been
doing so ever since' – particularly in his films when emerging
from some disaster or other. It was used as the title of one of these
films in 1941 (as well as being the punchline of it) and as the title
of a song.

it's what your right arm's for! slogan for Courage Tavern (ale),
current in the UK by the early 1970s. Although the line became a
popular catchphrase – referring to the lure of drinking – it risked
being applied to rival products as well. Possibly of earlier origin.

it's worse than a crime, it's a blunder! from a remark uttered in
connection with the execution of the Duc d'Enghien in 1804.
Napoleon, suspecting the duke of being involved in royalist con-
spiracies against him, had him captured and executed, an act that
hardened opinion against the French Emperor. But who said it?
Comte Boulay de la Meurthe (1761–1840) has been credited
with the remark, but among other names sometimes linked to it
are Talleyrand, Joseph Fouché and Napoleon himself. In French,
the remark is usually rendered as: *'C'est pire qu'un crime; c'est une
faute!'*

J
j

Jack Robinson   *see* **before you can say...**

Jesus saves, (but) Moses invests   one of several graffiti or lapel-button type jokes popular in the early 1980s. Known in the US and the UK, this particular example was current by 1979. 'Jesus saves' is still a common slogan of the more evangelistic type of Christian.

joke('s) over!   either said by the teller of a joke that has misfired or by the person to whom it has been told. By the 1920s.

jolly good show!   very English phrase of approbation, in use by the 1930s. Terry-Thomas (1911–90), the gap-toothed British comedian certainly said it, as also **oh, good show!** in his late 1940s and early 1950s monologues.

jolly hockey sticks!   exclamation of a certain type of girl or woman who is public school, gushing, games-playing and enthusiastic. 'Jolly hockey sticks' is also used adjectivally to describe such a person. Apparently the phrase was coined by the British actress Beryl Reid when playing the schoolgirl 'Monica' in the BBC radio series *Educating Archie* (1950s).

Judy...Judy...Judy!   impersonators always put this line in the mouth of Cary Grant, the English-born film actor (1904–86), though Grant always denied that he had ever said it and had a check made of all his films (in which, presumably, if he was referring to Judy Garland in character, he wouldn't have been calling her by her actual name, anyway). According to Richard Keyes, *Nice Guys Finish Seventh* (1992), Grant once said: 'I vaguely recall that at a party someone introduced Judy by saying, "Judy, Judy, Judy", and it caught on, attributed to me.'

jumpy as a one-legged cat in a sand-box, as   *see* **as busy as a...**

jury is still out on..., the   mostly a journalistic cliché, noticeable from the late 1980s, meaning that no final conclusion can be drawn, minds are not yet made up. Compare **a question-mark still hangs over...**

just fancy that!   often ironical exclamation after a revelation has been made which, to the speaker, was eminently predictable given what was known about the person/people involved beforehand. Since the 1880s.

just like that!   said in gruff tones and accompanied by small paddling gestures, this was the catchphrase of the British comedian Tommy Cooper (1922–84) – and a gift to mimics. It was not a premeditated catchphrase, he said. He only noticed it when impressionists and others singled it out from his mad 'failed conjuror' act. Inevitably, the phrase was used by Cooper as the title of his autobiography. There was also a song incorporating it.

just one of those things, (it was)   meaning, 'it was something inexplicable or inevitable' and is not to be taken too seriously. Ensured of immortality by its use as the title of a Cole Porter song (1935), but the form of words had been in existence by the 1870s.

just the facts, ma'am   *see* **all we want is the facts, ma'am!**

just what the doctor ordered   phrase of approval applied to anything that is just right or eminently agreeable – and by no means restricted to medicinal matters, healthy foods, etc. Known in the US and UK by the 1910s.

K
k

keep it under your hat! (or **keep it under your stetson!**) security slogans from the Second World War for the UK and US, respectively. Perhaps it meant that if information was retained within one's head, no one inappropriate would be able to get at it. The basic expression was known in the UK by the 1880s. *Under Your Hat* had been the title of a Cicely Courtneidge/Jack Hulbert musical comedy in London's West End (1938).

keep on truckin'! persevere, keep on 'keeping on', do your own thing – the slogan of a cartoon character created by the US 'underground' artist Robert Crumb in the 1960s. Possibly derived from 'the truck' or 'trucking', a jerky dance that came out of Harlem in the early 1930s. 'Trucking it' was also what tramps and hoboes were said to do, riding on or clinging to railroad trucks in the same period.

keep taking the tablets! traditionally what doctors advise patients to do to ensure that a complete cure is effected. Possibly turned into a catchphrase by the BBC radio *Goon Show* (1950s). Also the punchline of a joke (known by the 1970s) involving Moses and his tablets of stone.

keep up the good work! phrase of encouragement, the sort of thing likely to be uttered by any officer before, after, or instead of saying, 'Carry on, Sergeant!' Probably current in the UK before 1939. In the US, the phrase occurs in Eugene O'Neill's play *Long Day's Journey Into Night* (1953).

keep your legs together! (or **keep your legs crossed!**) jocular advice to a girl or woman in order that she can thwart sexual advances. Mostly in the US, by the 1930s, though 'Cross your legs' was what Billy Sunday, the American evangelist, used to advise the females in his audience in the 1890s, adding, when they had done so, 'Now the gates of hell are closed'.

keeping up with Joneses striving not to be outdone by one's neighbours. The expression comes from a comic strip by Arthur R. 'Pop' Momand entitled *Keeping up with the Joneses* which appeared in the New York *Globe* from 1913 to 1931. It is said that Momand had at first intended to call his strip 'Keeping up with the Smiths' but refrained because his own neighbours were actually of that name and some of the exploits he wished to report had been acted out by them in real life.

Kilroy was here the most widely known of graffiti slogans was brought to Europe by American GIs in the early 1940s and came to indicate that an American soldier had indeed been present at the place in order to be able to write it. As with most graffiti slogan writing, the underlying statement was 'I am here, I exist'. The phrase may have originated with James J. Kilroy (who died in 1962), a shipyard inspector in Quincy, Mass., who would chalk it up to indicate that a check had been made by him.

kind mother used to make, the like home cooking and thus very acceptable. This expression seems to have acquired figurative quotation marks around it by the early years of the twentieth century. As such, it is of American origin and was soon used by advertisers as a form of slogan (compare the US pop song of the Second World War, 'Ma, I Miss Your Apple Pie'). 'The kind mother used to make' was used as a slogan by New England Mincemeat' around 1900.

kindly leave the stage! *see* **I don't wish to know that!**

kipper's knickers *see* **bee's knees.**

kiss me, Hardy! jocular quotation of Lord Nelson's dying words, perhaps in order to poke fun at their inherent sentimentality. What exactly Nelson did say as he lay dying on HMS *Victory* at Trafalgar in 1805 has been the subject of some debate. It has been asserted that, according to the Nelson family, he was in the habit of saying 'kismet' (fate) when anything went wrong. It is therefore not *too* unlikely that he said, 'Kismet, Hardy' to his Flag

Captain, and that witnesses misheard, but there is no real reason to choose this version. In Ludovic Kennedy's *On My Way to the Club* (1989), he recalls his investigations into the matter: 'I was delighted to receive further confirmation from a Mr Corbett, writing from Hardy's home town of Portesham [in 1951]. He said that Nelson's grandson by his daughter Horatia had recently paid him a visit, at the age of over ninety. "He told me he had asked his mother what exactly had happened when Nelson was dying. She said she herself had asked Hardy, who replied, 'Nelson said, "Kiss me, Hardy" and I knelt down and kissed him" .'

kiss my grits!   meaning, 'to hell with you', a catchphrase from the American TV situation comedy *Alice* (1976–80). Uttered by 'Flo Castelberry', a Southern-born, man-hungry waitress (played by Polly Holliday), who later had her own series, *Flo* (1980–1). Presumably, 'kiss my arse' altered to sound like 'kiss my tits' ('grits' being, of course, the kind of American food made from coarsely ground grain that a waitress would serve).

kiss of death, the   either unwelcome support from an unpopular supporter (as for a politician) or the action or gesture that finally kills off a project. The original was the kiss of betrayal given by Judas to Christ which foreshadowed the latter's death. In the Mafia, too, a kiss from the boss is an indication that one's time is up. Compare *Kiss of Death*, the title of a gangster film (US, 1947). Known by the 1920s.

knock, knock!   catchphrase said to have been used by the British music-hall comedian Wee Georgie Wood (1895–1979). He used it in radio programmes in mid-1936, possibly as an imported American device to warn that a dubious joke was coming up. Later, 'knock, knock' was the name given to a type of (usually punning) joke popular in the US and the UK from the 1950/60s onwards, e.g.: 'Knock, knock!/Who's there?/Sam and Janet/Sam and Janet who?/Sam and Janet evening. . .'.

know what I mean?   *see* **nudge nudge, wink wink!**

know what I mean, 'Arry?   post-boxing match interview phrase supposedly used by the British fighter Frank Bruno to Harry

Carpenter, for many years BBC TV's chief match commentator. A catchphrase by the mid-1980s. Carpenter commented (1992): 'I only have to walk down the street or stand in a bar to have someone say to me: "Where's Frank?" or "Know what I mean, 'Arry?" (Strange how people always drop the aitch when they say that. Frank never does.)'.

L
l

last of the big spenders!, (ah), the ironic put-down, descriptive of someone who is being tight with his money. American, from the 1920s/30s.

late for your own funeral, you'd be admonition to someone who is chronically unpunctual. Origin and date unknown.

laugh all the way to the bank *see* **cry all the way to the bank.**

laugh? I thought I should have died (or . . .I thought I'd died) exaggerated expression to convey appreciation of a joke or, more usually, a comic happening. British use, since the 1880s. The line occurs in Albert Chevalier's song 'Knocked 'Em in the Old Kent Road' (1890s). Variants include . . .**I nearly bought my own beer!** and . . .**I nearly fell off the wife!**

laughing haversacks (I'll/he'll be) catchphrase indicative of anticipated pleasure, though also sometimes used simply as in 'I laughed haversacks. . .' The choice of 'haversacks' is puzzling. Could it mean, 'I'll laugh *loads*', especially when variants include 'laughing kitbags'? Mostly Forces' slang, since the 1930s.

lead on Macduff! meaning, 'you lead the way!; let's get started!', the expression is adapted from the line in Shakespeare's *Macbeth* (1606): '*Lay on*, Macduff;/And damn'd be he that first cries, "Hold, enough!"' ' There has also been a change of meaning along the way. Macbeth uses the words 'lay on' with the meaning 'deal blows with vigour, make vigorous attack'. The shape of the phrase was clearly so appealing that it was adapted to a different purpose.

let George do it! meaning, 'let someone else do it, or take the responsibility', this catchphrase was in use by 1910 and is probably of American origin.

let me have a word...   *see* **in your shell-like (ear)**.

let me tell you!   emphatic tag dating from the 1700s. During the Second World War, the BBC radio programme *Happidrome* featured Harry Korris as Mr Lovejoy, a theatre manager and Robby Vincent as Enoch, the call-boy. Enoch would say 'let me tell you, Mr Lovejoy', with every word emphasized, when revealing some startling fact.

let's do the show right here! (or **let's put on a show...**)   taken to be a staple line from films featuring the young Mickey Rooney and Judy Garland (1939 onwards). It had several forms: 'Hey! I've got it! Why don't we put on a show?'/'Hey kids! We can put on the show in the backyard!' In whatever form, the line has become a film cliché of youthful theatrical enthusiasm, now used only with amused affection.

let's get down to the nitty gritty   meaning, 'let's get down to the real basics of a problem or situation' (like getting down to brass tacks). Originally, a black American phrase, it seems to have had a particular vogue among Black Power campaigners in the early 1960s. In 1963, Shirley Ellis recorded a song 'The Nitty Gritty' to launch a new dance craze. The opening line of the record is, 'Now let's get down to the real nitty-gritty'. One theory is that the phrase originally referred to the grit-like nits or small lice that are hard to get out of one's hair or scalp, or to a black English term for the anus.

let's get on with it!   British husband and wife entertainers, Nat Mills and Bobbie, flourished in the 1930s and 1940s portraying 'a gumpish type of lad and his equally gumpish girlfriend'. Their catchphrase arose during the very early part of the Second World War and was taken from a works foreman whom they observed during a BBC radio *Workers' Playtime* broadcast from a factory in South Wales. Even Winston Churchill used the slogan to the troops during the early stages of the war.

let's get outta here!   staple line of American films. A survey of 350 feature films, made in the US between 1938 and 1985, revealed that the cry 'Let's get outta here!' was used at least once in 81 per cent of them and more than once in 17 per cent.

let's get this show on the road!   signal or encouragement to get started on any activity – originally in American show business. Perhaps originally from circus and travelling theatre use, it probably moved into the mainstream through the military and business. Certainly a catchphrase in the 1930s, and probably much earlier.

let's put on a show...   *see* **let's do the show right here!**

let's run it up the flagpole (and see who salutes it)!   in business and advertising circles, this construction is much used to indicate how an idea should be researched and tested, or rather, simply put to the public to see what the reaction will be. Some of the versions: **Let's put it on the porch and see if the cat will eat it/...put it on the train and see if it gets off at Westchester/...leave it in the water overnight and see if it springs any leaks/...pull something out of the hat here and see if it hops for us**. All these were known by the early 1980s and are largely American.

let's take a rain-check   *see* **I'll take a rain-check.**

licence to print money, it's a   said of any enterprise where there is easy money to be made. Roy Thomson (later Lord Thomson), the Canadian-born industrialist, said to a neighbour in Edinburgh just after the opening of Scottish Television (a commercial TV company he had founded) in 1957: 'You know, it's just like having a licence to print your own money.'

lie back and think of England   *see* **close your eyes and think of England.**

lies, damn lies and statistics, there are   statistics are the worst kind of lie. Although often attributed to Mark Twain – because it appears in his *Autobiography* (1924) – this should more properly be ascribed to Benjamin Disraeli, as indeed Twain took trouble to do. On the other hand, the remark remains untraced among Disraeli's writings and sayings.

life begins at forty   saying originated in 1932 by William J. Pitkin, a Professor of Journalism at Columbia University, New York. He published a book called *Life Begins at Forty* in which he dealt with 'adult reorientation' at a time when the problems of extended life and leisure were beginning to be recognized. It rapidly became a well-established catchphrase. Helping it along was a song with the title by Jack Yellen and Ted Shapiro (recorded by Sophie Tucker in 1937).

life is just a bowl of cherries   life is fun and full of delights. A modern proverbial expression that apparently originated in the song by Lew Brown (music by Ray Henderson), first heard in the American musical *Scandals of 1931*.

life is just one damned thing after another   view of life in which problems and difficulties 'come along in threes', just like buses. Known by the 1920s, when John Masefield even entitled a novel *Odtaa* (1926), an acronym made from the initials of the last few words of the phrase.

life isn't/wasn't meant to be easy   philosophical phrase (compare **life's unfair/life is hard**), but elevated to the status of political slogan in Australia when Malcolm Fraser was Liberal Prime Minister (1975–83). The phrase was very much associated with him and was used as the title of a biography by John Edwards in 1977. Douglas Aiton asked Fraser in an interview for the London *Times* (16 March 1981) if he had ever actually said it. Fraser replied, 'I said something very like it. It's from *Back to Methusaleh* by Bernard Shaw...A friend I was visiting in hospital asked me why I didn't give up politics and return to the good life [on his sheep farm]. I said life wasn't meant to be like that. That would be too easy. So that's what it grew from. I wouldn't mind a cent for every time it's been quoted or misquoted. It's the best thing I ever said.'

The derivation from Shaw was probably an afterthought. In a Deakin lecture on 20 July 1971, which seems to have been his first public use of the phrase, Fraser made no mention of Shaw. Referring rather to Arnold Toynbee's analysis of history, Fraser said: 'It involves a conclusion about the past that life has not been easy for people or for nations, and an assumption for the future that that condition will not alter. There is within me some part of the metaphysic, and thus I would add that life is not meant to be easy.'

In Shaw's play (1921), it appears in the form, 'Life is not meant to be easy, my child; but take courage: it can be delightful.' Even then, it was not, of course, a startlingly original view. In A.C. Benson's collection of essays *The Leaves of the Tree* (1912), he quotes Brooke Foss Westcott, Bishop of Durham, as saying: 'The only people with whom I have no sympathy . . . are those who say that things are easy. Life is not easy, nor was it meant to be.'

life's a bitch and then you die!   modern proverbial expression, probably of North American origin and current by the early 1980s. A development of it, known in both the US and the UK, is 'Life's a bitch, *you marry a bitch*, and then you die.' The punning **life's a beach** seems to have taken on a life of its own as a slogan in the early 1990s, especially in Australia.

life's too short. . . (or **life's short enough as it is**)   an excuse for not doing something. 'Life's too short for chess' occurs in Henry James Byron's play *Our Boys* (1874). 'Life's too short to stuff a mushroom' is the epigraph to Shirley Conran's home-help manual *Superwoman* (1975).

lift/elevator doesn't go to the top floor/all the way up   *see* **few vouchers short. . .**

light at the end of the tunnel, there is   meaning, there is a sign that some long-awaited relief – or a solution to some problem – is at hand. Mostly used in politics, British since the 1920s and American since the 1960s (especially with regard to the Vietnam War).

light the blue touch paper and retire immediately   said when doing something risky, though not necessarily physically dangerous: it could be no more than raising a contentious topic in conversation. From the instruction often to be found on fireworks. Popularized by Arthur Askey on BBC radio's *Band Waggon* (late 1930s).

light's on, but no one's in   *see* **few vouchers short. . .**

like a fart in a colander   indecisive; all over the place. British use since the 1920s at least. The complete expression, which makes

125

its meaning clear, may be something like: 'He's like a fart in a colander – can't make up his mind which hole to come out of!'

like a pork chop at a Jewish wedding (or . . .at a synagogue)   isolated, at a loose end, redundant, useless. Since the mid-twentieth century, because pork is a forbidden food as far as the Jews are concerned. Compare:

like a spare prick at a wedding, (standing about)   isolated, at a loose end, redundant, useless. By the mid-twentieth century and certainly by 1971 when John Osborne in *West of Suez* has 'like a professional spare prick at a wedding'. Compare the more polite **standing around like a lost lemon.**

like Brer Rabbit he lay low   he was reticent, kept out of the public eye. A fairly common conflation of what the American author Joel Chandler Harris actually wrote in 'The Wonderful Tar-Baby Story' from *Uncle Remus and His Legends of the Old Plantation* (1881): 'Tar-baby ain't sayin' nuthin', en Brer Fox, he lay low.' In fact, the phrase 'en Brer Fox, he lay low' is a phrase repeated rhythmically throughout the piece, as Frank Muir has noted, 'like a line in a Blues song'.

like something the cat's brought/dragged in, looking   bedraggled, a mess, a sight (sometimes concluded with . . .on a wet night). Possibly by the 1920s.

like the inside of a Turkish wrestler's jockstrap   *see* **mouth like the bottom of. . .**

like the man said   *see* **as the man said.**

like there was no tomorrow   desperately, as if this was the last chance to do something. Probably of American origin, noticed elsewhere in the 1970s.

likely as a snow-storm in Karachi, as   *see* **as busy as a. . .**

listen very carefully, I shall say this only once   line from the BBC TV comedy series *'Allo, 'Allo* (since 1984) about Resistance workers in occupied France during the Second World War. Used by Michelle, an agent of the Resistance, it somehow contrived to catch on. Jeremy Lloyd, one of the show's co-scriptwriters, used the line as the title of his autobiography (1993).

listen who's talking!   *see* **look who's talking!**

little of what you fancy does you good, a   nudging point of view from a song by Fred W. Leigh and George Arthurs. It was popularized, with a wink, by Marie Lloyd (1870–1922) in the 1890s.

live for ever!   *see* **true, O king!**

Lloyd George knew my father   even before the death of the British Prime Minister David Lloyd George in 1945, Welsh people away from home liked to claim some affinity with the Great Man. In time, this inclination was encapsulated in the singing of the words 'Lloyd George knew my father, my father knew Lloyd George' to the strains of 'Onward Christian Soldiers', which they neatly fit. The line may have been coined by Tommy Rhys Roberts QC (1910–75) whose father did indeed know Lloyd George.

loadsamoney!   'Loadsamoney' was the name of a character portrayed by the British comedy performer Harry Enfield, chiefly in the Channel 4 TV series *Friday Night Live* in 1987–8. He was intended to be a satirical embodiment of the money-worshipping philistinism of Margaret Thatcher's Britain but, regrettably, appeared to be savoured and loved. As sometimes happens, a satirical invention threatened to become a role model instead, and Enfield abandoned the character after a time.

long time no see!   farewell remark 'I have not seen you for a long time', as rendered in Chinese-sounding Pidgin English. Known by 1900. It appears fully formed in Raymond Chandler, *Farewell, My Lovely* (1940) and as a title in Ed McBain's *Long Time No See* (1977).

look, Ma, no hands!   American version of the British 'look, Mum, no hands!' or 'look, no hands!' when a child (usually) is demonstrating some feat to its elders, like riding a bicycle. Now used allusively about any activity to which the doer seeks to draw attention. Lesley Storm's comedy *Look, No Hands!* opened in London in July 1971, but the phrase probably dates back to the 1950s at least (when there was a joke about a German boy shooting his mother – 'Look, Hans – no Ma!').

look who it isn't!   facetious greeting of the **do you see who I see?** variety, uttered on spotting a friend or acquaintance. Mid-twentieth century.

look who's talking! (or **listen/hark...**)   derisive comment on someone who has just said something which they should not, because by their usual behaviour they contradict the sentiment they have just expressed. Mid-twentieth century.

looking like...   *see* **like something the cat's...**

looks like a million dollars   looks extremely attractive, as though a great deal of money has been spent on her. By the 1920s. Compare **I feel like a million dollars** – I feel on top of the world, couldn't be better.

looks like a wet weekend   looks grim, unappealing, about as much fun – and this may be the (Australian?) origin of the phrase – as a woman who is having a period and thus putting the damper on joint sexual activity. Since the 1930s/40s.

Luton Airport!, nah...   *see* **nice 'ere, innit?**

M
m

mail must get through, the some difficult task must be carried through to a successful conclusion. A slogan of probable North American origin referring to the Pony Express that briefly flourished *c* 1860. The mail-carrying riders had to battle through all kinds of dangers ranging from hostile Indians on the prairie to storms in the mountains. They were soon replaced by railway mail deliveries.

make love, not war a 'peacenik' or 'flower power' slogan of the mid-1960s. It was not just applied to the Vietnam War but was used to express the attitude of a whole generation of protest. It was written up (in English) at the University of Nanterre during the French student revolution of 1968. Coinage has been attributed to 'G. Legman', a sexologist with the Kinsey Institute, though this is also the name of the editor of *The Limerick* (1964/9).

makes you feel like a queen slogan for Summer County margarine, current in UK in the 1960s and before that in the US for Imperial Margarine. The idea of such elevation is not new. In November 1864, Tolstoy's wife Sonya wrote to him, 'Without you, I am nothing. With you, I feel like a queen' – though this is from a translation for an American edition of a French biography (1967).

makes you think! *see* **this is it!**

man who came in from the cold, the 'the —— who came in from the cold' is a journalistic format phrase derived from the title of John Le Carré's novel *The Spy Who Came In From the Cold* (1963), about a spy from the West getting even with his East German counterpart around the time of the erection of the Berlin

Wall. From then on, any people or any thing, coming in from any kind of exposed position, or returning to favour, might be described as 'coming in from the cold'.

man you love to hate, the   said of an attractive or alluring villain or hate-figure. A slogan originally applied to the Hollywood director Erich von Stroheim (1885–1957) when he appeared as an actor in the 1918 propaganda film *The Heart of Humanity*. In it, he played an obnoxious German officer who not only attempted to violate the leading lady but nonchalantly tossed a baby out of the window. At the film's première in Los Angeles, von Stroheim was hooted and jeered at when he walked on stage.

man's gotta do, what a man's gotta do, a   a man has to do what duty obliges him to do. Since the 1930/40s, American. The earliest printed reference so far found to a definite source for this phrase occurs in John Steinbeck's novel *The Grapes of Wrath* (1939): 'I know this – a man got to do what he got to do.'

marching to/hearing a...   *see* **different drummer.**

Martini – shaken not stirred, a   an example of would-be sophistication that became a running-joke in the immensely popular James Bond films of the 1960s and 70s. The idea stems from the very first of Ian Fleming's Bond books, *Casino Royale* (1953), in which Bond orders a cocktail of his own devising. It consists of one dry Martini 'in a deep champagne goblet', three measures of Gordon's gin, one of vodka – 'made with grain instead of potatoes' – and half a measure of Kina Lillet. 'Shake it very well until it's ice-cold.' From *Diamonds Are Forever* (1956): 'The waiter brought the Martinis, shaken and not stirred, as Bond had stipulated.' The characteristic was aped by the writers of the first Bond story to be filmed – *Dr No* (1962). A West Indian servant brings Bond a vodka and Martini and says: 'Martini like you said, sir, and not stirred.'

may the Force be with you!   fairly meaningless benediction/valediction from the film *Star Wars* (US, 1977). Compare 'The Lord be with you' from Morning Prayer in the Anglican Prayer Book.

may you live in interesting times! said to be an ancient Chinese curse, and popular in the UK from the early 1980s.

Me, Tarzan! – you, Jane! jungle love-talk, supposedly from the first sound Tarzan film – *Tarzan the Ape Man* (US, 1932), but not actually spoken in that film. Rather, Johnny Weissmuller, as Tarzan, whisks Maureen O'Sullivan as Jane to his tree-top abode and indulges in some elementary conversation with her. Thumping his chest, he says, 'Tarzan!'; pointing at her, he says, 'Jane!' Nor does the famous line occur in the original novel, *Tarzan of the Apes* (1914) by Edgar Rice Burroughs, not least because, in the jungle, Tarzan and Jane are only able to communicate by writing notes to each other.

means never having to say you're sorry, [something] an adaptation of the dubious sentiment expressed in Erich Segal's film script (and novel) *Love Story* (1970) and as a promotional tag for it. Ryan O'Neal says it, quoting his student wife (Ali MacGraw) who has just died. In the novelization of the story, the line appears as the penultimate sentence, in the form 'Love means *not ever* having to say you're sorry'.

From the *Independent* Magazine (1992): ' "We tried to introduce scuppies, which are socially conscious yuppies. But...nobody wanted to know." Well, of course not. Yuppie means never having to say you're sorry'; the *Spectator* (1992): ' "Politicians don't do that sort of thing [admit to having genuine human feelings of regret]", was the dismissive retort of a Conservative MP...Politics means never having to say you're sorry.'

meanwhile back at the ranch phrase used in imitation of the rapidly changing storylines of the early movies. A caption/subtitle/intertitle from the days of the silent cinema but also possibly used in US radio 'horse operas', when recapping the story after a commercial break.

Meredith, we're in! triumphant exclamation on making any kind of breakthrough. It originated in a British music-hall sketch called 'The Bailiff' (or 'Moses and Son'), performed by Fred Kitchen, the leading comedian with Fred Karno's company. The sketch was first seen in 1907 and the phrase was uttered each time a bailiff and his assistant looked like gaining entrance to the house.

mind boggles!, the   one is astonished at hearing of such an absurdity! 'The mind boggles...' wrote the *Observer* in an editorial headed 'New World' after the death of Stalin in early 1953.

mind how you go!   look after yourself, take care of yourself! A kindly caution since the 1940s, given a new lease of life by 'PC George Dixon' (Jack Warner) at the conclusion of countless editions of BBC TV's police series *Dixon of Dock Green* (1955–76) – the sort of phrase that all real policemen ought to say, even if not all of them do.

Miss Otis regrets...   parody of a statement of regret as contained in the song 'Miss Otis Regrets She's Unable To Lunch Today' (1934) by Cole Porter, in which a butler catalogues the reasons why this particular woman cannot – chief among which is that she has shot her lover and been hanged for it. In *Graffiti 3* (1981) there appeared this addition to a notice in York: 'LIFT UNDER REPAIR. USE OTHER LIFT. – This Otis regrets it is unable to lift today.'

missing you already!   *see* **have a nice day!**

money for jam!   *see* **piece of cake.**

more power to your elbow!   every encouragement to your endeavours. Since the 1830s. From archery, gambling, weight-lifting or drinking? Impossible to say, and the phrase may be no more than a connection between 'elbow' and 'effort', as in the expression 'to apply a little elbow-grease'. Perhaps also there is a connection with writing – vigorous movement of the elbow when scribbling in long-hand.

more —— than you can shake a stick at   anything in uncountable numbers – as in, 'Hell, there's more deer in those woods than you can shake a stick at'. From the US originally – e.g. the Lancaster, Pa., *Journal* (5 August 1818): 'We have in Lancaster more Taverns as you can shake a stick at.'

morning after the night before, the   denoting the effects of a drinking bout on the person who is suffering from them. Early twentieth century.

mother know you're out?, does your   chat-up line now addressed to a seemingly under-aged girl but, originally, to a foolish person of either sex who betrays signs of youthful innocence. From the title of a comic poem published in the *Mirror* (28 April 1838) but popular even before that.

mother of all ——, the   the ultimate (anything). Popular in English since the start of the Gulf War (January 1991) when the Iraqi president, Saddam Hussein said, 'The great, the jewel and the mother of battles has begun.' Although, as a result, 'the mother of ——' became a format phrase in the West, Hussein was simply using the commonplace Arabic 'mother of' construction. A review by Anita Brookner in *The Spectator* (11 May 1991) of Margaret Forster's book *The Battle for Christabel* was headed 'The battle of all mothers'.

mouth like the bottom of a parrot's cage, (I've got a)   one of a number of common similes for the effects of a hangover or other form of alcoholic indulgence. Since the 1920s. Another: **like the inside of a Turkish wrestler's jockstrap.**

move 'em on, head 'em up!   (. . .'head 'em up, move 'em on,/Move 'em on, head 'em up. . .Rawhide!') *Rawhide*, the American Western TV series (1959–66), was notable for its Frankie Laine theme song over the credits.

Mr Sharp from Sheffield, straight out of the knife box   *see* **you're so sharp!**

much chance as a fart in a wind-storm, as   *see* **as busy as a. . .**

much use as a one-legged man at an arse-kicking contest, as   *see* **as busy as a. . .**

music, maestro, please!   stock phrase of the British band leader Harry Leader, who broadcast from 1933 onwards, and now addressed jocularly to any musician about to play. Leader had had two signature tunes before he adopted this one while he was resident at the Astoria, Charing Cross Road, in 1943. It appears to have come from a song with the title by Herb Magidson and Allie Wrubel, featured by Flanagan and Allen in the revue *These Foolish Things* (1938).

must you go, can't you stay?   an invitation to remain in company, but also capable of being used to provoke the opposite: G.W.E. Russell in his *Collections and Recollections* (1898), gives it as a helpful remark of Dr Vaughan, Head Master of Harrow, designed to get rid of boys he had entertained at breakfast. 'When the muffins and sausages had been devoured...and all possible school-topics discussed, there used to ensue a horrid silence...Then the Doctor would approach with cat-like softness, and, extending his hand to the shyest and most loutish boy, would say, "Must you go? Can't you stay?" and the party broke up with magical celerity.'

It was later twisted to, 'Must you *stay*? Can't you *go*?' – for example, as the caption to a *Punch* cartoon in the edition dated 18 January 1905. The Governor of Madagascar is saying it, referring to the prolonged stay of the Russian Admiral Rodjestvensky at Madagascar when on his way to meet the Japanese Fleet.

mutton dressed as lamb   phrase used to describe something old got up to look like something younger – most often a woman wearing clothes that are ridiculously and noticeably too young for her. Since the late nineteenth century.

my dog has fleas   inconsequential title of a little tune that gives you the tuning notes (A, D, F♯, E) for a ukelele or banjo. It has been called the 'international call-sign of the ukelele-player'.

——, my hero!   the quintessential cry of the female in romantic fiction when her beau has just rescued her or overcome some formidable obstacle to their love. Seldom used seriously. P.G. Wodehouse has it in *Aunts Aren't Gentlemen* (1975), and Raina says it a number of times in Shaw's *Arms and the Man* (1894), but that is really a parody, too.

my husband and I!   phrase spoken in imitation of Queen Elizabeth II. Her father, King George VI, had quite naturally spoken the words 'The Queen and I' but something in Elizabeth's drawling delivery turned her version into a joke. It first appeared during her second Christmas broadcast (made from New Zealand) in 1953 – 'My husband and I left London a month ago' – and still survived in 1962: 'My husband and I are greatly looking forward to visiting New Zealand and Australia in the New Year.' By 1967, the phrase had become 'Prince Philip and I'. At a Silver Wedding banquet in 1972, the Queen allowed herself a little joke: 'I think on this occasion I may be forgiven for saying "My husband and I".'

my lips are sealed!　meaning, 'I am not going to say anything, nor give anything away by talking.' Deriving originally perhaps from the expression to seal up *another* person's lips or mouth, to prevent betrayal of a secret. Current by the 1780s. In a debate in the House of Commons on the Abyssinia crisis (10 December 1935), the British Prime Minister Stanley Baldwin said: 'I shall be but a short time tonight. I have seldom spoken with greater regret, for my lips are not yet unsealed.' In the speech, he was playing for time with what, he admitted, was one of the stupidest things he had ever said. The cartoonist Low portrayed him for weeks afterwards with sticking plaster over his lips.

my name is mud!　an acknowledgement that one has made a mistake, is held in low esteem and one is going to have to pay for it. When John Wilkes Booth was escaping from the Washington DC theatre in which he had just assassinated President Lincoln in 1865, he fell and broke his leg. A country doctor called Dr Samuel Mudd tended Booth's injury without realizing the circumstances under which it had been received. When he did realize, he informed the authorities, was charged with being a co-conspirator, and sentenced to life imprisonment.

However, 'mud' in the sense of scandalous and defamatory charges, goes back to a time well before the Civil War. There had been an expression 'the mud press' to describe mud-slinging newspapers in the US before 1846, so it seems most likely that the expression was well established before Dr Mudd met his unhappy fate.

135

my wife doesn't understand me! spoken by a man seeking sympathy for the unhappy state of his marriage and – often – seeking solace in the arms of the woman to whom the line is addressed. By the 1920s/30s at least.

N
n

name of the game   *see* —— **is the name of the game.**

name your poison!   'What would you like to drink?' Mostly British use, by the 1950s.

natives are hostile/restless!, the   what someone might say, with literal meaning, in British imperial fiction – but probably best known through parodies of same. Could now be used to convey that any group of people is hostile or impatient or whatever – a queue in a canteen, an audience in a theatre. The 'hostile' version is uttered in *Target for Tonight* (UK, 1942), a film about RAF Bomber Command.

naughty but nice!, (it's)   alliterative temptation. The phrase was used in British advertisements for fresh cream cakes in the early 1980s, and also for National Dairy Council cream advertisements in the late 1980s. But the phrase has been much used elsewhere. It was the title of a 1939 US film about a professor of classical music who accidentally wrote a popular song. Earlier, in the 1890s, it may have been a covert allusion to sex.

Navy's here!, the   'rescue is at hand, everything is going to be all right, be assured'. From an actual use of the words during the Second World War. On the night of 16 February 1940, 299 British seamen were freed from captivity aboard the German ship *Altmark* as it lay in a Norwegian fjord. The destroyer *Cossack*, under the command of Captain Philip Vian, had managed to locate the German supply ship and a boarding party discovered that British prisoners were locked in its hold. As Vian described it, Lieutenant Bradwell Turner, the leader of the boarding party, called out: 'Any British down there?' 'Yes, we're all British', came the reply. 'Come on up then,' he said, 'The Navy's here.'

137

The identity of the speaker is still in some doubt, however. *The Times* on 19 February 1940 gave a version from the lips of one of those who had been freed and who had actually heard the exchange: 'John Quigley of London said that the first they knew of their rescue was when they heard a shout of "Any Englishmen here?" They shouted "Yes" and immediately came the cheering words, "Well, the Navy is here." Quigley said – "We were all hoarse with cheering when we heard those words".'

neither (one thing) nor (the other)   format for a series of expressions giving a sense of 'in-between, indeterminate, falling between two stools', e.g. **neither arm'ole nor watercress; neither breakfast-time nor Wednesday'**; (doesn't know whether it's) **Pancake Tuesday or half-past breakfast-time.**

never darken my door again   meaning, 'never cross the threshold of my house again'. In England since the seventeenth century. Shakespeare does not use the phrase, but Benjamin Franklin is using it in the US by 1729.

never-ending battle for truth, justice and the American way, a   stated aims of the hero in *Batman* – as an American comic-strip hero, from the 1930s, and on radio from the 1940s.

never explain and never apologize   said to be a Royal Navy maxim of the early 1900s, but known before then. Admiral Lord Fisher wrote to *The Times* (5 September 1919): 'Never contradict. Never explain. Never apologize. (Those are the secrets of a happy life!).' According to an article in the *Oxford Chronicle* (7 October 1893), a favourite piece of advice given to young men by Benjamin Jowett, who became Master of Balliol College, Oxford, in 1870, was, 'Never regret, never explain, never apologize'. Each must, however, have been referring back to, or at least echoing, Disraeli who was quoted as having said 'Never complain and never explain' (specifically about attacks in Parliament) in John Morley's *Life of Gladstone* (1903).

never give a sucker an even break   don't pass up the opportunity to take advantage of a fool. This saying has been attributed to various people (Edward Francis Albee and P.T. Barnum among them) but has largely become associated with the American comedian W.C. Fields. He is believed to have ad-libbed it in the musical *Poppy* (1923) and certainly spoke it in the film version (1936). The words are not uttered, however, in the film with the title *Never Give a Sucker an Even Break* (1941).

never mind the quality, feel the width!   supposedly the sort of thing a street-tradesman (or Jewish tailor) might say. Perhaps once used literally in the early twentieth century, in more serious contexts. Used as the title of a British 'multi-ethnic' TV comedy series (1967–9) about 'Manny Cohen' and 'Patrick Kelly', a Jew and an Irishman, running a tailoring business in the East End of London.

never say die!   meaning, 'never give in'. Much used by Charles Dickens in his writings, starting with 'Greenwich Fair' in *Sketches by Boz* (written 1833–6) – though it was probably a proverbial expression before him.

nice 'ere, innit?   conversational gambit but, in this form, alluding to a British TV advertisement of 1976: on a balcony in Venice, an elegant-looking girl sipped Campari and then shattered the atmosphere by saying in a rough Cockney voice, 'Nice 'ere, innit?' In the follow-up advertisement, a smooth type asked the same girl, 'Were you truly wafted here from Paradise?' She replies: '**Nah. . .Luton Airport.**' These two phrases were the making of the actress, Lorraine Chase, who went on to record a song called 'It's Nice 'Ere, Innit?' (1979). Cats UK recorded 'Luton Airport' the same year.

nice guys finish last   in the struggle of life, only the ruthless win the race. A saying attributed to Leo Durocher when manager of the Brooklyn Dodgers baseball team (1951–4), but probably earlier. In his autobiography with the title *Nice Guys Finish Last* (1975), Durocher recalled that what he had said to reporters concerning the New York Giants in July 1946, was: 'All nice guys. They'll finish last. Nice guys. Finish last.' However, Frank Graham of the New York *Journal-American* had written down something slightly different: 'Why, they're the nicest guys in the world! And where are they? In seventh place!'

nice little earner, a a small but profitable source of income, applied to a job or sideline, but a touch shady with it. Much used by George Cole in the character of 'Arthur Daley' in British TV's *Minder* series (from the late 1970s on). 'Earner' on its own, for 'money earned' (often shadily), may go back to the 1930s.

nice little place you got here... *see* **nice place you got here.**

nice one, Cyril! a classic example of the near-meaningless catchphrase for which any number of uses were found. Originally a line from a British TV advertisement for Wonderloaf in 1972, it caught on, was all the rage and was as suddenly discarded. Two bakers were shown discussing individual loaves of bread and suggesting that though Wonderloaf might seem to be mass-produced, they thought they could tell who baked it.

Hence, 'Nice one, Cyril!' which, as a catchphrase, had a sibilant ease; it was fun to say. More importantly it could be used in any number of situations, not least sexual ones. In 1973, the phrase was taken up by Tottenham Hotspur football supporters who were fans of the player Cyril Knowles. They even recorded a song about him which went: 'Nice one, Cyril/Nice one, son./Nice one, Cyril,/Let's have another one.'

nice place you got here (or **nice little...**) film cliché of the 1930s/40s, spoken by a 'heavy' who has come to deliver a warning. In admiring the owner's 'place', he often breaks a small object, adding (or implying), '...it'd be a pity if anything were to...happen to it...'.

Used, too, in a non-threatening, admiring way about a property which is impressively grand or – ironically – about one which is rather a dump.

nice——, shame about the—— format phrase derived from 'Nice Legs, Shame About Her Face', the title of a briefly popular song recorded by The Monks in 1979. Originally a way of decrying the mixed attributes of a female, it then came to be applied to anything: 'Nice video, shame about the song'; 'Nice face, shame about the breath'; 'Good tune, shame about the words'; 'Nice prints, shame about the books'.

nice work if you can get it! approving, if not envious, phrase about a particular type of employment – a job which takes the person addressed to exotic places, for example. Most probably from the title of the song 'Nice Work If You Can Get It' (1937) by George and Ira Gershwin. The latter admitted that he might have found the phrase in the caption to a *Punch* cartoon that had been rejected as not being suitable for publication – in it, two men had been discussing the daughter of a third, who had become a whore.

night is young!, the the sort of thing one says when attempting to justify another drink. From Frank Brady, *Citizen Welles* (1989): 'At three in the morning, when a few people decided to leave, Orson, stepping into the role of clichéd host from a Grade B movie, would not hear of it: "You're not leaving already, my friends. The night is still young. Play, Gypsies! Play, play, play!" ' Probably taken from the titles of two songs: 'The Night Is Young (And So Are We)' (1935) by Oscar Hammerstein II and Sigmund Romberg and included in the film *The Night is Young*; and 'The Night is Young (and You're So Beautiful)' by Billy Rose and Irving Kahal (1936).

nil carborundum! *see* **illegitimi(s) non carborundum.**

ninepence to the shilling *see* **few vouchers short. . .**

'no answer' came the stern reply! ironic comment on the fact that no one has replied or said a word. Known by the 1930s but in various forms, including: **'No answer, no answer' came the loud reply** and **'shrieks of silence' was the stern reply.** If these are quotations, the original source has not been identified.

no, but you hum it and I'll pick up the tune *see* **do you know. . .?**

no can do! *see* **can do!**

no comment! humorously dismissive phrase, when people in the news are being hounded by journalists. Probably American in origin, say from the 1920s/30s. Winston Churchill appears only to have become aware of it in 1946. After a meeting with President Truman, he said, 'I think "No Comment" is a splendid expression. I got it from Sumner Welles.' Also in 1946, British critic C.A. Lejeune's entire review of the US film *No Leave, No Love* was 'No comment'.

no, I'm/we're with the Woolwich!/(are you with me?)   'are you with me?' – meaning, 'do you understand?' has been current since the 1920s, at least. It was coupled with the response 'no, I'm/we're with the Woolwich' in a once prominent advertising campaign for the Woolwich Building Society in the UK (1970s).

no more Mr Nice Guy!   'Mr Nice Guy' is a nickname applied to 'straight' figures (especially politicians) who may possibly be following someone who is palpably not 'nice' (Gerald Ford after Richard Nixon, for example). They then sometimes feel the need to throw off some of their virtuous image, as presidential challenger Senator Ed Muskie did in 1972, hence his aides declaring, 'No more Mr Nice Guy'. The origin probably lies in America of the 1950s.

no names, no packdrill!   meaning, 'I am not going to betray any confidences by mentioning names.' This alludes to a one-time British army punishment when soldiers were made to march up and down carrying a heavy pack. Known by the First World War, the expression is probably a short form of saying, 'As long as I don't give away any names, I won't get punished for it – that's why I am not telling you.'

no one likes us – we don't care   a defiant line sung by fans of Millwall football club to the tune of Rod Stewart's song 'Sailing'. Millwall fans are famous in London for their vocal and physical forcefulness. *No One Likes Us, We Don't Care* was, consequently, the title given to a Channel 4 TV documentary about them in January 1990.

no peace/rest for the wicked!   light-hearted exclamation by someone who is being harried by demands from other people or snowed under with work. By the nineteenth century, possibly in imitation of certain biblical passages, e.g. Isaiah 48:22: 'There is no peace, saith the Lord, unto the wicked' and 57:21: 'There is no peace, saith my God, to the wicked'.

no pun intended! *see* **if you'll excuse the pun!**

no way, Jose! firm refusal, in imitation of the way an American might speak to a Hispanic. By the early 1980s.

no way to run a whelk stall! *see* **couldn't run a whelk-stall!**

nobody's perfect! pleasant way of excusing one's own or another's failings. By the nineteenth century. The last lines of the film *Some Like It Hot* (US, 1959) have Tony Curtis (in drag) explaining to a potential husband why they should not marry: 'she' is not a woman. Unflustered by this, Joe E. Brown as an old millionaire says, 'Nobody's perfect'.

noise and the people!, the mock exclamation of dismay at crowded conditions, derived from what a certain Captain Strahan said supposedly said after the Battle of Bastogne (1944) or, more probably, after the evacuation of Allied forces from Dunkirk (1940). Often introduced with, 'Oh, my dear fellow...!', with the inference that the speaker has a blasé attitude to the dangers and a disdain of the common soldiery he is being forced to mix with. It was already being quoted in 1942.

noofter! *see* **yer plonker!**

——, not! cry tacked on to the end of a statement and instantly negating its meaning: e.g. 'I believe you – NOT!' Popularized by *Wayne's World*, a segment of the NBC TV show *Saturday Night Live* (from 1989) and then a feature film (1992). Based on American urban teenagers' use.

not a dry eye (in the house) exaggerated comment on an effective performance or speech that has palpably moved an audience to tears. Known, in its literal sense, by the 1850s.

not a lot! catchphrase of the British magician and comedian Paul Daniels since the 1970s. Used to modify a compliment so that it becomes slightly critical: 'I like your suit. Not a lot, but I like it.'

not a lot of people know that! *see* **not many people know that!**

not a pretty sight understatement when describing something that is ugly, horrible, a mess or simply something the speaker wishes to criticize. Possibly from parodies of old British imperial-speak. Known by the 1970s.

not all there *see* **few vouchers short. . .**

not bloody likely! an emphatic refusal and a famous quotation from George Bernard Shaw's play *Pygmalion* (1914): *Freddy*: 'Are you walking across the Park, Miss Doolittle? If so –.' *Liza*: 'Walk! Not bloody likely.' (*Sensation.*) The shock of the original was that it was uttered at a polite tea-party and the word 'bloody' had rarely, if ever, been uttered on the British stage. By the time *My Fair Lady* – the musical version – was filmed in 1964, the shock effect of 'bloody' was so mild that Liza was given the line 'Come on, Dover, move your ruddy arse!' in the Ascot racing sequence.

not for a big clock! 'I would not do it – not for a big inducement!' British use by the 1980s, a variant of the traditional '. . .not for all the tea in China.'

not in front of the children! request from one grown-up to another to desist from arguing or making a scene when there are young people present. In use since the 1920s, but now mostly jocularly. Spoken in French, *pas devant les enfants*, as it sometimes is, the phrase is a rather more discreet way of achieving what the speaker wishes.

not many people know that! (or **not a lot of people. . .**) humorous addition following the imparting of bizarre, platitudinous or inconsequential information. In imitation of the habit ascribed to the British actor Michael Caine by Peter Sellers in a BBC TV chat show (1972): ' "Not many people know that". . .this is my Michael Caine impression. . .You see Mike's always quoting from *The Guinness Book of Records*. At the drop of a hat he'll trot one out. "Did you know that it takes a man in a tweed suit five and a half seconds to fall from the top of Big Ben to the ground? Now there's not many people know that"!' It had caught on in a big way by the early 1980s.

not playing with a full deck *see* **few vouchers short. . .**

not quite enough coupons. . . *see* **few vouchers short. . .**

not the full shilling   *see* **few vouchers short. . .**

not tonight, Josephine!   way of declining to do something, in imitation of Napoleon Bonaparte's alleged rebuff to the Empress Josephine's sexual demands. An established catchphrase by the 1930s and probably originating in nineteenth-century music-hall sketches.

not waving but drowning   comment on the possible confused understanding of a gesture, cry for help or other signal. A quotation from a poem with the same title (1957) by the British poet Stevie Smith.

not with a bang but a whimper   phrase of anticlimax, derived from T.S. Eliot's poem *The Hollow Men* (1925): 'This is the way the world ends/Not with a bang but a whimper.' Frequently alluded to: from Richard Aldington, *The Colonel's Daughter* (1931): 'I wish you'd all shoot yourselves with a bang, instead of continuing to whimper.' From *The Times* (16 December 1959): 'Here the world ends neither with a bang nor a whimper, but with a slow, resigned sigh at its own criminal imbecility.'

now I've seen/heard everything!   mostly good-humoured expression of wonder or amazement at being told a piece of news. Since the 1940s.

now you see it, now you don't!   said about anything that quickly disappears, especially as a result of trickery or deception. From conjuror's patter, since the 1930s?

now you're talking!   meaning, 'now you are saying something worth considering or useful (and not just waffling)'. Since the 1880s.

nudge nudge, wink wink!   phrase used when confiding in another person or assuming shared knowledge (especially of sexual matters), following Eric Idle's use of the words as a prurient character in the BBC TV series *Monty Python's Flying Circus* (in 1969). He also used the phrases **know what I mean?** and **say no more!** in a similarly nudging fashion.

nuff said!   *see* **enough said!**

145

O

o

off with his head – so much for Buckingham!   the second phrase is a wonderfully dismissive addition by the playwright Colley Cibber to his 1700 edition of Shakespeare's *Richard III*. The extension of Shakespeare's simple 'Off with his head' proved a popular and lasting emendation. In 'Private Theatres' (1835), one of the *Sketches by Boz*, Charles Dickens describes the roles on offer to amateur actors who at that time could pay to take certain roles in plays: 'For instance, the Duke of Glo'ster is well worth two pounds. . .including the "off with his head!" – which is sure to bring down the applause, and it is very easy to do – "Orf with his ed" (very quick and loud; – then slow and sneeringly) – "So much for Bu-u-u-uckingham!" Lay the emphasis on the "uck"; get yourself gradually into a corner, and work with your right hand, while you're saying it, as if you were feeling your way, and it's sure to do.'

The extra phrase was also included in Laurence Olivier's film of Shakespeare's play (1955). The simple 'Off with his head!', as an abrupt command, has probably been more associated latterly with the Queen in Lewis Carroll's *Alice's Adventures in Wonderland* (1865).

often/always a bridesmaid, but never a bride   always the runner-up never the winner, always the helper never the helped. From a slogan for Listerine mouthwash, in the US (1920s) but containing more than an echo of the British music-hall song 'Why Am I Always the Bridesmaid?' (1917) made famous by Lily Morris.

oh, good show!   *see* **jolly good show!**

oh, la! la! (pronounced 'oo-la! la!')   exclamation in imitation of a French speaker, but also used to describe anything sexy. 'She is very, you know, *oh, la! la!*' By the time of the First World War.

oh, Moses! catchphrase of the British actor Derek Nimmo, playing Noot, the Bishop's chaplain, in a late 1960s BBC TV sitcom about clerical folk, *All Gas and Gaiters*. In fact, what he said was 'Moses!' but this is how the phrase is remembered. Subsequently, the actor went on to play another ecclesiastical character in *Oh, Brother!* (set in a religious institution). **Oh, brother!** had, however, been an American exclamation since the 1890s without any religious connotations.

oh no, there isn't!/oh yes, there is! in British pantomime, there is always a scene in which an actor speaks to the audience with his back to someone or something which he denies exists. A ritual exchange then takes place: 'There isn't a bear behind me, is there, children?' Audience: 'Oh yes, there is!' 'Oh, no there isn't!' and so on. There will also be cries of **behind you!** Since the nineteenth century.

oh, you kid! *see* **I love my wife but, oh, you kid!**

oil and water don't mix two people with different characteristics will not get on well with each other. A proverbial saying, known especially in the US since the 1780s but ignored by the main British proverb collections.

OK, yah! an agreeing noise characteristic of the – especially female – Sloane Ranger, a sub-species of upper-middle-class life remarked upon and celebrated in the mid-1980s. The London *Evening Standard* wrote of the show *The Sloane Ranger Revue* at the Duchess Theatre, 'OK Yah, that's brill!'

okey-pokey *see* **hokey pokey penny a lump!**

old as my tongue and a little older than my teeth, as what nannies (and other older folk) traditionally reply when asked how old they are by the inquisitive young. Jonathan Swift has it already in *Polite Conversation* by the 1730s.

old soldiers never die: they simply fade away a line from a British Army song of the First World War, itself a parody of the gospel hymn 'Kind Words Can Never Die'. J. Foley copyrighted a version of the parody in 1920. Recalled in his farewell speech by General

Douglas MacArthur in 1951 when he had been sacked from his command of UN forces in Korea for repeatedly criticizing the administration's policy of non-confrontation with China. He chose a slightly different version, however, for his peroration: 'I still remember the refrain of one of the most popular barrack ballads of that day, which proclaimed, most proudly, that old soldiers never die. They just fade away. And like the old soldier of that ballad, I now close my military career and just fade away...'

It is an observation that has appealed to many jokers over the years. From the early 1980s come these examples: 'Old soldiers never die, just their privates'; 'Old professors...just lose their faculties'; 'Old golfers...just lose their balls'; 'Old fishermen never die, they just smell that way'.

on a scale of one to ten   popular system of rating things – also used allusively, e.g 'a ten', 'a two'. American origin, 1970s. In a West Coast party scene in the film *Annie Hall* (US, 1977), a character says of a woman, 'She's a ten', indicating that she is his ideal. This usage was further popularized by the film *10* (1979) in which the sexual allure or performance of the hero's girlfriends was so rated. Possibly derived from the Richter scale of measuring the severity of earthquakes (1 to 10), named after Charles F. Richter who began devising the scale in 1932, or simply from the old school habit of marking things out of ten.

on behalf of the working classes   at first a phrase used literally by people purporting to represent the case of this sector of society; Robert Owen, the social reformer, used the title *Two Memorials on behalf of the Working Classes* in 1816. Later, the phrase became the bill matter of the British music-hall comedian Billy Russell (1893–1971).

on one's/my shit list, he's/you're   meaning, 'he's in my bad books, has offended me in some way and is in line for retribution.' Since the 1940s, and possibly derived from 'hit list' and 'short list'.

on with the motley!   let's press on as though nothing has happened, in spite of the difficulties. Alluding to the Clown's cry – '*vesti la giubba*' – in Leoncavallo's opera *I Pagliacci* (1892). The

Clown has to 'carry on with the show' despite having a broken heart. So it might be said jokingly nowadays by anyone who has to proceed with something in spite of difficulties.

'*Giubba*' in Italian means simply 'jacket' (in the sense of costume), and 'motley' is the old English word for an actor's or clown's clothes, originally the many-coloured coat worn by a jester or fool.

on your bike! meaning 'go away' or 'be off with you', this phrase may have been current in Britain in the 1960s. However, it was given an interesting twist by opponents of the British Conservative politician Norman Tebbit. Having just been appointed British Employment Secretary, Tebbit addressed the Conservative Party Conference on 15 October 1981. He related how he had grown up in the 1930s when unemployment was all around and commented: '[My father] did not riot. He got on his bike and looked for work. And he kept on looking till he found it.' This was interpreted as suggesting that the unemployed should get on their bikes and go away though Tebbit later pointed out that he had not been suggesting that the unemployed should literally get on their bikes.

once a ——, always a ——! format phrase deriving from an old series of proverbial expressions, 'Once a knave/whore/captain, always a...' (known since the early 1800s). Latterly, Mary O'Malley wrote a play called *Once a Catholic* (1971), the title being based on the saying 'once a Catholic always a Catholic' which had been known since the 1940s.

once aboard the lugger and the girl is mine! male catchphrase expressing lusting intent, now only used jocularly and in imitation of nineteenth-century use in nautical melodramas.

once upon a time. . . the traditional start to fairy tales has existed as a general story-teller's phrase since the sixteenth century. No fewer than thirteen of the twenty-four *Classic Fairy Tales* collected in their earliest English versions by Iona and Peter Opie (1974) begin with these words. Mostly the versions are translations from the French of Charles Perrault's collected *Histories, or Tales of Past Times* (1697), beginning '*Il estoit une fois*'.

one apple short of a full load *see* **few vouchers short. . .**

one brick/a few bricks short of a (full) load *see* **few vouchers short. . .**

one card short of a full deck *see* **few vouchers short. . .**

one day all this will be yours, my son! spoken by a proud father, gesturing proprietorially over his property. Possibly nineteenth-century in origin. From Rudyard Kipling's story 'The Brushwood Boy' (1895) comes this: ' "Perfect! By Jove, it's perfect!" Georgie was looking at the round-bosomed woods beyond the home paddock, where the white pheasant-boxes were ranged. . .Georgie felt his father's arm tighten in his.

' "It's not half bad – but *hodie mihi, cras tibi* [what's mine today will be yours], isn't it?" '

one foot in the grave, (with) meaning 'near to dying'. Known since the early seventeenth century. Used as the title of a BBC TV comedy series *One Foot in the Grave* (1993–) about a man having to endure premature retirement.

one for the book, that's a saying, exaggeration or claim, which is so remarkable that it ought to be consigned to the book that used to be kept for just this purpose in RAF messes since the 1920s. But also said to have been applied to a joke that was so good it deserved putting in the famous book *Joe Miller's Jests* (1739).

one grape short of a bunch *see* **few vouchers short. . .**

one more for the Gipper!, (win) sporting turned political slogan. Bridging his film and political careers, Ronald Reagan used a saying that echoed George Gipp, a character he played in *Knute Rockne – All-American* (1940). Gipp was a real-life football star who died young. At half-time in a 1928 army game, Rockne, the team coach, had recalled something Gipp had said to him: 'Rock, someday when things look real tough for Notre Dame, ask the boys to go out there and win one for me.' Reagan used the slogan countless times.

one of its legs is both the same *see* **because the higher the fewer!**

one pork pie/two sandwiches short of a picnic *see* **few vouchers short. . .**

one small step for ——, one giant leap for —— format phrase derived from what the American astronaut Neil Armstrong claimed he said when stepping on to the moon's surface for the first time in 1969: 'That's one small step for a man, one giant leap for mankind'. The indefinite article before 'man' was, however, completely inaudible, thus ruining the sense. Nevertheless, Armstrong launched a seemingly imperishable format phrase.

one step forward two steps back phrase indicating that progress is slow to non-existent. The Russian revolutionary Lenin wrote a booklet with the title (*Shag vpered dva shaga nazad*, in Russian, 1904) about 'the crisis within our party'. However, in *Conducted Tour* (1981), Bernard Levin refers to Lenin's 'pamphlet' under the title *Four Steps Forward, Three Steps Back*. Vilmos Voigt pointed out in *Proverbium Yearbook of International Proverb Scholarship* (1984) that just after the publication of his work, Lenin talked of the 'current German form, *Ein Schritt vorwärts, zwei Schritte zurück* [one step forwards, two steps back]', and Voigt wondered what precisely the source of Lenin's phrase was and in which language.

one that (almost) got away, the journalistic cliché based presumably on 'this was the fish that almost got away'. A British film with the title *The One That Got Away* (about an escaped prisoner) was released in 1957.

only her hairdresser knows for sure *see* **does she or doesn't she?**

only in America! observation based on amazement or astonishment or plain acceptance that something (possibly inspirational) has happened that could have occurred nowhere else but in the US. By the 1950s?

only in the mating season! *see* **do you come here often?**

only the names have been changed. . . *see* **all we want is the facts, ma'am!**

only time will tell cliché especially of broadcast news journalism and used by reporters to round off a story when they cannot think of anything else to say. Noticed by the 1980s, but the proverbial expression had existed since 1539.

. . .only when I laugh excusatory phrase in answer to the question 'Does it hurt?' Used as the title of novel (1968; film UK, 1968) by Len Deighton and as the title of an ITV comedy series *Only When I Laugh* (1979–84), set in a hospital, and of a film (US, 1981) which was released in the UK as *It Hurts Only When I Laugh* – which points to its origin. There is an old joke about an English soldier in Africa who gets pinned to a tree by an assegai. When asked if it hurts, he replies with this stiff-upper-lip statement.

onwards and upwards! now a humorously uplifting phrase, designed to encourage, deriving possibly from the religious notion of striving onwards and upwards through the everlasting night. Since the nineteenth century, in its literal sense. Late twentieth century for the ironic use, as especially in theatrical circles.

oompah, oompah, stick it up your jumper! dismissive phrase that could be used in response to a stupid suggestion (like 'why don't you just go and stuff it. . .?') but really no more than a meaningless exclamation. 'Oompah, oompah' is, of course, imitative of the noise made by a brass musical instrument such as a euphonium or tuba. Since the 1920s, and possibly quoting a line from a song.

oooh, you are awful. . .but I like you [wallop]! catchphrase of the British comedian Dick Emery. In a TV series of the 1970s, one of the characters he played was that of Mandy, a man-hungry spinster. The last word of the phrase was followed by a quick bash with her handbag. Also the title of a song and of a feature film (1980).

open the box! contestants in the old British TV quiz *Take Your Pick* – which ran on ITV for almost twenty years from 1955 – were given the option of opening a numbered box (which might either contain something valuable or something worthless) or accepting a sum of money which might turn out to be worth more – or less – than what was in the box. The studio audience would chant its advice – 'take the money' or, more usually, 'open the box!'

open the door, Richard! equivalent of 'open up!', taken from the title line of a popular American song (1947).

opera ain't over till the fat lady sings, the modern proverb warning 'not to count your chickens before they are hatched' or simply 'it isn't over till it's over'. In this form, the saying seems to have arisen in American basketball circles in the mid-1970s, though a widely shared view is that it has something to do with Kate Smith, a handsomely proportioned American singer of the 1930s and 1940s whose rendition of Irving Berlin's 'God Bless America' signified the end of events like the political party conventions and World Series baseball games. Hence, possibly, the alternative version: **the game's not over till the fat lady sings.**

Almost certainly, however, both these versions are pre-dated by similar expressions of the same thought: 'The game's not over until the last man strikes out'; 'Church is not out 'til they sing'; and 'Church ain't out till the fat lady sings'.

our reporter made an excuse and left two-faced line dating from the rise of mass-circulation British newspapers when reporters sought to depict vice and crime in a titillating way while protecting themselves by righteous condemnation and crusading zeal. The *People* (founded in 1881) was one of those muck-raking papers that developed a method of reporting sexual scandals which sometimes involved a reporter setting up a compromising situation – e.g. provoking prostitutes and pimps to reveal their game – and then making it clear that, of course, he himself had taken no part in what was on offer. Probably from the 1920s onwards.

ours is a nice 'ouse ours is! *see* **I'm dreaming...**

out of your tiny Chinese little minds meaning, 'mad'. Gratuitously offensive, and probably dating from the 1950s, at the earliest. The simpler 'out of your tiny mind' *may* be the older expression, though it is not recorded until the mid-1960s (compare **damn(ed) clever these Chinese**).

over the moon joyously victorious, especially after a sporting achievement. In about 1978, two cliché expressions became notorious in Britain if one wished to express either pleasure or dismay at the outcome of anything, but especially of a football match. The speaker was either 'over the moon' or **sick as a parrot**. It probably all began because of the remorseless post-game analysis by TV football commentators and the consequent need for players and managers to provide pithy comments. 'Sick as a parrot' was already in use at the time of the 1978 Football League Cup Final.

'Over the moon' is probably the older of the two phrases and was known by the 1850s. 'Sick as a parrot' may be connected with psittacosis or parrot disease/fever. In about 1973, there were a number of cases of people dying of this in West Africa. Or perhaps it comes from an earlier expression, 'as sick as a parrot with a rubber beak', meaning that the bird was incapacitated without a sharp weapon, as also in the saying, 'no more chance than a cat in hell with no claws'.

over Will's mother's way   *see* **black over Bill's mother's. . .**

overpaid, (overfed) oversexed and over here   said of American troops in Britain during the Second World War. Sometimes ascribed to the British comedian Tommy Trinder.

'ow do, 'ow are yer?   typical English North Country greeting, almost reduced to self-parody when used by Wilfred Pickles in the course of the folksy BBC radio show *Have A Go* (1946–67).

P
p

Pancake Tuesday or half-past breakfast-time *see* **neither one thing nor the other.**

panic stations! light-hearted use of the naval term 'be at panic stations', meaning 'be prepared for the worst' (and current from the beginning of the Second World War). Nowadays, it may mean no more than 'don't get in my way, I've got a crisis on!'

pardon my French! (or **excuse. . .**) said after using bad language or language that might be taken for such. The use of 'French' to mean 'bad language' was known by the 1890s. 'Pardon my French' was current in the 1930s. Possibly the use of this British and American phrase followed the forces' use of it in France during the First World War.

pardon the pun! *see* **if you'll excuse the pun!**

pas devant les enfants! *see* **not in front of the children!**

pass! 'I don't know, next question!' In BBC TV's *Mastermind* quiz (since the early 1970s), contestants used this word so as not to waste valuable time when answering questions against the clock . It is not the most obvious of things to say. 'Next question' or 'I dunno' would spring more readily to mind but, so deep has this phrase penetrated the public consciousness that it is now what is said in any remotely similar circumstances.

pass the sickbag, Alice! *see* **I think we should be told!**

patter of tiny feet, the rather fey euphemism when inquiring about the expected arrival of a baby, as in 'And when shall we be hearing the patter of tiny feet?' British and American use since about the 1920s.

155

peasants are revolting, the As with the **natives are hostile/ restless**, this is a jocular way of describing almost any form of unrest among people. It also harks back to what imperialist Britons (or medieval tyrants) *might* be supposed to have said, if only in historical fiction. Since the 1940s. The actual Peasants' Revolt (against taxes) took place in southern England in 1381.

Sometimes there is a riposte: 'Revolting? They're nauseating!'

penny's dropped, the belated realization that something has happened or that someone has understood something – as though a slow-moving coin-in-the-slot machine has at last produced results. Since the 1920s, at least.

perfick! a Kentish dialect pronunciation of 'perfect' as found particularly in H.E. Bates, *The Darling Buds of May* (1958) and subsequent stories. In that first book, Pa Larkin talks, for example, of 'perfick wevver' for 'perfect weather'. The expression 'perfick!' again had a vogue in the spring of 1991 when the stories were dramatized for British TV with great success.

pick on someone your own size! advice on how to quarrel offered to someone who has been picking on an easy victim. Of American origin, since the late nineteenth century.

picture is worth a thousand words, a a famous observation sometimes said to be a Chinese proverb. However, its origin is more prosaic. It originated in an American paper *Printers' Ink* (8 December 1921) in the form 'one look is worth a thousand words'. It was later reprinted in the better-known form in the same paper (10 March 1927) and there ascribed by its actual author, Frederick R. Barnard, to a Chinese source ('so that people would take it seriously', he told Burton Stevenson in 1948).

piece of cake, (it's a) meaning, 'simple, no bother, easily achieved'. Comparisons are inevitable with other food phrases like **'easy as pie'** and **'money for jam'**, but the general assumption seems to be that it is a shortened form of 'it's as easy as eating a piece of cake'. Possibly of American origin in the 1930s but especially popular in the RAF during the Second World War.

pin back your lug 'oles! *see* **I'm dreaming, oh my darling love, of thee!**

piss-up in a brewery *see* **couldn't run a whelk-stall!**

pistols for two, breakfast (or **coffee**) **for one!** parody of duellists' talk, source untraced, but known by the 1980s.

place is alive! *see* **shut that door!**

play it again, Sam! 'encore!, let's hear it again!' in emulation of Humphrey Bogart and Ingrid Bergman in the film *Casablanca* (1942) who were supposed to have said this to 'Sam' (Dooley Wilson) about the sentimental song 'As Time Goes By'. But, as almost everyone knows by now, they do not actually use these precise words.

All one needs to say is that the saying was utterly well established by the time Woody Allen thus entitled his play (1969; film US, 1972) about a film critic who is abandoned by his wife and obtains the help of Bogart's 'shade'.

please give generously/all you can! *see* **all contributions gratefully received!**

plot thickens!, the jokingly used expression to point up any turn of events that appears to be significant or which betrays some complicating feature. Used seriously in nineteenth-century melodramas. In *The Rehearsal* by George Villiers (1671), a character said, perhaps for the first time, 'Ay, now the plot thickens very much upon us.'

point Percy at the porcelain, (I must go and) euphemistic announcement of male urination introduced to Britain by the Australian Barry Humphries through the 'Barry Mackenzie' strip cartoon in *Private Eye* magazine. Early 1970s.

point taken! phrase used to show acceptance of an argument or point of view in conversation. Since the 1940s/50s.

praise the Lord and pass the ammunition! a somewhat dubious conflation of worldliness and godliness, though it may be used good-humouredly to suggest that you have to keep on with practicalities in difficult circumstances. As a catchphrase of religious pragmatism, it was actually said in 1941, and subsequently used as the title of a song by Frank Loesser (1942), though the authorship of this saying is disputed. It may have been said by an American naval chaplain during the Japanese attack on Pearl Harbor. Lieut. Howell M. Forgy (1908–83) is one candidate. He was on board the US cruiser *New Orleans* on 7 December 1941 and encouraged those around him to to keep up the barrage when under attack. His claim is supported by a report in the *New York Times* (1 November 1942).

Another name mentioned is that of Captain W.H. Maguire. At first Captain Maguire did not recall having used the words but a year later said he might have done. Either way, the expression actually dates from the time of the American Civil War.

promises, promises! an expression either mocking another person's undertaking to do something or the simple promoter of a *double entendre*. For example, if one person were to say, 'If you pop round later this evening, I can give you one', then the other might say... *Promises, Promises* was the title of a musical (Broadway, 1968) based on the Billy Wilder film *The Apartment*, and may have encouraged the use of the phrase.

Public Enemy No. 1 name given to anyone the speaker does not care for, anyone undesirable. The American killer and bank robber John Dillinger was the first officially designated 'Public Enemy No. 1' and was so dubbed by the Attorney General, Homer Cummings. In fact, Dillinger was the *only* person ever so named. The FBI's 'Ten Most Wanted Men' list did not give a ranking.

The coining of the term 'Public Enemy' in this context has been attributed to Frank Loesch, president of the Chicago Crime Commission, who had to try to deal with Al Capone's hold over the city in 1923. The idea was to try and dispel the romantic aura such gangsters had been invested with by the popular press. James Cagney starred in a gangster film called *The Public Enemy* in 1931.

pull the other one – it's got bells on it! 'I don't believe you – you're pulling my leg!' A reponse to any far-fetched or preposterous statement or story. Possibly since the 1920s. Clearly related to 'pulling someone's leg' in the sense of teasing, but quite how the bells come into it is not clear – except that bells are obviously something that one pulls as well as other people's legs. Or perhaps there is an allusion to the bells that a court jester would wear on his costume?

put a sock in it! 'shut up!, shut your mouth!, stop talking!' addressed to a noisy or talkative person. Since the 1910s and possibly a development of the earlier **put a bung in it** – as in a bath or any sort of leak. But why should not a sock inserted in the human mouth be the origin? It would be reasonably effective. The theory that the phrase comes from inserting an article of clothing in an old wind-up, 'acoustic' gramophone (where the sound emerged from a horn) to control the level of sound coming out, is fanciful but far-fetched.

put a tiger in your tank! 'get a move on, acquire a bit of oomph!' Originally, a slogan for Esso petrol in the US, mid-1960s, and eventually used all over the world. Perhaps it owed something to the Muddy Waters song '(I Want to Put a) Tiger in Your Tank' (by W. Dixon) which he was performing by 1960 and which gave double meanings to a number of motoring phrases (not least in the title).

put her/him down you don't know where (s)he's been! jocular remark addressed to a person showing sexual interest in another, since the 1950s. After the domestic catchphrase addressed to a child about an object – 'Put it down, dear, you don't know where it's been.'

put it down to experience *see* **chalk it up to experience.**

put that in your pipe and smoke it! a retort used after having advanced what the speaker feels is a crushing argument. 'Digest that, if you can!' Since the early nineteenth century. Possibly alluding to the calming and soothing properties of tobacco.

put up or shut up! 'either make good your argument or stop talking about it'. In America, this translates as 'put up your money (as though for a bet)' but in Britain, 'put up your fists (as though for a fight)'. Both uses probably dating from the nineteenth century.

A possible third interpretation is 'put up with things or shut up about them', along the lines of the pro-government American slogan in the Vietnam War (1960s): '**America: love it or leave it!**'

put your pudden/puddings out (or **up**) **for treacle**   an encouragement to people to put themselves forward (as though in order to receive sauce on their dessert), though it may be used to suggest a double meaning. In May 1994, Teresa Gorman MP accused the British minister Michael Heseltine of disloyalty to Prime Minister John Major by saying that he was 'putting his puddings out for treacle'. Mrs Gorman subsequently explained her expression to Alan Watkins in the *Independent on Sunday* (12 June 1994): '[It] was used in our neighbourhood about any woman considered to be putting herself forward for attention – or suspected of paying the tradesmen's bills in "kind"!'

Q
q

queen for a day   phrase describing a woman who is being given a special treat. It derives from the title of an American radio programme of the 1940s in which contestants were granted a wish. When Radio Luxembourg adopted the format (from 1955), the title was changed to *Princess for a Day*.

queer as a clockwork orange   'odd'; said to be a Cockney expression of the mid-1950s, according to Anthony Burgess, author of the novel *A Clockwork Orange* (1962; film UK, 1971). 'Queer' in the sense of 'homosexual' does not appear to be the meaning here and homosexuality is not a feature of the novel which tells of an official attempt to punish its criminal hero, Alex, by turning him into a 'mechanical man' through forms of therapy and brainwashing. The following passage hints at a reason for the choice of title: 'Who ever heard of a clockwork orange?...The attempt to impose upon man, a creature of growth and capable of sweetness, to ooze juicily at the last round the bearded lips of God, to attempt to impose, I say, laws and conditions appropriate to a mechanical creation, against this I raise my sword-pen.'

queer as a coot   pejorative phrase that has been applied to 'queers' in the homosexual sense (and was so recorded in the 1950s), but is probably no more than an alliterative version of the older 'stupid as a coot'. Coots are probably no stupider or queerer than any other bird, but the name sounds funny – hence also **bald as a coot/bandicoot.**

queer as Dick's hatband, as (or **funny as...**and sometimes completed with **it went round twice and then didn't fit/meet**)   dismissive phrase for anything odd or peculiar. Mostly Northern or Midlands English dialect use (in various forms) since the eighteenth century. One explanation as to who Dick was is Richard

161

Cromwell (1626–1712), who succeeded Oliver, his father, as Lord Protector in 1658 and did not make a very good job of it. Hence, 'Dick's hatband' was his 'crown'.

question-mark still hangs over, a   *see* **jury is still out.**

quick and dirty   phrase applied to a job or piece of work accomplished fast and with the minimum of fuss – probably not very well done, too, but cheap. Probably American in origin, since the 1950s.

R
r

rabbit, rabbit! phrase emulating talkative women. 'To rabbit', meaning 'to talk', comes from rhyming slang ('rabbit and pork'). The Cockney singers Chas and Dave popularized this old phrase when using it in one of their commercials for Courage Best Bitter in the UK, early 1980s.

rain-check, let's take a *see* **I'll take a rain-check.**

rare as rocking horse shit/manure that is, rare to the point of being non-existent. By the 1970s and possibly from British forces' slang. A 1986 advertisement for Qantas, the Australian airline, was cajoling passengers with: 'You'll agree a better deal [than Qantas offer] is about as likely as rocking-horse manure'. Modern version of **rare as hen's teeth.**

read any good books lately? what you might say to someone who, for no obvious reason, is staring at you or as a way of changing the subject in conversation. This last use was much in evidence in the BBC radio show *Much Binding in the Marsh* (1940s): *Kenneth Horne*: 'One of the nicest sandwiches I've ever had. What was in it, Murdoch?' *Richard Murdoch*: 'Well, there was – er – have you read any good books lately?' *Horne*: 'I thought it tasted something like that.' Well-established by the 1930s, it had once, presumably, been used in all seriousness as a conversational gambit.

read my lips! 'listen to what I am saying – I mean it.' Although popularized by George Bush in his speech accepting the Republican presidential nomination in 1988, the phrase is rooted in 1970s rock music. The British actor/singer Tim Curry used the phrase as the title of an album of songs in 1978. Curry said he took it from an Italian-American recording engineer who used it to mean, 'Listen and listen very hard, because I want you to hear what I've got to say.'

re-arrange the following into a well-known phrase or saying instruction often to be found in competitions and puzzles. The actual game of re-ordering the words on a board to make up a sentence was almost certainly played in the 'Beat the Clock' segment of the ITV show *Sunday Night at the London Palladium* (1950s/60s). From the 1970s, a graffito: 'Arrange the following words into a well-known phrase or saying: Off Piss.'

Reds under the bed (there are) a watchword of anti-Bolshevik scares and current within a few years of the 1917 October Revolution in Russia. A red flag was used in the 1789 French Revolution and the colour had come to be associated with revolutionary movements during the nineteenth century before being adopted by Communists and their sympathizers. It was said that originally the flag had been dipped in the blood of victims of oppression.

—— **refreshes the parts other** —— **cannot reach** format taken from a slogan for Heineken lager beer in the UK, since the mid-1970s: 'Heineken refreshes the parts other beers cannot reach.' From a political speech: 'When I think of our much-travelled Foreign Secretary [Lord Carrington] I am reminded of...the peer that reaches those foreign parts other peers cannot reach' (Margaret Thatcher, Conservative Party Conference, 1980). Compare the American proverb first recorded by Gelett Burgess in *Are You a Bromide?* (1907): 'The Salvation Army reaches a class of people that churches never do.'

rejoice! rejoice! cry of victory, subsequently likely to be disapproved of. Margaret Thatcher is still being reported as having said it to newsmen outside 10 Downing Street on 25 April 1982 following the recapture of South Georgia by British forces during the Falklands War. What the British Prime Minister *actually* said was: 'Just rejoice at that news and congratulate our forces and the Marines. Goodnight. Rejoice!' But in the following day's *Daily Telegraph* this had already become: 'A triumphant Prime

Minister declared "Rejoice, rejoice" last night ...'. Much later, Julian Critchley MP wrote in the *Observer* (27 June 1993): 'Shortly after Mrs Thatcher's defenestration in November 1990, I ran into [Sir Edward] Heath in a Westminster corridor. I quoted a Spanish proverb: if you wait by the river long enough, the body of your enemy will float by. Heath broke into a broad grin: "Rejoice, rejoice", was his reply.'

Either way, might one detect signs of Mrs Thatcher's Methodist upbringing in her remark? Although 'Rejoice, rejoice!' is quite a common expression, each verse of Charles Wesley's hymn 'Rejoice! the Lord is King' ends: 'Rejoice, again I say, rejoice.' There is also a nineteenth century hymn (words by Grace J. Frances), 'Rejoice, Rejoice, Believer!' The phrase occurs as well in Handel's oratorio *Messiah* ('Rejoice, rejoice, rejoice greatly, O daughter of Zion') based on Zechariah 9:9. The ultimate source may equally be Philippians 4:4: 'Rejoice in the Lord alway: and again I say, Rejoice.'

remember the ——! a common form of sloganeering, particularly as a way of starting conflicts or keeping them alive, especially in the US. Probably the first was **remember the River Raisin!** – a war cry of Kentucky soldiers dating from the War of 1812. In the Raisin River massacre, 700 Kentuckians, badly wounded trying to capture Detroit, were scalped and butchered by Indians who were allies of the British. Then came **remember the Alamo!** after the siege of 1836. **Remember the *Maine*!** helped turn the sinking of the battleship *Maine* in Havana harbour (1898) into an excuse for the Spanish-American War (as well as for the contemporary graffito: 'Remember the Maine/To hell with Spain/Don't forget to pull the chain'). **Remember the *Lusitania*!** followed the sinking of another ship (in 1915). **Remember Belgium!** was originally a recruiting slogan of the First World War. It eventually re-emerged with ironic emphasis amid the mud of Ypres, encouraging the rejoinder: 'As if I'm ever likely to forget the bloody place!' **Remember Pearl Harbor!** followed from the 1941 incident and **remember the *Pueblo*!** commemorated the capture of the USS *Pueblo* by North Korea in 1968.

Most of these phrases – particularly 'Remember the Alamo!' –

are now recalled with but a very hazy idea of their original signifi-
cance. Their value is simply that they did stand for something
once.

remember there is a war on   *see* **don't you know there's a war on?**

rest is history!, the   an ending to a biographical anecdote, that
enables the teller to fast-forward to the conclusion. Alan Bennett
played delightfully with the phrase in *Oxford Today* (Michaelmas
1988), having described his transition from Oxford history don
to Broadway revue artist: 'The rest, one might say pompously, is
history. Except that in my case the opposite was true. What it
had been was history. What it was to be was not history at all.'
Now, in less felicitous hands, a cliché.

retreat? Hell, no, we only just got here!   'no, we're not giving up,
we've only just started' – from an unconfirmed quotation of
what US Captain Lloyd S. Williams said when advised by the
French to retreat, shortly after his arrival at the Western Front
during the First World War (in June 1918). Margaret Thatcher
quoted it at a Confederation of British Industry dinner in 1980, a
year after she took office.

rhubarb, rhubarb!   what actors mumble in crowd scenes to give
the impression of speech, as a background noise, without
actually producing coherent sentences. One wonders whether
the adoption of the word 'rhubarb' in the English version has
anything to do with its slang use to denote the male (and
occasionally female) genitals. Or could there have been some
rhyming slang phrase, i.e. rhubarb (tart) = fart (akin to rasp-
berry tart = fart)? It is impossible to date the start of this
expression.

right monkey!   *see* **cheeky monkey!**

rowing with one oar in the water   *see* **few vouchers short. . .**

——— rules OK!   a curious affirmative, said to have begun in gang-
speak of the late 1960s in Scotland and Northern Ireland,
though some would say it dates back to the 1930s. Either a gang

or a football team or the Provisional IRA would be said to 'rule OK'. Later, around 1976, the format phrase became an almost unstoppable cliché, but also a joke with numerous variations – 'Queen Elizabeth rules UK', 'Rodgers and Hammerstein rule OK, lahoma', and so on.

S
s

sausages are the boys! *see* **if you want me, Thingmy...**

say hey! a characteristic expression of Willie Mays, the American baseball star of the 1950s/60s. He would say it when he was excited and it somehow caught on.

say it ain't so, Joe! phrase used when expressing pained disbelief – the archetypal remark when youthful innocence is confronted with the possibility of corruption in an admired hero. It originated with the question reputedly addressed by a small boy to the American baseball player 'Shoeless Joe' Jackson as he came out of a grand jury session in 1920 about corruption in the 1919 World Series. Jackson, of the Chicago White Sox, had been accused with others of deliberately losing the Series at the behest of gamblers. A journalist reported a boy asking, 'It ain't so, Joe, is it?' and Jackson's reply, 'Yes, kid, I'm afraid it is.' Over the years, the words re-arranged themselves into the more euphonious order. Ironically, Jackson denied that the exchange had ever taken place – using any set of words.

say it, don't spray it! *see* **spray it again, will you?**

say it with flowers 'say it nicely' – from a slogan devised for the Society of American Florists, and invented in 1917 for its chairman, Henry Penn of Boston, Massachusetts. Major Patrick O'Keefe, head of an advertising agency, suggested: 'Flowers are words that even a babe can understand' – a line he had found in a poetry book. Penn considered that too long. O'Keefe, agreeing, rejoined: 'Why, you can say it with flowers in so many words.' Later came several songs with the title.

say no more! *see* **nudge nudge, wink wink!**

scarce as rocking-horse manure, as *see* **as busy as a...**

Scout's honour! 'honestly, I'm telling the truth!' – possibly said with an accompanying two-fingered (together) salute to the forehead. Joining the Boy Scout movement, founded by Robert Baden-Powell in 1908, involved a simple oath-taking ceremony, after which it was assumed that a Scout would not lie. The first item of the ten-point 'Scout Law' is 'A Scout's honour is to be trusted'.

scratch my breech and I'll claw your elbow *see* **you scratch my back…**

screw loose *see* **few vouchers short…**

see a man about a dog, (I must go and) the best-known of the numerous (male) euphemisms for going to the lavatory, though it is possible that originally it was an excuse for visiting a woman for a sexual purpose. Impossible to date but possibly by 1900.

see you in church! jocular farewell – usually among non-churchgoers. American origin, by the mid-twentieth century. Compare **see you in court,** a rather more menacing farewell, perhaps hinting that someone is up to no good. Also American, by the 1920s/30s.

see you later, alligator! farewell remark but so meaningless as to be used in almost any situation. On its own 'see you later', as a form of farewell, entered American speech in the 1870s. By the 1930s, it had some 'jive use' in 'see you later, alligator'. To this was added the response, 'In a while, crocodile'. The exchange became known to a wider public through the song 'See You Later, Alligator', sung by Bill Haley and his Comets in the film *Rock Around the Clock* (1956), which recorded the origins of rock-'n'roll. The next stage was for the front and back of the phrase to be dropped off, leaving the simple 'Lay-tuh' as a way to say goodbye.

seen one, seen 'em all! now a loosely applied reason for not going to see something (a film or sporting event or whatever) but, originally, perhaps said by one sex about the sexual organs of the other. By the 1970s but probably much earlier.

send in the clowns! *see* **show must go on!**

sex rears its ugly head!   an explanation for something that has happened, usually in a relationship between two people, and equivalent to the expression *cherchez la femme*. Also used as a complaint about the intrusion of sex in books, TV programmes, etc. where the speaker would rather not find it.

And how curious. Why? Because the penis rises? If so, then why ugly? A very odd usage, except that the construction 'to raise/rear its ugly head' was probably used about other matters before sex. The image is presumably of a Loch Ness-type monster, perhaps, emerging from the deep. Since the 1930s.

shave and a hair cut, five bob!   *see* **hi-tiddly-i-ti!**

she knows, you know!   catchphrase of the diminutive Northern English comedienne Hylda Baker (1908–86). She used to say it in sketches with or in monologues about Cynthia, her mute giraffe-like partner – who was actually a man in drag. Baker's other phrase **be soooon!**, which she pronounced with stuck-out lips, was used as the title of a TV series in the 1950s.

she should lie back and enjoy it!   a politically incorrect view of rape or other form of forced sexual intercourse. Sometimes given as a 'mock-Confucianism' in the form: 'If rape is inevitable, lie back and enjoy it' and therefore probably of simple American origin. Mid-twentieth century? Compare **close your eyes and think of England.**

she wasn't around when the looks were given out   *see* **wrong side of the hedge when. . .**

she who must be obeyed   tag applied to a fearsome woman. The original 'she' in the novel *She* (1887) by H. Rider Haggard was the all-powerful Ayesha, who 'was obeyed throughout the length and breadth of the land, and to question her command was certain death'. From that we get the use of the phrase by barrister 'Horace Rumpole' with regard to his formidable wife in the 'Rumpole of the Bailey' stories by John Mortimer (in TV plays since 1978, and novelizations therefrom). Hence, too, one of the many nicknames applied to Margaret Thatcher when British Prime Minister (1980s).

she's got legs right up to her bum admiring description of an attractive girl whose long legs are her main feature. Say by the 1950s. Later variations might include, **she's got legs that go on for ever** and (even) **she's got legs that go right up to her armpits/ the lobes of her ears.**

she's got round heels 'she's anybody's, she's an easy lay' – a delightfully descriptive expression which suggests that a woman's heels are so curved that the slightest push from a man would put her on her back and in a position to have sexual intercourse. From the mid-twentieth century?

she's joined the club! 'she's pregnant', especially when the woman in question is unmarried. The club referred to – with a far from exclusive membership – was known in the nineteenth century as the 'Pudding' or 'Pudden Club' (where 'pudden' was seminal fluid). The expression has also been used to describe a girl's first menstrual period.

she's my best friend and I hate her! phrase imitative of a child's mixed loyalties and feelings. Originally, 'Priscilla – she's my best friend and I *hate* her!' and spoken by the schoolgirl character 'Monica' (Beryl Reid) in BBC radio's *Educating Archie* (1950s).

shepherd before sheep! *see* **age before beauty!**

shit before shovel! *see* **age before beauty!**

shit hits the fan, when the probably a 1930s/40s forces' phrase for when the reckoning is due in any situation – when for example, a person in authority discovers some misdeed and erupts with terrible temper (and, to mix metaphors, **there'll be blood all over the walls**). A colourful and much used image. Alluded to delightfully in January 1989 when the Nottingham Forest football manager, Brian Clough, administered buffets, clouts and clips round the ear to his team's fans who had invaded the pitch (and got into trouble for it).

shock, horror! jocular reaction to anything surprising expressed in parody of tabloid newspaper-speak, from the 1970s onwards.

In form, it is similar to 'Shock, horror, probe, sensation!' promoted since the 1960s by *Private Eye* as a stock sensational newspaper headline.

shoot first and ask afterwards   cynical instruction to, say, soldiers on sentry duty or to policemen in riot situations. The epitome of rough and summary justice – but all too often leading to injustice. Since the nineteenth century, in the Wild West perhaps?

show must go on!   like **send in the clowns**, this seems to have been originally a circus phrase, though apparently no one can turn up a written reference much before 1930. It was the title of a film in 1937 and of an Ira Gershwin/Jerome Kern song in *Cover Girl* (1944). In 1950, the phrase was spoken in the film *All About Eve* and, in the same decade, Noël Coward wrote a song which posed the question '*Why* Must the Show Go On?'

'shrieks of silence' was the stern reply   *see* **'no answer' came...**

shut that door!   catchphrase of the camp British entertainer Larry Grayson (1923–95) who came to prominence as a comedy personality on TV in the 1970s. The first time he used the phrase was on stage at the Theatre Royal, Brighton in 1970, 'when I felt a terrible draught up my trouser legs. I turned to the wings and said it. I really meant it.' Also in the 1970s, Grayson had any number of camp phrases like **what a gay day!**, **the place is alive!** and **I just don't care any more!**

sick as a parrot   *see* **over the moon.**

silly Billy!   said to a foolish person, the phrase was in widespread general use by the 1850s. The most notable person to be given it as a nickname was William Frederick, 2nd Duke of Gloucester (1776–1834), uncle of William IV. In the 1970s, Mike Yarwood, the British TV impressionist, put it in the mouth of the Labour politician Denis Healey, because it went rather well with the Healey persona and distinctive vocal delivery.

since nineteen-hundred-and-frozen-to-death   a somewhat arch way of avoiding giving a person's (or one's own) age. Rather dated in its own way, but heard still in the UK in the 1980s. Another version is **since nineteen-hundred-and-mind-your-own-business.**

sir, you are speaking of the woman I love!   pompous assertion on behalf of a woman who has been spoken ill of. From dramas (almost melodramas) of the 1880s/90s and now used as a conscious archaism.

sixty four thousand dollar question, the   (sometimes simply **the sixty-four dollar question**) meaning, 'the question which would solve all our problems if only we knew the answer to it'. Originally, 'the sixty-four dollar question' was the highest award in a CBS radio quiz called *Take It or Leave It* (1940s) in which the value of the prize doubled every time the contestant got a right answer (in the progression 1–2–4–8–16–32–64 – hence the title *Double Your Money* given to the first of the British TV versions). Subsequently, in the US TV version of the show (1955–7), the top prize did go up to $64,000 – though, cunningly, when ITV imported the show for British viewers shortly afterwards, the title was simply *The 64,000 Question* or *Challenge*, making no mention of the denomination of currency involved.

small, but perfectly formed   slightly twee compensatory remark, as in, 'You are a lovely audience. . .small, yes, but *perfectly formed*.' As such one might have suspected a theatrical, possibly American showbiz, origin. However, in *A Durable Fire – The Letters of Duff and Diana Cooper 1913–50*, the phrase appears in a letter from Duff to Diana in October 1914: 'That is the sort of party I like. . .You must think I have enjoyed it too, with your two stout lovers frowning at one another across the hearth rug, while your small, but perfectly formed one kept the party in a roar.' As such, it would seem to be fashionable slang or smart talk of the period.

smarter than the average bear   said of himself by Yogi Bear to his sidekick, Booboo, in the American Yogi Bear cartoon TV series (started 1958).

smashing, lovely, super!   a *real* catchphrase based on the enthusiastic mutterings of the British comedian Jim Bowen when hosting a darts-orientated TV game called *Bullseye* (since 1981). The order of the words was variable and when Bowen appeared in poster advertisements for Skol Lager (1993–4), the copy line was 'Great, smashing, super'.

smile when you say that!   warning given to someone who has just said something that otherwise could lead to a fight. Originally, a quotation from Owen Wister's novel *The Virginian* (1902): "Therefore Trampas spoke. "You bet, you son-of-a——". The Virginian's pistol came out, and...he issued his orders to the man Trampas: – "**When you call me that, *smile*!**" ' Popularized by the film version (1929) in which Gary Cooper says, standing up to Walter Huston: 'If you want to call me that, smile.'

smile, you're on *Candid Camera*!   said when a practical joke or hoax has been revealed as such. This is what Allen Funt would say to members of the American public who had been victims of his practical joke TV show *Candid Camera* (1948–78) – earlier, on radio, it had been *Candid Microphone*.

snap a wrist!   *see* **break a leg!**

snug as a bug in a rug   well-fitting and/or extremely warm and comfortable. Usually ascribed to Benjamin Franklin, the American writer and philosopher, who mentioned a type of epitaph in a letter to Miss Georgiana Shipley (26 September 1772) on the death of her pet squirrel, 'Skugg': 'Here Skugg lies snug/As a bug in a rug.' But there are earlier uses. In an anonymous work *Stratford Jubilee* (commemorating David Garrick's Shakespeare festival in 1769) we find: 'If she [a rich widow] has the mopus's [money]/I'll have her, as snug as a bug in a rug.' Probably, however, it was an established expression even by that date, if only because in 1706 Edward Ward in *The Wooden World Dissected* had the similar 'He sits as snug as a Bee in a Box' and in Thomas Heywood's play *A Woman Killed with Kindness* (1603) there is 'Let us sleep as snug as pigs in pease-straw.'

so poor (s)he didn't have a pot to piss in, (s)he was   self-explanatory North American phrase, sometimes extended to include: '...and **not even a window to throw it out of**'. 1980s, and the likely source of the word 'potless' to describe the poverty-stricken.

so stupid he can't chew gum and walk (straight) at the same time an American test of extreme dumbness. The notion became popular when Gerald Ford became President in 1974 on account of his verbal infelicities and physical unsteadiness. Lyndon Johnson was quoted as having said: 'That Gerald Ford. He can't fart and chew gum at the same time.' This is the correct version of the oft misquoted, 'He couldn't walk and chew gum at the same time', according to J.K. Galbraith, *A Life in Our Times* (1981).

so what's new? *see* **'twas ever thus!**

sock it to me! spoken by the English actress Judy Carne who became known as the Sock-It-To-Me Girl on *Rowan and Martin's Laugh-In* (NBC TV, 1960s). She would appear and chant the phrase until – ever unsuspecting – something dreadful happened to her. She would be drenched with a bucket of water, fall through a trap door, get blown up, or find herself shot from a cannon.

The actual phrase was taken from a hit record entitled 'Respect' (1967) recorded by Aretha Franklin, which featured a chorus repeating 'Sock it to me' quite rapidly in the background. The phrase 'to sock it to someone' originally meant 'to put something bluntly' (and was used as such by Mark Twain). Black jazz musicians gave it a sexual meaning, as in 'I'd like to sock it to *her*.'

sod/fuck this for a game of soldiers! *see* **fuck this/that for a lark!**

soft as a brush *see* **daft as a brush.**

softly, softly, catchee monkey 'gently does it, subtlety will get results.' From what has been described as a 'negro proverb'. Hence, the title *Softly Softly* of a BBC TV police drama series (1966–76), which came, more particularly, from the use of the saying as the motto of the Lancashire Constabulary Training School which inspired the series.

some like it hot 'some people like things – especially music and sex – to be exciting' – a phrase chiefly familiar as the title of a film (US, 1959) about two unemployed musicians who are accidental witnesses of the St Valentine's Day Massacre and flee to Miami disguised as members of an all-girls jazz band. So the 'hotness' comes from the jazz and the position they find themselves in. An allusion, if at all, is intended towards the nursery rhyme 'Pease porridge hot' (first recorded about 1750), of which the second verse goes: 'Some like it hot/Some like it cold/Some like it in the pot/ Nine days old.'

some mothers do 'ave 'em! *see* **don't some. . .**

some of my best friends are —— (most commonly **Jews/Jewish**) a self-conscious (and occasionally jokey) disclaimer of prejudice. The Jewish sense was predominantly the one used in the 1930s but the phrase seems to have been in existence in a general way by 1931 when the Marx Brothers film *Monkey Business* included the line, 'Some of my best friends are *housewives*'. Hence, the expression has been adapted, jokingly, to accommodate any group to which the speaker may be thought not to belong or stand aloof from.

someone/somebody up there likes me an expression of faith in heavenly powers either on the grounds that the speaker has experienced good fortune or, especially, been spared from death or injury in some unfortunate circumstance. *Somebody Up There Likes Me* was the title of a 1956 film written by Ernest Lehman. It starred Paul Newman and was based on the life of the World Middleweight Boxing Champion of 1947–8, Rocky Graziano whose autobiography bore the same title.

something is rotten in the state of Denmark all is not well in this country or in this organization. A quotation from Shakespeare's *Hamlet* (I.iv.90) where the line is spoken by Marcellus concerning the corruption that is spreading out from the royal court at Elsinore.

somewhere to the right of Genghis Khan a cliché description of someone's politics, if they are thought to be right-wing or fascist. Popular in the UK, by the early 1980s. Genghis Khan (*c* 1162–1227) was a Mongol ruler who conquered large parts of Asia and, rightly or not, his name is always equated with terror, devastation and butchery. Occasionally, the similar Attila the Hun has his name substituted in the expression.

South will rise again!, the 'the (American) South is not finished yet and has a future' – a slogan referring to the aftermath of the Civil War and which presumably came out of the period that followed it known as Reconstruction. Somewhat tainted in that it has also been used as a rallying cry of segregationists.

speak softly and carry a big stick 'There is a homely adage – "Speak softly and carry a big stick – you will go far".' On 2 September 1901, just a few days before the assassination of President McKinley, Vice President Theodore Roosevelt said this at Minnesota State Fair. He went on, 'If the American nation will speak softly and yet build and keep at a pitch of the highest training a thoroughly efficient navy, the Monroe Doctrine [which sought to exclude European intervention in the American continent] will go far.' Note that he did not claim the 'adage' to be original.

spray it again, will you? pointed remark to the sort of person who 'sprays' when speaking – i.e. produces spittle and saliva on pronouncing certain letters of the alphabet. Since the 1940s. Also **say it, don't spray it!** (which has also been seen as an anti-graffiti graffito – London, early 1980s).

squeeze till the pips squeak meaning 'extract the most [usually, money] from anything or anyone'. Apparently coined by Sir Eric Geddes, a British Conservative politician, shortly after the end of the First World War. On the question of reparations, Geddes said in an election speech in Cambridge (10 December 1918): 'The Germans, if this Government is returned, are going to pay every penny; they are going to be squeezed as a lemon is squeezed – until the pips squeak. My only doubt is not whether we can squeeze hard enough, but whether there is enough juice.' The previous night, Geddes, who had lately been First Lord of the Admiralty, said the same thing in a slightly different way as part of what was obviously a stump speech: 'I have personally no doubt we will get everything out of her that you can squeeze out of a lemon and a bit more. . .I will squeeze her until you can hear the pips squeak. . .I would strip Germany as she has stripped Belgium.'

stairs do not reach all the way to the attic   *see* **few vouchers short**...

stand up and be counted!   'declare openly your allegiance or beliefs'. Of American origin, by the early 1900s.

standing about like a lost lemon   *see* **like a spare prick at a wedding**.

standing prick has no conscience   *see* **stiff prick has**...

steady the Buffs!   self-admonitory phrase, meaning 'brace up, be careful, hold on, keep calm'. The Buffs was the name given to the Royal East Kent Regiment (on account of their buff-coloured tunics). The phrase was originally a military command given to them to hold their position and not to fire. Commonly used by the 1880s.

stick it, Jerry!   phrase of encouragement (i.e. 'stick at it...'), originating in the early years of the twentieth century. It was a line from a sketch involving Lew Luke, the Cockney comedian. Playing a burglar, he would say it to his companion when they were throwing missiles at policemen pursuing them. The phrase was popular during the First World War but, apparently, this is not how the name 'Jerry' came to be applied to refer to Germans.

stiff prick has/hath no conscience, a   a proverbial view (sometimes completed with **and an itching cunt feels no shame**, according to some sources) has been confidently ascribed to St Augustine of Hippo, the North African Christian theologian (AD 354–430). Or so John Osborne would have us believe in *Almost a Gentleman* (1991). Indeed, it would not be surprising given Augustine's interesting activities prior to conversion (compare 'Give me chastity and continency – but not yet!' from his *Confessions*, AD 397–8). But confirmation is lacking and one can only say that its proverbial status was evident by the 1880s when 'Walter' in *My Secret Life* (Vol. I, Chap. 12) wrote: 'I thought how unfair it was to her sister, who was in the family way by me...but a standing prick stifles all conscience.' Indeed **a standing prick has no conscience** is an equally well-known version.

still going strong, like Johnnie Walker an allusion to the slogan for Johnnie Walker whisky – 'Born 1820 – still going strong' (itself in use since 1910). From Randolph Quirk, *Style and Communication in the English Language* (1983): 'English lexicography knocks Johnnie Walker into a tricuspidal fedora. Over four hundred years, and going stronger than ever.'

stop me if you've heard it/this one... apologetic preamble to a joke. Since the 1920s.

stop messing about! (pronounced **stop messin' abaht!**) catch-phrase of the British comic actor Kenneth Williams. Originally used in BBC radio's *Hancock's Half-Hour* (mid-1950s), it stayed with Williams and was later used as the title of a radio show of which he, by that time, was the star.

stop the world I want to get off! meaning 'I'm tired of life' and taken from the title of a musical written by Anthony Newley and Leslie Bricusse (1961). They, in turn, apparently took it from a graffito.

story of my life!, that's the exclamation when reacting to a piece of misfortune – usually fairly minor, like losing a parking space. Second half of the twentieth century.

straight from/out of Central Casting applied to a person who conforms to type or is exactly what you would expect. From the Central Casting office set up and maintained by all major Hollywood studios in 1926 as a pool for supplying extras for films. David Niven, for example, claimed to have been listed on its books in the mid-1930s as 'Anglo-Saxon Type No. 2008'.

strictly for the birds meaning 'of no consequence', this is an American expression (by the 1950s), alluding to horse manure which is only good for picking over by small birds.

such is life! a reflective exclamation when the inevitable happens. Since the eighteenth century. The last words of Ned Kelly, the Australian outlaw, who was hanged in Melbourne in 1880 at the age of 25, are said to have been: 'Ah well, I suppose it has come to this!. . .Such is life!' The British pop singer and political clown 'Lord' David Sutch felicitously entitled his autobiography *Sutch is Life* (1992).

suck it and see   meaning 'try it out', presumably from what you would say about a sweets or candy – 'suck it and see whether you like the taste of it'. It was used as a catchphrase by Charlie Naughton of the British Crazy Gang (1940s/50s), though it is possibly of earlier music-hall origin.

Sunday, *bloody* Sunday!   expression of frustration or boredom at the traditional inactivity of the Sabbath, since the nineteenth century. The film title *Sunday Bloody Sunday* (1971) follows this, without great relevance to its story. Later (1973) the UK/US group Black Sabbath had a record album with the title 'Sabbath Bloody Sabbath'.

support your local sheriff   *see* **your friendly neighbourhood ——** .

surprise, surprise!   what you say when giving someone an unexpected present or when arriving unexpectedly to see people. Possibly of American origin, 1950s. In the 1990s, a British TV show with the title *Surprise, Surprise* was built on the premise of surprising members of the public who had merited this treatment.

swinging!   *see* **dodgy!**

T
t

take me to your leader! traditional line spoken in cartoons by Martians who have just landed on earth, or in science fiction by earth persons landing on some other planet. Echoing what explorers or invaders might have said when encountering a tribe in some distant land in imperial days. Very 1950s.

take the money and run meaning 'settle for what you've got and don't quibble or hang about', as though giving advice to a bank robber that he should take what he has got rather than look for more and risk being caught. Or it might be advice given to a person worried about the value of a job. In which case, one might say, 'I should just take the money and run, if I were you'. Mid-twentieth century. The title of a Woody Allen film was *Take the Money and Run* (1968).

talking about Uganda *see* **discussing Ugandan affairs.**

tall, dark, and handsome description of the standard attributes of a romantic hero, as likely to be found especially in women's fiction. By the 1900s. Cesar Romero played the lead in the 1941 film *Tall, Dark and Handsome* which no doubt helped fix the phrase in popular use.

ta-ta for now! *see* **T.T.F.N.!**

tell it like it is! injunction to tell the truth or the facts as you see them, popular in the 1960s when it was addressed to speakers at American Civil Rights demonstrations. But equally a simple verbal encouragement to keep on talking.

tell it/that to the Marines! 'I don't believe that, though others may; don't expect us to believe that' – this apparently dates from the days, in Britain, when Marines were looked down upon by

181

ordinary sailors and soldiers. Working on land and sea, the Marines were clearly neither one thing nor the other, and thus stupid. So perhaps they would believe a piece of unbelievable information. The phrase was current by the early 1800s. The phrase is also well-known in the US. Sometimes it takes the form, 'Tell that to the *horse*-marines'.

tennis, anyone?   *see* **anyone for tennis?**

T.G.I.F.! (short for '**Thank God It's Friday!**') an expression of relief, especially among office workers and schoolteachers, by the 1960s at least.

thank you for sharing that with us!   mild and ironic put down after being told an unwelcome piece of news or a poor joke. Mostly American use, since the 1960s.

thank you for those few kind words!   slightly ironic acceptance of a complimentary remark – especially if it was somewhat double-edged. By the 1910s.

thanking you!   *see* **I'm dreaming...**

thanks, but no thanks!   polite refusal, but perhaps indicating that the offer is not worth much anyway. Mostly American use, since the 1950s.

that'll be the day!   response to a statement or promise that something unlikely is going to occur. 'He says he's going to buy us all a drink this time' – 'That'll be the day...'. Since the 1910s? 'That'll Be the Day' later became the title of a song made famous by Buddy Holly (1957) and, from that, a film (1973).

that'll do nicely, sir!   obsequious acquiescence – a fawning line from an American Express TV advertisement of the late 1970s, especially in the UK. It was in answer to an enquiry as to whether the establishment accepted the credit card in question.

that's all, folks!   announcement of the end of show or similar. Famously, it was the concluding line – not spoken, but written on the screen – of *Merry Melodies*, the Warner Bros. cartoon series, from 1930 onwards.

that's life! exclamation of the *c'est la vie*, **that's show business, such is life** type, used to cover disappointment at the inevitable happening. Probably established by the 1950s. *That's Life* was the title of a BBC TV programme (1975–94) that combined folksy human-interest items with consumerist campaigning.

that's my story and I'm sticking to it! 'I really mean it' – but also indicating a stubborn unwillingness to drop whatever explanation is at issue. By the 1940s.

that's show business/showbiz! exclamation used to cover disappointment at bad luck or the failure of anything, and as such not limited to use in or about the world of entertainment. Certainly current by the early 1960s, the expression is akin to **that's life!** The similar-sounding 'That's Entertainment' (but without any inference of fate's inevitability) was used by Howard Dietz and Arthur Schwarz as the title of a song in the film *Band Wagon* (1953) and as the title of two films (US, 1974; 1976).

that's the stuff to give the troops! welcoming remark as food is placed on the table or after consuming it. Since the First World War. May also be used to mean 'that's the idea, that's what we want', and not necessarily about food.

that's the way the cookie crumbles! meaning, 'that's the way it is, that's the way things turn out, there's no escaping it'. Very 1950s and American (hence 'cookie' rather than 'biscuit'). It was, however, given a memorable twist in Billy Wilder's film *The Apartment* (1960). The main characters make much use of the suffix '-wise', as in 'promotion-wise' and 'gracious-living-wise'. Then Miss Kubelik (Shirley MacLaine) says to C.C. Baxter (Jack Lemmon): 'Why can't I ever fall in love with somebody nice like you?' Replies Baxter: 'Yeah, well, **that's the way it crumbles, cookie-wise.**' A showbiz variant heard in the 1980s is **that's the way the mop flops**.

that's what —— is all about journalistic cliché appearing most frequently in sporting contexts. The basic notion is 'winning is what it's all about' which is often ascribed to Vince Lombardi, coach and general manager of the Green Bay Packers pro-football team from 1959, in the form 'Winning isn't everything, it's the only thing', though of earlier 1950s origin.

that's what *you* think!   'that's what you think', with the inference that the person addressed is wrong and that the speaker knows best. Mid-twentieth century.

that's yer lot!   *see* **aye, aye, that's yer lot!**

that's your actual French!   catchphrase of 'Sandy' (Kenneth Williams) in sketches involving two very camp gentlemen in the BBC radio series *Round the Horne* (1960s). It pointlessly underlines that a French phrase has been spoken: e.g. *Sandy:* 'Mr Horne, we are in the forefront of your *Nouvelle Vague*. That's your actual French.' *Julian*: 'It means we are of the New Wave.' *Sandy*: 'And very nice it looks on you, too.'

   The meaninglessly emphatic **your/yer actual** was also a very 1960s British turn of phrase.

that's your/yer lot!   *see* **aye, aye...**

there ain't gonna be no war!   optimistic catchphrase or anti-war slogan. As Foreign Secretary to British Prime Minister Eden, Harold Macmillan attended a four-power summit conference at Geneva where the chief topic for discussion was German reunification. Nothing much was achieved but the 'Geneva spirit' was optimistic and on his return to London he breezily told a press conference on 24 July 1955, 'There ain't gonna be no war'. Was this a conscious Americanism? There had been, at some time prior to December 1941, an American song (by Frankl) called, precisely, 'There Ain't Gonna Be No War':

> We're going to have peace and quiet
> And if they start a riot
> We'll just sit back and keep score.
> The only place you'll go marching to
> Will be the corner grocery store.
> So rock-a-bye, my baby
> There ain't gonna be no war.

But Macmillan was, without doubt, quoting directly from a *c* 1910 music-hall song, which was sung in a raucous cockney accent by a certain Mr Pélissier (1879–1913) in a show called 'Pélissier's Follies' during the reign of Edward VII:

> There ain't going to be no waar
> So long as we've a king like Good King Edward.
> 'E won't 'ave it, 'cos 'e 'ates that sort of fing.
> Muvvers, don't worry,
> Not wiv a king like Good King Edward.
> Peace wiv honour is 'is motter [snort] –
> Gawd save the King!

there ain't/is no such thing as a free lunch meaning 'there's always a catch' or 'don't expect something for nothing'. In the US the concept of the 'free lunch' dates back to at least the 1840s. It might have amounted to no more than thirst-arousing snacks like pretzels in saloon bars, but even so it was not strictly speaking 'free' because you had to buy a beer to obtain it. It is hard to say when the catchphrase formalizing the thought that free lunches have hidden costs arose. In the epilogue to his *America* (1973) Alistair Cooke ascribes to 'an Italian immigrant, when asked to say what forty years of American life had taught him' – 'There is no free lunch'.

The American economist Milton Friedman gave the saying new life in the 1970s, using it in articles, lectures and as the title of a book (1975) to support his monetarist theories which were enthusiastically embraced by Ronald Reagan and Margaret Thatcher. But he did not coin the phrase either, even if it came to be much associated with him.

there are no pockets in shrouds *see* **you can't take it with you!**

there is no alternative political catchphrase and unofficial slogan of the British Conservative government led by Margaret Thatcher. By the early 1980s, everyone in Britain knew the phrase, but how did it arise? In a speech to the Conservative Women's Conference (on 21 May 1980), marking the end of her first year in office, Mrs Thatcher declared: 'There is no easy popularity in that [harsh economic measures already set in train by the government] but I believe people accept there is no alternative.' The famously nannyish phrase became a rallying cry of the Thatcher

185

government. The acronym TINA, said to have been coined by Young Conservatives, was flourishing by the time of the Party Conference in September 1981. Compare the old Hebrew catchphrase *ain breira* ('there is no choice').

there must be easier ways of making a living!   exasperated comment made in the midst of carrying out a difficult or distasteful or ludicrous task. By the 1940s.

there you go!   phrase of excuse, approbation, thanks, or simply courtesy. Known in the US by 1844 and very common in Australia (for example, when said by a waitress putting a dish in front of a customer). In Britain, in the late 1970s, it was noted as a fairly meaningless filler phrase used by Tony Blackburn, the disc jockey, as well as a widely used phrase when handing purchases to customer, for example.

there'll be blood all over the walls   *see* **shit hits the fan, when the**

there'll be dancing in the streets tonight   cliché of reporting – to signify elation at some victory, certainly by the 1960s. Tom Stoppard in an extended parody of sports journalism in the play *Professional Foul* (1978) has: 'There'll be Czechs bouncing in the streets of Prague tonight as bankruptcy stares English football in the face.'

there's a cheque in the post   customary unbelieved excuse/ response to a demand that an overdue payment be forthcoming. By the 1970s, definitely.

there's a lot of it about!   useful, but fairly meaningless and facetious, rejoinder. Originally, perhaps, what you would say when someone remarked 'I've got the 'flu' (or some other medical complaint). Title of, and running gag in, a Spike Milligan series on BBC TV in 1982.

there's a sucker born every minute (or **there's one born every minute**)   meaning, 'there are lots of fools waiting to be taken advantage of'. There is no evidence that P.T. Barnum, the American circus magnate (1810–91) ever used this expression – not least, it is said, because 'sucker' was not a common term in his day. He did, however, express the view that, 'The people like to be humbugged', which conveys the same idea. There was also a song of the period, 'There's a New Jay Born Every Day' (where 'jay' = 'gullible hick'). By whatever route, Barnum took the attribution.

there's always a first time!   *see* **I'll try anything once!**

there's gold in them thar hills!   meaning 'there are opportunities where indicated'. Presumably this phrase was established literally in US gold-mining by the end of the nineteenth century. It seems to have had a resurgence in the 1930s/40s, probably through use in Western films. Frank Marvin wrote and performed a song with the title in the 1930s. A Laurel and Hardy short called *Them Thar Hills* appeared in 1934. The phrase now has a jokey application to any enterprise which contains a hint of promise.

there's life in the old dog yet!   said of or about the unexpected possessor of some power when that person is thought to be 'past it' (especially when referring to the person's love life). It was used as the title of a painting (1838) – precisely 'The Life's in the Old Dog Yet' – by Sir Edwin Landseer, which shows a Scottish ghillie rescuing a deerhound which, unlike a stag and two other hunting dogs, has not just plunged to its death over a precipice.

there's more where that came from   *see* **and there's more. . .**

there's no answer to that!   phrase used to escape creating a *double entendre*. In the BBC TV *Morecambe and Wise Show* (1970s) it was Eric Morecambe's standard innuendo-laden response to such comments as: *Casanova (Frank Finlay):* 'I'll be perfectly frank with you – I have a long felt want. . .'

there's no such thing as bad publicity   *see* **all/any publicity is good publicity**

these foolish things   best known as the title of a popular song ('These foolish things/Remind me of you', lyrics by Eric Maschwitz, 1936), picked up by Michael Sadleir for a book called *These Foolish Things* in 1937 and by Bertrand Tavernier as the title of a film (1990) which included the song on the soundtrack.

they all look the same in the dark   contemptuous male view of women as sexual objects. Ovid in his *Ars Amatoria* says much the same thing more diplomatically: 'The dark makes every woman beautiful.' Compare: **seen one, seen 'em all!**

they don't make ——/write songs like that any more!   reactionary cry, possibly dating from the 1920s/30s – also applied to people of a type thought no longer to exist. Especially applied in the form, 'They don't write songs like that any more!' – to which the joke response is, 'Thank goodness!'

they laughed when I sat down at the piano. But when I started to play...   a slogan for the US School of Music piano tutor, from 1925. It gave rise to various jokes: 'They laughed when I sat down to play – someone had taken away the stool/how did I know the bathroom door was open/etc.' John Caples, the copywriter, also came up with, 'They grinned when the waiter spoke to me in French – but their laughter changed to amazement at my reply' (presumably on behalf of another client).

In the film *Much Too Shy* (UK, 1942) there is a song 'They Laughed When I Sat Down at the Piano', inspired by the slogan.

they're playing our tune, (darling)!   a phrase from romantic fiction when (presumably married and ageing) lovers hear a tune that makes them nostalgic. From the 1930s/40s? A musical *They're Playing Our Song* (by Marvin Hamlisch and Carole Bayer Sager) was staged in New York in 1979.

things ain't what they used to be!   reactionary moan, revived in the title of the Frank Norman/Lionel Bart musical *Fings Ain't Wot They Used T'be* (London, 1959). Earlier, however, there had been a song by Mercer Ellington and Ted Persons, published in 1939, and actually called 'Things Ain't What They Used To Be'.

things I've done for England!, the   statement of disillusion or disgust at having to perform some unpleasant or disagreeable task in the course of one's job or duties. A quotation. In Sir Alexander Korda's film *The Private Life of Henry VIII* (1933), Charles Laughton as the King is just about to get into bed with one of his many wives when, alluding to her ugliness, he sighs: 'The things I've done for England!'

In 1979, Prince Charles on a visit to Hong Kong sampled curried snake meat and, with a polite nod towards his forebear (however fictionalized), exclaimed, 'Boy, the things I do for England...'.

things were done better in my/our day reactionary phrase of regret. 'Things were done better in *my* day' was said by Alice Keppel, who had been King Edward VII's mistress, on the day of King Edward VIII's abdication. What she presumably meant to convey was, 'The King didn't have to abdicate in order to carry on. He married properly and then took whomever he fancied as mistresses.' The remark has also been attributed to Miss Maxine Elliott, the Edwardian actress and another former mistress of Edward VII, in the form, 'We did it better in my day'. According to Andrew Barrow, *Gossip* (1978), Elliott said it to Winston Churchill at a dinner with the Duke and Duchess of Windsor near Cannes on 7 January 1938.

Compare the similar lament from Laurence Sterne, *A Sentimental Journey* (1768): 'They order, said I, this matter better in France', which, by 1818, had become in Lady Morgan's *Autobiography* (not published until 1859): 'So you see, my dear Olivia, they manage these things better in France.' In a letter to former President Eisenhower (20 July 1965), the former British Prime Minister Harold Macmillan lamented: 'Naturally, people consult me, but they never take my advice, so I give it without much sense of responsibility. Yes, indeed, we managed things much better in our time.'

this hurts me more than it hurts you! *see* **hurts me more than it's hurting you, this**

this is/it's a free country! argument advanced when trying to assert one's right to do what one likes. Probably since the nineteenth century and mostly British.

this is Liberty Hall! *see* **anything goes...**

this is it! phrase of agreement and occurring where a simple 'yes' or 'I agree' would do, or when drawing attention to a key point in argument. Kenneth Tynan reviewing an idiomatic modern translation of *Medea* by Euripides (1948) noted Medea's reaction to Creon's notice of expulsion, 'This is *it*.' The 'I agree with you' version acquired catchphrase status through BBC Radio's satirical *Week Ending* show from about 1977 when two pub bores (played by David Jason and Bill Wallis) conversed on current topics. One would ritually say 'this is it!', followed by **makes you think!**

this is the age of the train   *see* **we're getting there!**

this is/was war!   meaning, 'this is very serious, and justifies the particular course adopted'. 1970s/80s. Compare this earlier version from President Nixon on 15 September 1972: 'We are all in it together. This is a war. We take a few shots and it will be over. . .I wouldn't want to be on the other side right now. Would you?' (*The White House Transcripts*, 1974).

this is where we came in   meaning, 'I am/you are beginning to repeat myself/yourself. This is where we should stop whatever it is we are doing.' Or, 'we have been here (at this point) before, haven't we?' From the remark uttered in cinemas when continuous performances were the order of the day – from the 1920s to the 1970s. From 'Cato', *Guilty Men* (1940): 'When the news of the appointment [of Sir Samuel Hoare re-appointed as Minister of Air in 1940] became known, an aged opponent of the administration rose from his seat, "This is where I came in", he said.'

this is your captain speaking!   mock pompous phrase (as though spoken by an airline or ship captain) when introducing any announcement concerning instructions or decisions made. Since the 1970s?

this one will run and run!   a promotional cliché from *Private Eye*'s collection of phrases (1960s/70s). This one (said of anything, but especially of a political dispute or a strike) was originally the sort of extract taken from critics' notices that theatrical managements liked to display outside their theatres to promote shows. Said originally to have derived from a theatrical review by Fergus Cashin of the *Sun*.

this tape will self-destruct in ten seconds   originally, 'this [audio] tape [of instructions] will. . .' in the American TV spy thriller *Mis-*

sion Impossible (1966–72). Each episode began with the leader of the Impossible Missions Force listening to tape-recorded instructions for an assignment. The voice on the tape would say: 'Your mission, Dan, should you decide to accept it, is...As always, should you or any member of your I.M. Force be caught or killed, the secretary will disavow any knowledge of your actions. This tape will self-destruct...'.

A lavatorial graffito quoted from West Germany in *Graffiti Lives OK* (1979) was, 'This cubicle will self-destruct in ten seconds which will make your mission impossible'.

this thing is bigger than both of us   i.e. 'this love we share', a Hollywood film cliché of the 1940s and 50s. In the 1976 re-make of *King Kong*, with the giant ape brushing against the side of the house they are sheltering in, Jeff Bridges as 'Jack Prescott' says to Jessica Lange as 'Dwan', 'He's bigger than both of us, know what I mean?'

this town ain't big enough for both of us/the two of us   cliché of Western films where it might be said by the villain to the sheriff or to anyone else who is trying to bring him to book. He is, of course, suggesting that the other person will have to get out of the town in order to make room...By the 1940s?

this week's deliberate mistake   *see* **did you spot...**

thought you'd never ask!, I   response to a long-awaited question of the 'Would you like a drink?' variety. By the 1980s.

time marches on!   meaning, 'it's getting on, time is moving forward, time flies...'. Although the phrase 'the march of time' was known by the 1830s, this catchphrase or slogan was possibly not coined until a hundred years on. 'Time...Marches On' was a line used in – and to promote – the 'March of Time' news-documentary-dramas which ran on American radio for fourteen years from 1931. The programmes were sponsored by *Time* magazine.

tired and emotional   a euphemism for 'drunk' and ideally suited to British newspapers which have to operate under libel laws effectively preventing any direct statement of a person's fondness for the bottle. The expression 't. and e.' (to which it is sometimes abbreviated) is said to have arisen when *Private Eye* printed a spoof Foreign Office memo suggesting it was a useful way of describing the antics of George Brown when he was British Foreign Secretary (late 1960s). Peter Paterson entitled his biography of Brown, *Tired and Emotional* (1993).

to boldly go where no man has gone before! *see* **beam me up, Scotty!**

to coin a phrase originally a phrase used literally, meaning to invent a phrase or give it 'currency', and known by 1840. But, in the twentieth century, people have also taken to saying the whole phrase as an ironic way of excusing a cliché, banal statement or *double entendre* they have just uttered. 'Well, it certainly looks as if I need to have it out with my secretary. . .to coin a phrase. . .'

today ——, tomorrow ——! ambitious, all-conquering slogan, indicating a progression from the minor to the major, from the local to the global. The concept can be glimpsed in embryo in the slogan for the German National Socialist Press in the early 1930s: '*Heute Presse der Nationalsozialisten, Morgen Presse der Nation*' [Today the press of the Nazis, tomorrow the nation's press]. This reaches its final form in '*Heute gehört uns Deutschland – morgen die ganze Welt*' [Today Germany belongs to us – tomorrow the whole world] which may actually have been uttered by Hitler in September 1939. This phrase seems to have come from the chorus of a song in the Hitler Youth 'songbook'. It has the title '*Es zittern die morschen Knochen*' [The Rotten Bones Are Trembling] and was written by Hans Baumann in 1932.

A variation: from the black British MP Paul Boateng's victory speech in his Brent South constituency (June 1987): 'Brent South today – Soweto tomorrow!' (where a black person's achievement in one place is turned into a promise of a greater breakthrough in a key South African township).

tonight's the night! 'something important is about to happen!' Used as the title of a musical 'sketch' show (1900) by George Le Brunn, this phrase has also been used to indicate that a sexual conquest is imminent.

'too late! too late!' the Captain cried – and shook his wooden leg
(or 'it's come too late!' the lady cried, as she waved her wooden
leg and passed out)   nonsense catchphrases known in Britain
by the mid-twentieth century – also proverbial expressions
known in the US, according to Wolfgang Mieder, *A Dictionary of
Wellerisms* (1994). He includes two relevant citations: from
Anon., Idaho (1966): ' "Aha!" she cried, as she waved her
wooden leg and died'; and, from Anon., Kentucky (*circa* 1950):
' "Hurrah!" as the old maid shouted waving her wooden leg.'

There may conceivably be some connection with the line 'Too
late! too late!' spoken in a high falsetto, in the joke about the
unhappy fellow who lost his manhood in a shark-infested sea just
before someone arrived to rescue him.

too many chiefs and not enough Indians   phrase suggesting that
in some confused situation there are too many leaders and not
enough led, or that there are too many people giving orders and
instructions but not enough people to carry them out. American
in origin? An alternative title of the film *Who Is Killing the Great
Chefs of Europe?* (US/W. Ger., 1978) was *Too Many Chefs* – which
also neatly alludes to the proverb 'too many cooks spoil the
broth'.

Toto, I have a feeling we're not in Kansas any more!   a line from
the film *The Wizard of Oz* (1939) rather than from Frank L.
Baum's original book, but one that has achieved catchphrase
status. Judy Garland as Dorothy says it on arrival in the Land of
Oz, concluding, 'We must be over the rainbow'. It is used when
speakers want to express bewilderment at the new circumstances they find themselves in.

tree fell on him!, a   stock phrase from one of Spike Milligan's *Q*
comedy series on BBC TV, in the early 1980s. For example: 'Q. Is
he Jewish?' 'A. No, a tree fell on him.'

trouble at t'mill   a key phrase supposedly taken from English
North Country dramas (especially set in the nineteenth century)
but best-known as a humorous allusion to the kind of line
thought to be uttered in same. It might be used now by someone

who is departing to sort out some problem but does not wish to spell out exactly what it is.

Allusively, the phrase was known by the 1960s. An actual example, though not as it happens from a North Country novel, can be found in *John Halifax, Gentleman* (1856) by Mrs Craik (Dinah Maria Mulock): ' "Unless you will consent to let me go alone to Enderley!" She shook her head. "What, with those troubles at the mills?" '

true, O king! phrase of agreement but also something of a put down. It might be said to someone who has just come out with an obvious or pompous or provocative statement that does not merit a proper answer. Possibly taken from the biblical story of Nebuchadnezzar and the gentlemen who were cast into the burning fiery furnace (Daniel 3:24). 'Did not we cast three men bound into the midst of fire?' Nebuchadnezzar asks. 'They answered and said unto the king, True, O king.'

Sometimes the phrase '**Live for ever**' is added.

T.T.F.N.! (short for '**Ta-ta for now!**') the farewell remark of the charlady 'Mrs Mopp' (Dorothy Summers) in the BBC radio comedy show *ITMA* (1940s).

tuppence short of a shilling *see* **few vouchers short...**

'twas ever thus! an exclamation meaning almost the same as the more modern **so what's new?** and used nowadays as a self-conscious anachronism. From the early nineteenth century.

two sticks short of a bundle *see* **few vouchers short...**

U
u

'ullo, 'ullo, 'ullo! (what's this?)   catchphrase from the BBC radio comedy series *Take It From Here* (1940s to 50s). Jimmy Edwards used to say it as 'Pa Glum' when interrupting son 'Ron' as he attempted to kiss fiancée 'Eth'. It also, of course, echoes the traditional inquiry of a policeman encountering something suspicious going on.

unaccustomed as I am to public speaking...   now an unforgivably clichéd way of starting a speech. Recognized as a standard formula for such by the 1840s, it did not escape Winston Churchill's clutches when he made his very first political speech at a Primrose League gathering near Bath in 1897. He started: 'If it were pardonable in any speaker to begin with the well worn and time honoured apology, "Unaccustomed as I am to public speaking," it would be pardonable in my case...'.

unhand me, villain!   jocular version of 'take your hands off me!', echoing the appeal made by a lady to a villain in late nineteenth-century drama. Alternatively, **unhand me, sir!**

up in Annie's room behind the clock, it's (or ...**behind the wall-paper**)   explanatory phrase for when something disappears unaccountably about the house (usually). It may have originated as a services' catchphrase before the First World War, in reply to a query concerning someone's whereabouts.

up Shit Creek without a paddle   irretrievably stuck or in any sort of difficult quandary. Since the 1920s. Possibly an elaboration of the phrase **up the creek**, popular especially in the US.

up to a point, Lord Copper!   phrase conveying only qualified agreement, where there is an unwillingness to offend. It is employed, for example, when disagreeing with someone it is prudent not to differ with. It is a quotation from Evelyn Waugh's novel about journalists, *Scoop* (1938): 'Mr Salter's side of the conversation was limited to expressions of assent. When Lord Copper [a newspaper proprietor] was right he said, "Definitely, Lord Copper"; when he was wrong, "Up to a point".'

up to my neck in muck and bullets catchphrase used by the British comedian Arthur Haynes (1914–66), in his tramp character in ITV shows of the 1960s. Sometimes remembered as 'mud and bullets'.

useless as a chocolate kettle, as *see* **as busy as a...**

V

very interesting. . .but stupid! (or . . .but stinks! or some other variant) catchphrase from *Rowan and Martin's Laugh-In* (1960s), spoken in a thick German accent by Arte Johnson as a bespectacled soldier wearing a helmet and peering through a potted plant. Hence, *Very Interesting. . .But Stupid!*, a book of catchphrases from the world of entertainment (1980) by the present author.

vote early and vote often! cynical slogan of political corruption and of certain American origin. 'Josh Billings' (pseudonym of Henry Wheeler Shaw, the American humorist, 1818–85) wrote that it was 'the Politishun's golden rule' in *Josh Billings' Wit and Humour* (1874), which seems merely to be recalling an adage. Indeed, earlier, William Porcher Miles had said in a speech to the House of Representatives (31 March 1858): ' "Vote early and vote often", the advice openly displayed on the election banners in one of our northern cities.' Another version is that the original joker was John Van Buren, a New York lawyer (*d* 1866), who was the son of President Martin Van Buren.

vous pouvez cracher ('you may spit!') the 1940s BBC Radio show *ITMA* did occasional skits on pre-war Radio Luxembourg and called it 'Radio Fakenburg'. '*Ici Radio Fakenburg,*' the announcer would say, '*mesdames et messieurs, défense de cracher*' (no spitting). Each episode would end: '*Mesdames et messieurs, vous pouvez cracher!*'

W
W

wait and see! an admonition to be patient, always associated with H.H. Asquith, the British Liberal Prime Minister, who said it to a persistent enquirer about the Parliament Act Procedure Bill, in the House of Commons in April 1910. In fact, this was the fourth occasion on which Asquith had said 'Wait and see'. Roy Jenkins commented in *Asquith* (1964): 'It was a use for which he was to pay dearly in the last years of his premiership when the phrase came to be erected by his enemies as a symbol of his alleged inactivity.'

In consequence, Asquith acquired the nickname 'Old Wait and See', and during the First World War French matches which failed to ignite were known either as 'Asquiths' or 'Wait and sees'.

wake up, England! a reprimand delivered by the speaker to himself for not having spotted something fairly obvious. Also, according to Iona and Peter Opie, *The Lore and Language of School-children* (1959), a phrase used to greet a bearer of bad news. In origin it is a misquotation or, rather, a phrase that was not actually spoken. The future King George V made a speech at the Guildhall, London, on 5 December 1901, as the Duke of York (only four days before he was created Prince of Wales). Returning from an Empire tour, he warned against taking the Empire for granted: 'To the distinguished representatives of the commercial interests of the Empire. . .I venture to allude to the impression which seemed generally to prevail among our brethren overseas, that the old country must wake up if she intends to maintain her old position of pre-eminence in her Colonial trade against foreign competitors.' This statement was encapsulated by the popular press in the phrase 'Wake up, England!' but George did not say precisely that himself.

wakey-wakey! rousing wake-up call such as might be shouted by an army sergeant to a hut full of raw recruits. Used at the start of *The Billy Cotton Band Show* on British radio and TV for over twenty years from the late 1940s and shouted by Cotton, the band-leader, himself. When the show first started it was broadcast live at 10.30 a.m. on a Sunday and rehearsals began at 8.45 a.m. – not the best time to enthuse a group of musicians who had been on the road all week. Hence, the cry.

was it good for you too? what the uncertain lover is supposed to say to his sexual partner after intercourse. Indications that the phrase had caught on came when Bob Chieger so entitled a book of quotations about love and sex (1983).

water under the bridge, that's all (or ...**over the dam/under the dyke/under the mill**) dismissive phrase of anything that it is no longer worth worrying about or spending time over. Certainly by the 1960s.

way up 'a 'ky! *see* **I've failed!**

we aim to please slogan of the sort that used automatically to be inscribed over British shops or any institution offering a service. From the 1920s/30s. Not long after, there arrived the graffito written up in men's urinals: 'We aim to please; you aim, too, please.'

we are just good friends clichéd way of expressing to a newspaper (say) that your relationship with another person is not romantic. The phrase probably established itself in the US during the 1930s, though in the film of Cole Porter's musical *Silk Stockings* (US, 1957), the phrase is used several times as if not clichéd yet. Now only used as a consciously humorous evasion, *especially when not true*. A BBC sitcom current in 1984 was called *Just Good Friends* and several songs about that time also had the title.

we are not amused! a put down, rebuffing a joke or a piece of behaviour, and echoing the words attributed to Queen Victoria. The subject was raised (after the Queen's death) in the 1919 *Notebooks of a Spinster Lady* written by Miss Caroline Holland: '[The Queen's] remarks can freeze as well as crystallize...there

199

is a tale of the unfortunate equerry who ventured during dinner at Windsor to tell a story with a spice of scandal or impropriety in it. "We are not amused", said the Queen when he had finished.'

Interviewed in 1978, Princess Alice, Countess of Athlone, said she had once questioned her grandmother about the phrase – 'I asked her...[but] she never said it' – and affirmed what many have held, that Queen Victoria was 'a very cheerful person'.

we are the unwilling, led by the unqualified, doing the unnecessary for the ungrateful a lament of the down-trodden is said to have been seen written on GI helmets in Vietnam in the 1960s/70s. In the June 1980 issue of the magazine *Playboy* there was a slightly different version from 'the Ninth Precinct': 'We the willing, led by the unknowing, are doing the impossible for the ungrateful. We have done so much for so long with so little, we are now qualified to do anything with nothing.' Somebody bitter about police salaries had amended the last line to read, 'To do anything for nothing'.

we be doomed, we all be doomed! *see* **doomed I am, doomed!**

we can't go/keep on meeting like this! possibly a line taken from a fictional love story where the lovers are only able to meet under difficult conditions, but now only used as a joking comment when two non-lovers meet again within a short space of time or encounter each other again in the same unromantic situation like a bus queue or public convenience. Since the 1920s?

we did it once at Bannockburn! the Scots entertainer Alec Finlay often portrayed an old Scots Home Guard sergeant (1940s/50s). If doubts were expressed about his company's abilities, he would reply: 'Dinna worry – we did it once at Bannockburn, we can do the same again!'

we got back on a wing and a prayer meaning, 'we survived despite difficult circumstances'. 'Comin' In On a Wing and a Pray'r' was the title of a song (1943) which was very popular in the Second World War. It derived from an alleged remark by a real pilot who was coming in to land with a badly damaged plane. Harold Adamson's lyrics (to music by Jimmy McHugh) include the lines:

Tho' there's one motor gone, we can still carry on
Comin' in on a wing and a pray'r.

A US film (1944) about life on an aircraft carrier was called simply *Wing and a Prayer*.

we had one of those but it died!   *see* **had one (of those) but the wheel...**

we have met the enemy and he is us   'if you are looking for the cause of all our problems, look no further than us' – a philosophical point of view formulated by the American cartoonist Walt Kelly in his syndicated comic strip featuring a possum called Pogo. Variously stated but in his introduction to *The Pogo Papers* (1953), he wrote: 'Resolve then, that on this very ground, with small flags waving and tinny blasts on tiny trumpets, we shall meet the enemy, and not only may he be ours, he may be us.'

we have ways (and means) of making you talk!   the threat by an evil inquisitor to his victim appears to have come originally from 1930s Hollywood villains and was then handed on to Nazi characters from the 1940s onwards. In *Lives of a Bengal Lancer* (US, 1935), the evil Mohammed Khan says, 'We have ways of making *men* talk' (he means by forcing slivers of wood under the fingernails and setting fire to them...). A typical 'Nazi' use can be found in the film *Odette* (UK, 1950) in which the French Resistance worker (Anna Neagle) is threatened with unmentioned nastiness by one of her captors. Says he: 'We have ways and means of making you talk.' Then, after a little stoking of the fire with a poker, he urges her on with: 'We have ways and means of making a woman talk.'

Latterly, the phrase has only been used in caricature, on TV shows like *Rowan and Martin's Laugh-In* (1960s) – but invariably pronounced with a German accent. Frank Muir presented a comedy series for London Weekend Television with the title *We Have Ways of Making You Laugh* (1968).

we name the guilty men   cliché of campaigning, exposé journalism. From the *Observer* (16 April 1989): 'Like all the best Sunday journalists, I name the guilty men, and one guilty woman, if we include Mrs Shirley Williams.' *Guilty Men* was the title of a tract written under the pseudonym 'Cato' in July 1940, taunting the appeasers who had brought about the situation where Britain had had to go to war with Germany.

we wuz robbed! a notable reaction to (usually) sporting defeat. Originally it was spoken by Joe Jacobs, American manager of the boxer Max Schmeling. Believing his man to have been cheated of the heavyweight title in a fight against Jack Sharkey in 1932, Jacobs shouted his protest into a microphone.

On another occasion, in October 1935, Jacobs left his sick-bed to attend the World Series (ball game) for the one and only time in his life. Having bet on the losers, he opined: **I should of stood in bed.**

we'll let you know! *see* **don't call/ring us, we'll call you.**

we're getting there! a somewhat debatable slogan for British Rail, current in 1985. In 1980, the organization had been promoted by the even more questionable **this is the age of the train**, which it undoubtedly was not (attracting the comments: 'Yes, it takes an age to catch one', 'Ours was 104', etc).

we've got a right one 'ere! comment from one person to another about a stupid third. In about 1959 it was the catchphrase of Dick Emery as 'Mr Monty' in BBC radio's *Educating Archie*. However, it is a common phrase also employed at one time and another by Tony Hancock, Frankie Howerd, Bruce Forsyth and other British comedians.

weekend starts here!, the slogan for the Associated-Rediffusion TV pop show *Ready, Steady, Go* (from 1964) which was transmitted live on Friday evenings in the UK. It caught on and has been used by other programmes since.

well, Brian... a response associated with British TV sports interviews and post-game analysis – because the interviewer of verbally challenged players and managers on ITV football coverage (since 1967) has often been Brian Moore. However, the phrase may have caught on independently of Moore as a result of a sketch on *Monty Python's Flying Circus* (in 1969) when a very unintelligent footballer replied either 'Good evening, Brian' or 'Well, Brian' to every question he was asked by a pretentious TV interviewer.

well, he would, wouldn't he?   comment on an obvious or expected statement by another person. A quotation. When Mandy Rice-Davies was called as a witness at a magistrates' court during the British political scandal known as the Profumo Affair (1963), she was questioned about the men she had had sex with. When told that Lord Astor – one of the names on the list – had categorically denied any involvement with her, she replied, chirpily: 'Well, he would, wouldn't he?' The court burst into laughter, the expression passed into the language, and is still resorted to because – as a good catchphrase ought to be – it is bright, useful in various circumstances, and tinged with innuendo.

well, I'll go to the foot of our stairs!   'I'm amazed!' – an old northern English expression suggesting, presumably, that the short walk to the place mentioned will allow the speaker to recover equanimity. Used by Tommy Handley in the BBC radio show *ITMA* (1940s) and elsewhere.

well to the right of Genghis Khan   *see* **somewhere to the right of. . .**

wham, bam, thank you ma'am!   phrase representing the style of a man who heartlessly has sex with a woman and then throws her over. Probably from forces' use in the 1940s.

what a gay day!   *see* **shut that door!**

what a performance!   catchphrase of the British comedian Sid Field (1904–50), spoken in 'sullen, flattened tones'. Used as the title of a play celebrating Field which was written by William Humble and featured David Suchet in the old routines (1994).

what a turn-up for the book(s)!   expression of surprise or pleasure at an unexpected outcome. The 'books' here are those kept by bookies to maintain a record of bets placed on a race. Does the bookie have to turn up the corner of a page if a race has an unexpected outcome? No, the phrase merely means that something unexpected has 'turned up'.

what a way to run a railway/road! exclamation expressing dismay at mismanagement or chaos of any kind. Possibly originally from the caption to a cartoon said to have appeared in the American *Collier's* magazine (though *Ballyhoo* in 1932 has also been suggested) showing two trains about to collide. A signalman is looking out of his box, saying: 'Tch-tch – what a way to run a railroad!'

The Boston & Maine railroad picked up this line when it sought a statement which would explain some of the problems of the railroad in times of inclement weather. It took the 'stock railroad phrase', derived from the cartoon, and put it between each paragraph of the advertisement in the form, 'That's A H**l of a Way to Run a Railroad!'

More general uses: 'What a way to run a country!' (1968); 'No way to run a revolution!' (1989).

what about the workers? (usually written, **wot abaht...?**) the traditional proletarian heckler's cry during a political speech. Almost a slogan in its own right, but now only used satirically. It occurs along with other rhetorical clichés during the 'Party Political Speech' (written by Max Schreiner) on the Peter Sellers comedy album *The Best of Sellers* (1958). Also in the 1950s, Harry Secombe as 'Neddie Seagoon' on the BBC radio *Goon Show* would sometimes exclaim (for no very good reason), '**Hello, folks, and what about the workers?!**'

Manny Shinwell, the veteran Labour MP, told John Mortimer in *Character Parts* (1986): 'I remember Bonar Law, future Prime Minister and Conservative Member of Parliament for the Gorbals, giving a speech in Glasgow [*c* 1904], and it was all about Free Trade or something and they were applauding him! Unemployed men were applauding Bonar Law! So I shouted out, "What about the workers!" ...I got my picture in the papers.'

what are you doing after the show? chat-up line, presumably of show-business origin. *What Are You Doing After the Show?* was the title of a long-forgotten British ITV comedy show (1971). The previous year's Swedish film, *Rötmanad*, had been given the English title *What Are You Doing After the Orgy?*

what did Gladstone say in ——? good-humouredly meaning-less heckle aimed at political speakers in the late nineteenth, early twentieth century. J.B. Priestley in his *English Journey* (1934) chooses '1884' to complete the catchphrase.

what did you do in the Great War, Daddy? catchphrase during and after the First World War derived from an actual slogan used on recruiting posters. These showed a little girl sitting on her father's knee and asking him, 'Daddy, what did *YOU* do in the Great War?' For his part, the father looks understandably ap-palled as he puzzles over what to reply. One suggestion was, 'Shut up, you little bastard. Get the Bluebell and go and clean my medals.' *What Did You Do in the War, Daddy?* was the title of a film (US, 1966).

what do you think of it/the show so far? Eric Morecambe's custo-mary enquiry of audiences animate or inanimate in BBC TV's *The Morecambe and Wise Show* (1970s). The audience would shout back 'Rubbish!' It first arose in a famous sketch about Antony and Cleopatra (featuring Glenda Jackson) in 1971.

what is a Beatle? *see* **who are the Beatles?**

what is that lady/gentleman *for*? phrase which is a convenient stick with which to beat anyone the speaker wishes to reduce in importance. It is particularly useful when taunting politicians and is spoken as though being asked by a child. For example, 'It was an anonymous little girl who, on first catching sight of Charles James Fox, is supposed to have asked her mother: "what is that gentleman for?" One asks the same question of Mr [Doug-las] Hurd. Why is he where he is in this particular government? He has never been wholly in sympathy either with Mrs Thatcher or with her version of Conservatism.' – Alan Watkins, the *Observer* (29 May 1988). Compare 'I am reminded of the small boy who once pointed at Hermione Gingold and asked, "Mummy, what's that lady for?" ' – Michael Billington (possibly quoting Kenneth Tynan) in the *Guardian* (21 July 1988). ' "What", a little girl is supposed to have asked her mother, point-ing at Sir John Simon, a pre-war Chancellor, "is that man for?"

What, she might now ask, pointing at the Labour faithful assembling in Brighton today, is that party for?' – editorial, the *Independent on Sunday* (29 September 1991).

The precise origin would appear to be the caption to a *Punch* cartoon (in the edition of 14 November 1906). Drawn by F.H. Townsend, it shows the remark being said by a small boy to his mother about a man carrying a bag of golf clubs. The caption is 'MUMMY, WHAT'S THAT MAN FOR?'

what is the difference between a chicken/duck?   *see* **because the higher the fewer!**

what larks, Pip!   an exclamation derived from the novel *Great Expectations* (1860–1) by Charles Dickens. It is a characteristic phrase of Joe Gargery, the blacksmith, who looks after his brother-in-law and apprentice, Pip, in the boy's youth. Chapter 13 has him saying 'calc'lated to lead to larks' and Chapter 57, 'And when you're well enough to go out for a ride – what larks!' The recent use of the phrase probably has more to do with the 1946 film of the book in which Bernard Miles played Joe. As he sees Pip off on a stage coach, he says, 'One day I'll come to see you in London and then, what larks, eh?' and similarly, after Pip's breakdown, 'You'll soon be well enough to go out again, and then – what larks!' Even here, the name Pip is not actually included in the phrase.

In *The Kenneth Williams Diaries* (1993) (entry for 30 August 1970), the actor writes: 'Tom played the piano and all the girls danced with us & I stuck me bum out and oh! what larks Pip!' Ned Sherrin dedicates his *Theatrical Anecdotes* (1991), 'For Judi [Dench] and Michael [Williams]: "What larks!" '

what no ——?   *see* **wot no ——?**

what the dickens!   an exclamation of incredulity. 'Dickens' has nothing to do with the novelist but is a euphemistic way of saying 'What the *devil*!' (and is perhaps a watered down version of 'devilkin', though this is not certain). Shakespeare has, 'I cannot tell what the dickens his name is' in *The Merry Wives of Windsor* (III.ii.16) in 1601.

what the well-dressed —— is wearing nowadays an ironical subject like 'tramp' or 'cart horse' is inserted where once something like 'man about town' might have been in a tailor's or couturier's slogan. Applied to any eccentric or scruffy choice of clothing, by the mid-twentieth century.

what time does the balloon go up? 'when does everything *get off the ground?* when does the excitement begin?' The notion of the 'balloon going up' was certainly current by the 1920s and may have derived from the barrage balloons introduced during the First World War to protect targets from air raids. The fact that these balloons – or observation ones – had 'gone up' would signal that some form of action was imminent.

what would you do, chums? a regular feature of BBC radio *Band Waggon* (late 1930s) was a tale told by the actor Syd Walker in the character of a junkman. He would pose some everyday dilemma and end with this query – or a variation upon it. It was used as the title of a film in 1939. George Orwell in his essay on 'The Art of Donald McGill' (1942) mentions a comic postcard he had seen which showed Hitler 'with the usual hypertrophied backside' bending down to pick a flower. The caption was: 'What would *you* do, chums?'

what you see is what you get (or **WYSIWYG**) an expression and acronym from computing, meant to suggest that what the operator sees on the computer screen is exactly how the material will appear when printed out (i.e. with correct type faces, artwork, etc.) In use by 1982. Additionally, now used to suggest that a person is not deceiving by appearances. President Bush said the full version on the first day of the Gulf War (in January 1991) when asked how he was feeling.

what's a nice girl like you doing in a joint/place like this? cliché of conversation or chatting up, and now used only in a consciously arch way. Possibly from Hollywood Westerns of the 1930s and certainly established as a film cliché by the 1950s.

what's it all about, (Alfie)? 'what is the meaning of life?' is a question about half as old as time. The phrase gained additional resonance from its use in Bill Naughton's *Alfie*, the 1966 film script of his stage and radio play: 'It seems to me if they ain't got you one way then they've got you another. So what's it all about, that's what I keep asking myself, what's it all about?' Subsequently, the phrase 'What's it all about, Alfie?' was popularized by Burt Bacharach and Hal David's song of that title. This was not written for the film but was later added to the soundtrack when it became a hit.

When Michael Caine, who played Alfie in the film, published his autobiography in 1992, it was naturally entitled *What's It All About?*

what's new, pussycat? playfully seductive enquiry from a man to a woman, along the lines of 'what have you been up to?', 'what gives?', 'what's going on around here?' Said to have been much used, if not coined, by the American actor Warren Beatty in the early 1960s. The film with the title (and the Tom Jones song therefrom) came out in 1965.

what's that got to do with the ——? meaning, 'what you have just said is irrelevant.' A very old form of this phrase is, 'What has that to do with Bacchus?' More recently **what has that got to do with the price of eggs?** (or **butter** or **fish**) has been more common – since the 1920s. **What's that got to do with the Prince of Wales?** – noted in the 1980s – is probably a mishearing of, or subconscious alteration of, 'the price of. . .'

what's the damage? 'how much is it?' – phrase used when asking for a bill (e.g. for drinks) or establishing who should pay it. In fact the word 'damage', meaning 'cost, expense', was in use by the 1750s. In 1852, 'What's the damage, as they say in Kentucky' appears in Harriet Beecher Stowe's *Uncle Tom's Cabin* (though not concerning drink). Presumably, the use derives from legal damages.

what's up, doc? characteristic enquiry of Bugs Bunny, the cartoon character, in the US film series which ran during 1937–63. It was addressed to Elmer Fudd, the doctor who devotes his life to attempting to destroy the rabbit. In full, the phrase, is 'Er, what's up, Doc?' – followed by a carrot crunch. Its origins may lie in an old Texan expression introduced to the films by one of the animators, Tex Avery.

Used as the title of a film starring Barbra Streisand and Ryan O'Neal (1972).

whatever happened to (old) ——? the conversational query about the well-being of former acquaintances occurs, for example, in Noël Coward's song 'I Wonder What Happened to Him?' (from *Sigh No More*, 1945) in the form, 'Whatever became of old Bagot...?' But the film title *Whatever Happened to Baby Jane?* (1962) fixed the phrase in the way most usually employed by journalists. Like **where are they now?** this became a standard formula for feature writers on a slack day.

whatever turns you on! latterly a jokey response to the announcement of any slightly odd (or, conceivably, sexy) enthusiasm. 'I like bathing in warm ass's milk' – 'Whatever turns you on, dear.' Originally, in the 1960s, it was part of a general encouragement to do one's own thing, particularly with regard to the drugs which succeeded in 'turning you on' best. Hence, 'You should do...whatever turns you on.'

when the going gets tough, the tough get going one of several axioms said to have come from the Boston-Irish political jungle or, more precisely, from President Kennedy's father, Joseph P. Kennedy (1888–1969). At this distance, it is impossible to say for sure whether this wealthy, ambitious businessman/ ambassador/politician originated the axiom, but he certainly instilled it in his sons.

Subsequently, it was used as a slogan for the film *The Jewel of the Nile* (1985) and a song with the title sung by Billy Ocean and the stars of the film was a No. 1 hit in 1986. The joke slogan **when the going gets tough, the tough go shopping** had appeared on T-shirts in the US by 1982.

when you call me that, *smile*! *see* **smile when you say that!**

when you got it, flaunt it Braniff Airline in the US used this headline over advertisements in *c* 1969 featuring flamboyant celebrities such as Sonny Liston, Andy Warhol and Joe Namath. Probably the line was taken from the 1967 Mel Brooks movie *The Producers* in which Zero Mostel as 'Max Bialystock' says to the owner of a large white limo: 'That's it, baby! When you got it, flaunt it! Flaunt it!' Later in the film he says, 'Take it when you can get it. Flaunt it! Flaunt it!'

where are they now? a popular journalistic formula when resurrecting people who have passed out of the headlines – compare **whatever happened to ——?** By the 1950s? *Where Are They Now?* was the title of a BBC radio play by Tom Stoppard in 1970.

——, where are you now? usually employed as an ironical, rhetorical plea to someone who has long since departed because the speaker considers that present circumstances are as bad as – or worse than – when the absent person was around. And so, one might have said during the Reagan Irangate scandal, 'Richard Nixon, where are you now?'

As such, it is a truncation of '...where are you now that your country needs you?' and an equivalent of **come back ——, all is forgiven** which, once upon a time, might have been said about a warrior who had retired to his farm and fallen out of favour. The graffito 'Lee Harvey Oswald [President Kennedy's assassin], where are you now that your country needs you?' appeared during the presidencies of both Lyndon Johnson and Richard Nixon.

where do we go from here? clichéd and pompous way of rounding off broadcasting discussions about the future of almost anything. Used as the title of a BBC TV inquiry in Scotland, 1968. 'Where Do We Go From Here?' was also the title of a song of the 1940s, popular for a while in the army.

Alternatively, the question is put to an individual (who has just been interviewed about his life and works) in the form, 'Well, where do you go from here?' A possible American origin was hinted at by Winston Churchill when, in a broadcast to the US from London in August 1939, he said: 'And now it is holiday again, and where are we now? Or, as you sometimes ask in the United States – where do we go from here?'

In politics, as a theme for debates, it tends to be put even more pompously (though now, with luck, only jokingly) in the form **whither ——?** (e.g. 'Whither Democracy?', 'Whither Europe?', 'Whither the Labour Party?'). The first episode of BBC TV's *Monty Python's Flying Circus* (1969) was sub-titled 'Whither Canada?'

where have all the —— gone? format phrase based on the title of the song 'Where Have All the Flowers Gone' by Pete Seeger (1961).

where have you been all my life? exaggerated question asked by a man of a woman whom he has just met and decided to woo. Since the 1920s. It is hard to believe it was ever said straightforwardly as a chatting-up line but stranger things have been known. Now only utterable as an obviously over-the-top bid for attention.

where it's at *see* —— **is where it's at.**

where were you when the lights went out? (or **where was Moses when the lights went out?**) nonsense questions. The first of these became the title of a film (US, 1968) inspired by the great New York blackout of 1965 when the electricity supply failed and, it was popularly believed, the birth-rate shot up nine months later. As such, the phrase echoed an old British music-hall song and/or the (American?) nonsense rhyme 'Where was Moses when the light went out?/Down in the cellar eating sauerkraut.' This last appears to have developed from the 'almost proverbial' riddle (as Iona and Peter Opie call it in *The Lore and Language of Schoolchildren*, 1959):

> *Q.* Where was Moses when the light went out?
> *A.* In the dark.

The Opies found this in *The Riddler's Oracle*, *c* 1821.

where's the beef? 'where's the substance to the argument?' – a classic example of an advertising slogan turning into a political catchphrase. The Wendy International hamburger chain promoted its wares in the US from 1984 with TV commercials, one of which showed three elderly women eyeing a small hamburger on a huge bun – a Wendy competitor's product. 'It certainly is a big bun,' asserted one. 'It's a very big fluffy bun,' the second agreed. But the third asked, 'Where's the beef?' The line caught on hugely. Walter Mondale, running for the Democratic presidential nomination, used it to question the substance of his rival Gary Hart's policies.

which would you rather be – or a wasp?   *see* **because the higher the fewer!**

which would you rather or go fishing?   *see* **because the higher the fewer!**

white man speak with forked tongue!   supposedly the way a Red Indian chief would pronounce on the duplicitous ways of the white man, in old Western movies. 1930s/40s, but no precise citations are available.

whither ——?   *see* **where do we go from here?**

who are the Beatles? (or **what is a Beatle?**)   the archetypal British judge's remark in court – often, of course, a question posed when the judge knows the answer, in order to further his reputation for fustiness and aloofness from the concerns of ordinary citizens. Or merely asked so that things may be properly clarified for the jury and no knowledge assumed on any one's part.

This actual query is probably apocryphal, though plenty of other similar ones have been recorded over the years: 'what is jazz?', 'what is the Grand National?', 'what is oomph?' and so on. However, a headline in the *Guardian* over a report of a copyright case on 10 December 1963 was '*What is a Beatle?*'

who do I have to fuck to get out of this show?   having, as legend would have it, had to fuck to get a part in a show or picture, the speaker is wondering how the process can be reversed – because the show or film is having problems or turns out to be no good. Bob Chieger in *Was It Good For You, Too?* ascribes to 'Shirley Wood, talent coordinator for NBC's *The Tonight Show* in the 1960s', the quotation: 'Who do you have to fuck to get *out* of show business?' The line 'Listen, who do I have to fuck to get *off* this picture?' occurs in Terry Southern's *Blue Movie* (1970).

Steve Bach in *Final Cut* (1985) ascribes 'Who do I fuck to get off this picture?' simply to 'Anonymous Hollywood starlet (circa 1930)'.

who do you think I am – Rockefeller? 'I'm not made of money, you know' – a claim to poverty invoking the legendary American multi-millionaire John D. Rockefeller (1839–1937). At any time since the 1930s but, curiously, still heard in the 1980s.

who he? popularized by *Private Eye* in the 1980s, this editorial interjection following the introduction of a little-known person's name shows some signs of catching on. No doubt Richard Ingrams, when editor of the *Eye*, consciously borrowed the phrase from Harold Ross (1892–1951), editor of the *New Yorker*. James Thurber in *The Years with Ross* (1959) describes how Ross would customarily add this query to manuscripts on finding a name he did not know (sometimes betraying his ignorance). He said the only two names everyone knew were Houdini and Sherlock Holmes.

A book with the title *Who He? Goodman's Dictionary of the Unknown Famous* was published in 1984.

who loves ya, baby? Telly Savalas created a vogue for this phrase of greeting (to a woman), as the lollipop-sucking New York police lieutenant in the TV series *Kojak* (1973–7). Inevitably, he also recorded a song with the title (in 1975).

who you lookin' at? yobbo or lout's challenge which caught on in the UK in the early 1990s.

who's for tennis? *see* **anyone for tennis?**

—— will never be the same again any change, however unremarkable, seems to require use of this journalistic cliché phrase. 'The Broadway musical would never be the same again' – TV promotion, New York 1983. 'Life for George Bush will never be the same again' – TV news (1989).

will the real ——, please stand up? question posed – often, indeed, of one's own self – when there is doubt as to the true identity and nature of some personality. In the American TV game *To Tell the*

Truth, devised by Goodson-Todman Productions and shown in 1956–66, a panel had to decide which of three contestants, all claiming to be a certain person, was telling the truth. After the panellists had interrogated the challenger and the 'impostors', they had to declare which person they thought was the real one. The MC Bud Collyer would then say: 'Will the real —— ——, please stand up!' and he or she did so. The game was revived in the UK as *Tell the Truth* in the 1980s.

Ian Carmichael, the actor, entitled his autobiography *Will the Real Ian Carmichael...* (1979). In March 1984, Elizabeth Taylor, the actress, was quoted as saying: 'I'm still trying to find the real Elizabeth Taylor and make her stand up.'

win one more for the Gipper! *see* **one more for the Gipper!**

wink wink, nudge nudge! *see* **nudge nudge...**

winning isn't everything, it's the only thing sporting catchphrase or slogan (but also common in American business and politics). Various versions of this oft-repeated statement exist. Vince Lombardi, the football coach and general manager of the Green Bay Packers team from 1959 onwards, claimed *not* to have said it in this form but, rather, 'Winning is not everything – but making the effort to win is' (interview, 1962). The first version of Lombardi's remark to appear in print was in the form, 'Winning is not the most important thing, it's everything'. One Bill Veeck is reported to have said something similar. Henry 'Red' Sanders, a football coach at Vanderbilt University, *does* seem to have said it, however, c 1948, and was so quoted in *Sports Illustrated* (26 December 1955). John Wayne, playing a football coach, delivered the line in the 1953 film *Trouble Along the Way*.

Compare 'Winning in politics isn't everything; it's the only thing' – a slogan for the infamous 'Committee to Re-Elect the President' (Nixon) in 1972.

wish you were here! *see* **having a wonderful time!**

with a little help from my/his/their friends suggestion as to how the world operates in terms of help from the 'old boy network', relatives, and old friends. But also hinting at how a person may 'get by' or 'cope' through use of drugs, alcohol and financial assistance. The phrase 'with a little help from my friends' (alluding specifically to drugs) was the title of a song written by Lennon and McCartney and included on the Beatles' *Sgt. Pepper's Lonely Hearts Club Band* album (1967).

...with difficulty! jocular reply to questions beginning with 'How...?' Since the 1950s/60s. 'Tell me, my dear, how did you manage to get into those jeans?' – 'With difficulty!' 'How do porcupines make love?' – 'With difficulty! (or perhaps, rather, 'Very carefully...').

with —— like that, who needs ——? format phrase, but most frequently encountered in the form 'with friends like that, who needs enemies?' – used in desperation after one has been betrayed by a supporter – the earliest example to hand is something Richard Crossman said of certain Labour MPs in 1969 – or ironically to others in difficulty. The *Daily Telegraph* used it as the headline over a picture spread of Richard Nixon's henchmen in August 1974, but it is of much older provenance. Charlotte Brontë said it, in a letter, concerning the patronizing reviewer of one of her books in the mid-nineteenth century.

with one bound/spring, he/Jack was free said of anyone who escapes miraculously from a tricky situation or tight corner. The phrase underlines the preposterousness of the adventures in which such lines can be 'spoken' – in cartoon strips, subtitles to silent films, or in *Boy's Own Paper*-type serials of the early twentieth century where the hero would frequently escape from seemingly impossible situations, mostly after he had been forced into them in a 'cliff-hanger'. Actually, the origin appears to be more recent – in an anecdote recounted by E.S. Turner in his book about this kind of literature, *Boys Will Be Boys* (1948): 'There is a delightful story, attributed to more than one publishing house, of the serial writer who disappears in the middle of a story. As he shows no sign of turning up, it is decided to carry on without him. Unfortunately he has left his hero bound to a stake, with lions circling him, and an avalanche about to fall for good measure (or some such situation). Relays of writers try to think of a way out, and give it up. Then at the eleventh hour the missing author returns. He takes the briefest look at the previous instalment and then, without a moment's hesitation, writes: "With one bound, Jack was free".'

with your thumb in your bum and your mind in neutral 'idle, vacant, empty-headed, not thinking'. A description popular in military circles by 1960.

without hesitation, deviation, or repetition! instruction to speakers in the BBC Radio panel game *Just a Minute* (1967–), devised by Ian Messiter, versions of which have been played in fifty-seven countries. Guests have to speak for one minute without transgressing any of these rules. In 1982, an MP stood up in the House of Commons and said of a guillotine motion, that he thought all speeches on the Bill should be 'like those in that radio game "without deviation, repetition and..." what was the other?' Prompts of: 'Hesitation!' from other MPs.

wogs begin at Barnet an ironic view of the North/South divide in Britain (Barnet being on the outer edge of north-west London), and clearly based on the old insular, foreigner-distrusting view that **wogs begin at Calais** (known by 1958). A motion for debate at the Oxford Union in 1964 took the form 'When going North, the wogs begin at Barnet'.

women and children first! catchphrase used jokingly in a situation where people might appear to be behaving as though caught in a shipwreck – in a crowded bus or train perhaps. It originated in the incident involving HMS *Birkenhead*, one of the first ships to have a hull of iron, in 1852. She was taking 476 British soldiers to the eighth 'Kaffir War' in the Eastern Cape of South Africa when she ran aground fifty miles off the Cape of Good Hope. It was clear that the ship would go under but only three of the eight lifeboats could be used and these were rapidly filled with the twenty women and children on board. According to tradition, soldiers remained calm and did not even break ranks when the funnel and mast crashed down on to the deck, with the loss of 445 lives. Thus was born the tradition of 'women and children' first. In naval circles, this is still known as the Birkenhead Drill.

women are like buses/streetcars: there'll be another coming along soon a turn of the century observation from the US, slightly later in the UK. Compare this allusion to the saying by Derick Heathcoat-Amory when British Chancellor of the Exchequer (1958–60): 'There are three things not worth running for – a bus, a woman or a new economic panacea; if you wait a bit another one will come along.'

wooden leg, waved her *see* 'too late! too late!'...

woofter! *see* **yer plonker!**

worse things happen at sea! consolatory phrase first recorded in 1829 (by Pierce Egan in *Boxiana*, in the form 'Worse accidents occur at sea!').

wot abaht...? *see* **what about the workers?**

wot no ——? the most common graffito of the past fifty years in Britain – apart from **Kilroy was here** (with which it was sometimes combined) – is the so-called figure of 'Chad', 'Mr Chad' or 'The Chad'. In Britain at least, there is no doubt Chad made his first appearance in the early stages of the Second World War, accompanied by protests about shortages of the time, such as, 'Wot no cake?', 'Wot no char?', 'Wot no beer?'.

The format was then used by Watneys London Ltd, the brewers, to promote their beer sometime in the 1940s or 50s. In 1933, at the end of Prohibition, Buster Keaton played in an American film farce with the title *What, No Beer?*

would you be shocked if I put on something more comfortable? a nudgingly provocative line, also rendered as, 'Do you mind if I put on something more comfortable?' and 'Excuse me while I slip into something more comfortable'. But the first is what Jean Harlow as 'Helen' actually says to Ben Lyon as 'Monte' in the US film *Hell's Angels* (1930). It is, of course, by way of a proposition and she duly exchanges her fur wrap for a dressing gown.

would you believe? used when making some exaggerated suggestion. 'One of the cringe-phrases of the age...You couldn't go an hour without hearing someone say it in Los Angeles' – Derek

Taylor, *It Was Twenty Years Ago Today* (1987). He attributes its popularity to the *Get Smart* TV show (1965–70), created by Buck Henry and Mel Brooks, and starring Don Adams. *The Complete Directory to Prime Time Network TV Shows* (1981) adds: 'Used whenever [a secret agent] of K.A.O.S. or someone on [Maxwell Smart's] own side didn't seem to accept one of his fabrications and he was trying to come up with a more acceptable alternative. That catch-phrase became very popular with young people in the late 1960s.'

would you buy a used car from this man?   meaning, 'this person is suspicious, untrustworthy', and used most famously in connection with Richard M. Nixon, long before he fell from grace as the American President. Although the coinage has been attributed by some to Mort Sahl and by others to Lenny Bruce, and though the cartoonist Herblock denied that he was responsible (*Guardian*, 24 December 1975), this is just a *joke* and one is no more going to find an origin for it than for most such. As to *when* it arose, this is Hugh Brogan, writing in *New Society* (4 November 1982): 'Nixon is a double-barrelled, treble-shotted twister, as my old history master would have remarked; and the fact has been a matter of universal knowledge since at least 1952, when, if I remember aright the joke, "Would you buy a second-hand car from this man?" began to circulate.' It was a very effective slur and, by 1968, when the politician was running (successfully) for President, a poster of a shifty-looking Nixon with the line as caption was in circulation.

Now, one might use the phrase about anybody one has doubts about. *The Encyclopedia of Graffiti* (1974) even finds: 'Governor Romney – would you buy a *new* car from this man?' In August 1984, John de Lorean said of himself – after being acquitted of drug-dealing – 'I have aged 600 years and my life as a hard-working industrialist is in tatters. Would you buy a used car from me?'

wreck of the *Hesperus*, the   as in, 'you look like/he or she looks like/I look or feel like. . .' In other words, 'a mess, in a sad state'. Known in the US and UK since the nineteenth century and alluding to Longfellow's famous poem 'The Wreck of the Hesperus'

(1842) about an actual incident involving a schooner off the coast of New England.

wrong side of the hedge when the brains were given away, he was the meaning, 'he is brainless or stupid'. Known since the nineteenth century in the UK and US. Compare **she wasn't around when the looks were given out** (said of an unattractive person).

WYSIWYG *see* **what you see is what you get.**

$$\frac{X}{X}$$

X marks the spot from the use of the letter X or a cross to show
the location of something (buried treasure perhaps) on a map.
Mostly in fiction? Since the early 1800s, at least.

Y
y

yabba-dabba-doo!   cry of delight from the US TV cartoon series *The Flintstones* (1960–6) which was a parody of suburban life set in the Stone Age and made by the Hanna-Barbera studios. It was used substantially in the promotion of the feature film *The Flintstones* (US, 1994) which used real actors in the cartoon roles. More than one critic of this film when advising audiences whether to go and see it, wrote, 'Yabba-dabba-don't!' But surely the phrase must have predated *The Flintstones* – in jazz perhaps?

ye gods and little fishes!   exclamation of contempt, derived from nineteenth-century drama.

yer plonker!   abusive epithet ('you idiot!') popularized by 'Del Boy' (David Jason) referring to his younger brother, Rodney, in the BBC TV comedy series *Only Fools and Horses* and current by 1986. In London dialect, 'plonker' = 'penis' (compare the epithets 'prick' and 'schmuck'). From the same series came the other abusive epithets **dipstick** (probably because rhyming with 'prick'), **noofter** and **woofter** (the last two rhyming with 'poofter' = homosexual).

yes, we have no bananas!   fairly meaningless cry, from the song 'Yes, We Have No Bananas' (1923), words by Irving Cohn to music by Frank Silver. According to Ian Whitcomb in *After the Ball* (1972), the title line came from a cartoon strip by Tad Dorgan and not, as the composers were wont to claim, from a Greek fruit-store owner on Long Island. Alternatively, it was a saying picked up by US troops in the Philippines from a Greek pedlar. In Britain, Elders & Fyffes, the banana importers, embraced the song and distributed 10,000 hands of bananas to music-sellers with the slogan: 'Yes! we have no bananas! On sale here.'

you ain't heard nothin' yet! meaning, 'the best (or worst) is yet to come'. It seems that when Al Jolson exclaimed this in the first full-length talking picture *The Jazz Singer* (1927), he was not just ad-libbing – as is usually supposed – but was promoting the title of one of his songs. He had recorded 'You Ain't Heard Nothing Yet', written by Gus Kahn and Buddy de Sylva, in 1919. In addition, Martin Abramson in *The Real Story of Al Jolson* (1950) suggests that Jolson had also uttered the slogan in San Francisco as long before as 1906. Interrupted by noise from a building site across the road from a café in which he was performing, Jolson had shouted, 'You think that's noise – you ain't heard nuttin' yet!' Listening to the film soundtrack makes it clear that Jolson did not add 'folks' at the end of his mighty line.

you ain't seen nothin' yet! an adaptation of the above which President Ronald Reagan appropriated as a kind of slogan in his successful 1984 bid for re-election. Or perhaps this is the commoner version? Both probably derive from about the same period, however.

you are awful but I like you! *see* **oooh...you are awful...**

you are Mr Lobby Lud and I claim... a circulation-raising stunt for British newspapers in the 1920s took the form of a challenge readers were encouraged to put to a man they were told would be in a certain place (usually a seaside resort) on a particular day. His description and a photograph were given in the paper and 'You are so-and-so and I claim my ten pounds' (or whatever the prize was) became the formula. The reader had, of course, to be carrying a copy of that day's paper. The first in the field was the *Westminster Gazette* in August 1927 and the correct challenge was: 'You are Mr Lobby Lud – I claim the *Westminster Gazette* prize' (which was initially £50, though if it was unclaimed it increased weekly). The name 'Lobby Lud' came from the *Gazette*'s telegraphic address – 'Lobby' because of the Westminster connection and 'Lud' from Ludgate Circus off Fleet Street. The stunt did nothing for the paper which closed the following year, but the idea was taken up by the *Daily News* and the *News Chronicle* and ran on for several years.

you('d) better believe it!   an emphatic 'yes'. Known in the US by 1865.

you can run but you can't hide!   threat or warning to an opponent. In the wake of the hijacking of a TWA airliner to Beirut in the summer of 1985, President Reagan issued a number of warnings to international terrorists. In October, he said that America had, 'sent a message to terrorists everywhere. The message: "You can run, but you can't hide." ' He was alluding to an utterance of the boxer Joe Louis who said of an opponent in a World Heavyweight Championship fight in June 1946, 'He can run, but he can't hide.' The opponent was Billy Conn – who was a fast mover – and Louis won the fight on a knock-out.

you cannot be serious!   exclamation in emulation of John McEnroe, the American tennis player and Wimbledon champion. By 1980, he had become celebrated for his 'Superbrat' behaviour towards umpires and linesmen – telling them 'You are the pits', and suchlike. 'You cannot be serious!' was elevated to catchphrase status through various showbiz take-offs, including Roger Kitter's record, 'Chalk Dust – The Umpire Strikes Back' (UK, 1982).

you can't make a soufflé rise twice!   meaning, 'it is pointless to try and make something happen again if it is unrepeatable'. Alice Roosevelt Longworth is supposed to have said it of Thomas E. Dewey's nomination as the Republican challenger in 1948 (Dewey had previously stood against F.D. Roosevelt in 1944). Paul McCartney has more than once used the phrase to discount the possibility of a Beatles reunion. Some chefs would say that making a soufflé rise twice is not actually impossible.

you can't take it with you   warning that when you are dead, money is of no use to you, so there is no point in holding on to it. *You Can't Take It With You* was the title of a play (1936; film US, 1938) by George S. Kaufman and Moss Hart. An early appearance of the phrase is in Captain Marryat's *Masterman Ready* (1841). An American version is 'You can't take your dough when you go.' Compare the proverb **there are no pockets in shrouds**.

'You can always take one with you' was a slogan suggested by Winston Churchill when invasion by the Germans threatened in 1940.

you can't win 'em all! self-consolatory phrase after defeat. Of American origin, by the 1940s.

you dirty old man! abusive term, usually coupled with some sexual accusation, and known by 1932. In the BBC TV comedy series *Steptoe and Son* (1964–73), the younger Steptoe (Harry H. Corbett) would shout it regularly at his father (Wilfred Brambell).

you dirty rat! although impersonators of the American film actor James Cagney always have him saying 'You dirty rat!', it may be that he never said it quite like that himself. In *Blonde Crazy* (1931) he calls someone a 'dirty, double-crossing rat' which amounts to much the same thing. In *Taxi* (1931) – which is about cabbies fighting off a mob-controlled fleet – he is supposed to have said: 'Come out and take it, you dirty yellow-bellied rat, or I'll give it to you through the door.'

you dirty rotten swine you! catchphrase of 'Bluebottle' (played by Peter Sellers) on the BBC radio *Goon Show* (1950s). Exclaimed by him/it on being visited by some punishment or disaster.

you don't have to be Jewish... ('...to love Levy's Real Jewish Rye') a slogan current in the US in 1967. The point was reinforced by the words being set next to pictures of patently non-Jewish people (Indians, Chinese, Eskimos). There had been a show of Jewish humour with the title *You Don't Have to be Jewish* running on Broadway in 1965, which is probably where it all started.

you know it makes sense! persuasive phrase from public service advertisements in the UK. It was the pay-off line to all British road safety advertisements from 1968 to 1970, but the phrase had been used with emphasis on BBC TV's *TW3* in 1963, so it must have been used somewhere else before this.

you lucky people! catchphrase of the British comedian Tommy Trinder (1909–89) who rode on a wave of publicity in the early

1940s. He even took space on advertising hoardings to declare, 'If it's laughter you're after, Trinder's the name. You lucky people!' The phrase (which came up first in concert-party work) was also used as the title of a film (UK, 1954).

you might think that; I couldn't possibly comment   fictional politician's catchphrase. Said to journalists by the British politician and Prime Minister, Francis Urquhart, in the political thrillers *House of Cards* and *To Play the King* by Michael Dobbs, adapted for television in 1990 and 1993, respectively, by Andrew Davies. The stock phrase, used repeatedly in the adaptations, was taken from the sort of comment politicians in government tend to make to inquisitive lobby journalists at Westminster. As a result of the serialization, actual politicians and Prime Minister 'poached' the phrase and used it self-consciously all the more.

you pays your money and you takes your choice   'it's up to you, the choice is yours' – proverbial expression current in the UK by the 1840s.

you scratch my back and I'll scratch yours!   promise of support in return for a favour. This occurs in Anthony Trollope's novel *The Way We Live Now* (1875) in the form: 'If I scratch their back, I mean them to scratch mine.' There have been several proverbial expressions of this idea, including: **scratch my breech and I'll claw your elbow** and **scratch me and I'll scratch thee**.

you should use stronger elastic!   catchphrase of the British comedian Ted Ray. At one time he was the first host of a BBC radio comedy show called *Calling All Forces* (1950 onwards). In the first show he had as a guest Freddie Mills, then world light heavyweight boxing champion. Mills – departing from his script – told of one punch he received when he momentarily lowered his boxing gloves: 'My trainer nearly fainted when he saw me drop 'em. I didn't mean to drop 'em.' Ted Ray immediately responded, 'You should use stronger elastic!'

Bob Monkhouse, the show's co-scriptwriter, soon engineered the return of this phrase, which really did catch on. Ray kept it in his stage act for many years.

you some kind of nut?, (what are you)   derisive question put to anyone who is acting or speaking strangely. American usage, especially, since the 1910s.

you talkin' to me?   assertive but cool phrase, apparently a quotation from the film *Taxi Driver* (1976) where it was spoken by Robert De Niro.

you, too, can have a body like mine!   a body-building slogan that, for some reason, caught on more than others. It was used to promote 'Charles Atlas' courses. 'Atlas' was born Angelo Siciliano in Italy in 1894 and died in America in 1972. He won the title of 'The World's Most Perfectly Developed Man' in a 1922 contest sponsored by Bernarr Macfaden and his *Physical Culture* magazine. Then he started giving mail-order body-building lessons. A famous promotional strip cartoon showed 'How Joe's body brought him FAME instead of SHAME.' 'Hey! Quit kicking sand in our face', Joe says to a bully on the beach. Then he takes a Charles Atlas course and ends up with a girl by his side who says, 'Oh, Joe! You are a real man after all!'

Like Joe, Atlas had himself been 'a skinny, timid weakling of only seven stone' (hence the expression **I was a seven stone weakling**). 'I didn't know what real health and strength were. I was afraid to fight – ashamed to be seen in a bathing costume.' But after watching a lion rippling its muscles at the zoo, he developed a method of pitting one muscle against another which he called 'Dynamic Tension'.

you're damned if you do and damned if you don't!   'on the horns of a dilemma; torn both ways; in a "Catch-22" situation' – probably American, early twentieth century.

you're going out there a youngster, you've got to come back a star!   not a cliché when new-minted in the film *42nd Street* (1933). Warner Baxter as a theatrical producer says the line to Ruby Keeler as the chorus girl who takes over at short notice from an indisposed star.

you're never alone with a Strand   slogan from a classic British advertisement for a brand of cigarettes from W.D. & H.O. Wills which caught the public imagination in 1960 and yet failed to sell the product. It was decided to appeal to the youth market by associating the product not with sex or social ease but with 'the loneliness and rejection of youth'. And so, a Frank Sinatra/James Dean clone was shown mooching about lonely locations in raincoat and hat. In no time at all he had his own fan-club and the music from the TV advertisement – 'The Lonely Man Theme' – became a hit in its own right. But the ads did not work. Viewers apparently revised the slogan in their own minds to mean, 'If you buy Strand, then you'll be alone'.

you're so sharp you'll be cutting yourself! rebuke to a sharp-tongued, waspish person. One of a number of phrases, perhaps dating from around 1900, on this theme, including **Mr Sharp from Sheffield, straight out of the knife-box!** (Sheffield having been for centuries the centre of the English cutlery trade). Earlier, Murdstone referred to David Copperfield (in Chapter 2 of Charles Dickens's novel, 1849) as 'Mr Brooks of Sheffield', to indicate that he was 'sharp'. There was indeed a firm of cutlery makers called Brookes of Sheffield.

you're the expert! 'I'll take your word for it' – a phrase respectful of someone who appears to be an authority on any subject. Since the 1930s/40s, like **you're the doctor!**

you've got a big red conk! the sort of catchphrase that runs into trouble with educationists as it so easily slips into schoolboy patois. Spoken by Ted Ray in the BBC radio show *Ray's A Laugh* (1950s). 'Conk' is British slang for 'nose'.

you've made an old man very happy! phrase spoken as though said by an old man to a woman for sexual favours granted, now a humorous way of expressing thanks about anything. Neatly inverted in the film *The Last Remake of Beau Geste* (1977). Terry-Thomas, as a prison governor, says to Ann-Margret, as a woman who has slept with him to secure an escape: 'Delighted you came, my dear, and I'd like you to know that you made a happy man feel very old.' From BBC radio *Round the Horne* (29 May 1966): 'Thank you. You are so kind. You've made an old fiendish master mind very happy'; (4 June 1967): 'Thank you. You've made an old volcano very happy.' In the film *It Happened One Night* (1934), the father of the runaway heiress gets to say to his daughter, 'You can make an old man happy' (by marrying the right man).

you've never had it so good   political slogan only employed at some risk to the politician or party involved. It is a phrase that will forever be linked in British politics with the name of Harold Macmillan (later 1st Earl of Stockton). In a speech in July 1957, he took pains to use the phrase not boastfully but as a warning: 'Let's be frank about it. Most of our people have never had it so good. Go around the country, go to the industrial towns, go to the farms, and you'll see a state of prosperity such as we have never had in my lifetime – nor indeed ever in the history of this country. What is beginning to worry some of us is "Is it too good to be true?" or perhaps I should say "Is it too good to last?" For amidst all this prosperity, there is one problem that has troubled us, in one way or another, ever since the war. It is the problem of rising prices. Our constant concern is: Can prices be steadied while at the same time we maintain full employment in an expanding economy? Can we control inflation?'

As **you never had it so good**, it had been a slogan used by the Democrats in the 1952 US presidential election.

young, gifted and ——   format phrase based on 'Young, Gifted and Black', the title of a hit song recorded by the Jamaican duo Bob and Marcia in 1970. In June 1989, British ITV was showing a comedy yarn about five young lads working on a Youth Training Scheme and called *Young, Gifted and Broke*.

your/yer actual   *see* **that's your actual French!**

your (back) wheel's going round!   *see* **hey – your back wheel's going round!**

your country needs *you*!   a recruiting slogan that has become an all-purpose catchphrase used whenever someone is being dragooned into carrying out a dangerous or unwelcome task. Originally, it was the caption to Alfred Leete's famous First World War recruiting poster showing Field Marshal Lord Kitchener pointing at *you* – a brilliant example of a slogan that is inseparable from a visual. It first appeared on the cover of *London Opinion* on 5 September 1914 and was taken up for poster use the following week. Earlier, a more formal advertisement bearing the words 'Your King and Country need you' with the royal coat of arms had been used. The idea was widely imitated abroad. In the USA, James Montgomery Flagg's poster of a pointing Uncle Sam bore the legend 'I want *you* for the US army'. There was also a version by Howard Chandler Christy featuring a woman with a mildly come-hither look saying, 'I want you for the Navy'.

your friendly neighbourhood ——— a usually ironic or facetious construction, possibly derived from the slogan 'Your friendly neighbourhood policeman' in a police public-relations campaign of the 1960s. Compare the American **support your local sheriff** established before the 1968 film *Support Your Local Sheriff* (which was followed three years later by *Support Your Local Gunfighter*). In 1969 there was a police bumper sticker in the US, 'Support your local police, keep them independent'.

your future is in your hands originally a slogan for the British Conservative Party in the 1950 General Election. The Conservatives were returned to power under Winston Churchill the following year. Churchill himself had used the idea in an address to Canadian troops aboard RMS *Queen Elizabeth* in January 1946: 'Our future is in our hands. Our lives are what we choose to make of them.' The slogan became a catchphrase as a result of being turned (inevitably) into a lavatorial joke, as in Keith Waterhouse, *Billy Liar* (1959): ' "No writing mucky words on the walls!" he called. I did not reply. Stamp began quoting, "*Gentlemen, you have the future of England in your hands*".'

your money or your life! the highwayman's/robber's traditional challenge turned into a joke. In one of the American comedian Jack Benny's most celebrated gags (playing on his legendary meanness), when the robber said this, Benny paused for a long time, and then replied, 'I'm thinking it over'. This was on American radio in the 1930s/40s.

'Your money *and* your life!' was an anti-smoking slogan in the UK in 1981.

your mother wouldn't like it! ironic warning against doing anything lest it incur parental disapproval. Used as the title of a rock-music programme on London's Capital Radio, presented by Nicky Horne, from 1973. The phrase seems to have been very much around at the time. The slogan 'Mother wouldn't like it' was used in MG motor advertisements (by April 1972) and W.H. Auden is reported by Stephen Spender as having said, 'Naughty! Naughty! Mother wouldn't like it!' to Philip Larkin, also in 1972. However, in Margaret Mitchell, *Gone With the Wind* (1936): 'There, [Scarlett] thought, I've said "nigger" and Mother wouldn't like that at all.'

your own, your very own! catchphrase often heard in 'old-time music-hall' from the Leeds City Varieties, a long-running BBC TV favourite during 1953–83. As its chairman, Leonard Sachs (1909–90) spoke in a florid way, presumably reproducing traditional music-hall phrases. Before banging his gavel to bring on the next act, he would describe 'your own, your very own' artistes with alluring alliteration. At the end, the audience (all in period costume) would join in a sing-song: 'To conclude, we assemble the entire company, ladies and gentlemen – the entire company, the orchestra, but this time, ladies and gentlemen, **chiefly yourselves!'**

your slip is showing! 'you are giving yourself away by saying or doing that' – a warning, current since the 1920s, indicating that a person is betraying himself (in however trivial a matter) just as a woman 'reveals' herself by letting her slip show under her dress.

you're far too wee! *see* **I've failed!**